THE UNIVERSITY OF LIVERPOOL
SYDNEY JONES LIBRARY

Please return or renew, on or before the last date below. A fine is payable on late returned items. Items may be recalled after one week for the use of another reader. Items may be renewed by telephone:- 0151 794 - 2678.

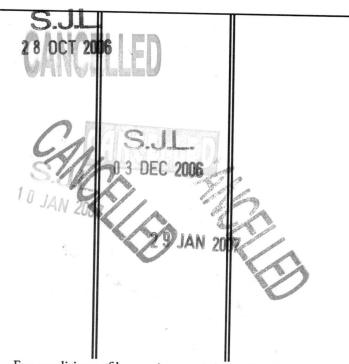
For conditions of borrowing, see Library Regulations

Transculturation

Critical Studies

Vol. 27

Amsterdam - New York, NY 2005

Transculturation

Cities, Spaces and Architectures in Latin America

Edited by

Felipe Hernández,
Mark Millington and
Iain Borden

Cover photograph:
Title: National Archive of Colombia
Architect: Rogelio Salmona.
Photographer and Year: Ricardo L. Castro ©1998

Cover design: Pier Post

The paper on which this book is printed meets the requirements of "ISO
9706:1994, Information and documentation - Paper for documents -
Requirements for permanence".

ISBN: 90-420-1628-0
©Editions Rodopi B.V., Amsterdam - New York, NY 2005
Printed in the Netherlands

Contents

Foreword

Most of essays collected in this volume were presented at the *Transcultural Architecture in Latin America* conference, which was held in Senate House, University of London, on the 9th and 10th of November 2001. The conference was organised by the Bartlett School of Architecture (UCL) and the Department of Hispanic and Latin America Studies of the University of Nottingham with the support of the Institute of Romance Studies (University of London).

    Transcultural Architecture in Latin America was an interdisciplinary conference that focused on the way inevitable processes of transculturation have affected, and continue to affect, Latin American cities, their urban spaces, and their architectures. The conference engaged with a broad range of cultural and architectural theory in order to embrace the whole spectrum of politics and social practices intrinsic to the development of cities and buildings in globalising culture.

    Despite the growing academic interest in issues related to Latin American culture, which has increased significantly during the last thirty years both within and outside Latin America, architecture has not received the same attention as other disciplinary areas. Not only has there been a lack of scholarship on Latin American architecture in general but it is also the case that research is carried out in a multitude of centres around the globe without appropriate outlets to disseminate the findings, with the result that those efforts remain isolated and largely inaccessible. *Transcultural Architecture in Latin America* was, therefore, an unprecedented attempt to congregate people from Latin America itself, the United States and Europe to discuss in one single forum the outcome of their work. The conference attracted scholars and practitioners from as diverse disciplines as architecture —history, theory and practice—, art history, cultural theory, urban studies and literature. All of whom gathered together for two very intense but stimulating days at Senate House, University of London, to present and scrutinise their most recent work.

    Although a large number of speakers and delegates were unable to attend the conference due to the unfortunate tragedy of September 11th in New York City, the breadth and depth of the papers that were presented made it clear that there are currently numerous people working on issues related to Latin American cities, their urban culture and their architectures. Not only are there many people carrying out research on Latin American architecture, but the quality of their work is also outstanding.

As the essays collected in this volume demonstrate, current approaches to Latin American cities and architecture no longer focus exclusively on the work of paradigmatic architects, nor do they use traditional architectural narratives to theorise and historicise architecture, but develop new methods of analysis that bring to light issues that had never been explored before. The very notion of transculturation, for example —as well as the use of terms such as hybridisation and translation—, which has been used by Latin Americanists for several years, but which has not permeated into architectural debates, seems to promote engagement with a new range of questions while facilitating interdisciplinary interaction between architecture and other areas of cultural theory. Thus, this book introduces new readings and interpretations of the work of well known architects, new analyses regarding the use of architectural materials and languages, new questions to do with minority architectures, gender and travel, and, from beginning to end, it engages with important political debates that are so rarely discussed within Latin American architectural circles.

Since the majority of papers here included were presented at the *Transcultural Architecture in Latin America* conference, we feel that this is an appropriate place to thank the UCL and The University of Nottingham for the financial support which they gave to the event as well as to acknowledge the Institute of Romance Studies for their logistic and administrative assistance. In particular, we are grateful to Jo Labanyi and Sarah Wykes who were director and administrative assistant, respectively, at the IRS at the time of the conference.

We are also indebted to Professor Mark Millington who, with the two of us, sat on the organising committee and Dr Jane Rendell who was on the Advisory Panel. We would like to extend our gratitude to the keynote speakers: Professor Román de la Campa, Professor Luis E Carranza and Enrique Browne, and to all the speakers and delegates who came from all over the world. Although we wrote these words together, I find it appropriate to also thank Professor Iain Borden for his enthusiastic support throughout the organisation and during the conference itself, as well as for his advice and assistance during the process of editing the book.

There were also numerous other people who have always remained anonymous but whose work helped to make both the conference and this book possible. Therefore, we are also grateful to the audiovisual technicians who managed to prepare all the equipment for what was a flawless aspect of the conference and to the anonymous referees who read the abstracts for the conference and the final papers during the preparation of this book.

For permission to re-publish some of the essays we would like to thank Gill Rye, Managing Editor of the *Journal of Romance Studies* and Berghahn Journals. Last, but by no means least, we are grateful to Rodopi for their interest in publishing this book from the outset and for their patience in seeing it finished.

Felipe Hernández
Iain Borden

Introduction:
Transcultural Architectures in Latin America

Felipe Hernández

The term transculturation, coined by the Cuban anthropologist Fernando Ortiz in the early 1940s, has been used in order to explore in a critical manner the dynamics of interaction between Latin American and other cultures around the world.[1] Particular attention has been paid to the effects that such a dynamic interaction has had in literature and other arts. However, the notion of transculturation has also been used in order to examine complex socio-political issues regarding processes of identity formation in Latin America. Despite its significance across so many disciplines, the term has not had a major impact on the study of Latin American architectures. Although the word itself has appeared within architectural discourses, it has never fully connected architecture with a broader range of cultural issues. Architects have used the notion of transculturation —and other terms such as hybridisation, syncretism, creolisation, etc.— only to describe the formal transformations that certain types of architecture undergo when they are translated to a new geographical context: Latin America. In so doing, architects ignore the complex social and political content implicit in terms such as transculturation.

Architectural studies in Latin America have traditionally relied heavily on the exclusive selection of paradigmatic buildings and their architects, in order to construct coherent, linear and homogenous architectural theories and histories. Thus, we find that architectural theorists and historians have focused their analyses mainly on the work of architects like Luis Barragán in Mexico, Oscar Niemeyer in Brazil, or Rogelio Salmona in Colombia. It is not a coincidence that, while the buildings designed by these architects are taken to represent Latin American architecture, they also comply with the parameters of modernist Euro-American architectural narratives. The work of these architects is celebrated because it reaches a high degree of refinement in comparison with that of other paradigmatic architects that are taken as referents. Such a generalisation offers only a partial view of the multiplicity and heterogeneity of the architectural practices that take place in Latin America. The fact that most of the projects

[1] We would like to thank the editors of the *Journal of Romance Studies* for permission to reproduce some sections of the article 'The Transcultural Phenomenon and the Transculturation of Architecture', originally published in *Journal of Romance Studies* (2002) 2.3, 1-15.

designed by the above-mentioned architects (Barragán and Salmona, in particular) were/are private houses or large institutional buildings implies that their work might not correspond to the conditions of poverty, unemployment and lack of education of the so-called minorities[2] and the less dominant members of the society.

It is clear that there is a lack of scholarship —and, therefore, of literature— on the architectures produced by minority groups in spontaneous settlements such as the *'favelas'* or *'invasiones'* that have developed in most Latin American cities. These architectures have been radically dismissed for not complying with hegemonic architectural narratives and, consequently, for disrupting the homogeneous growth of cities as imagined by architects. The paradox lies in the fact that the buildings produced by minority groups represent an average 70% of the fabric of Latin American cities. The fact that most architects and architectural theorists in the continent have refused to deal with such an overwhelming reality for the sake of constructing a coherent and homogeneous narrative renders the majority of existing architectural theories, and histories, inadequate and incomplete.

Considering that the notion of transculturation is intrinsically concerned with more complex socio-political processes, it is therefore paradoxical that the term has occasionally been used to support such a reductive view of Latin American architecture(s). Precisely because the term transculturation is loaded with an enormous socio-political content, it offers numerous possibilities to connect architecture with a broader range of cultural issues thus covering the entirety of architectural practices that take place in Latin American cities and not only those that comply with hegemonic narratives and exclusive referential structures. In other words, the use of the notion of transculturation within architecture requires us to challenge foundational, homogenising and hierarchical methods of architectural analysis. In this way, architectural practices that have so far been almost completely neglected, and whose values have been dismissed, such as the architecture(s) of the minorities, would be endowed with socio-political and architectural validity in the same way the work of paradigmatic architects such as Barragán, Niemeyer or Salmona is.

However, considering that the notion of transculturation has proved to be exceedingly polemical amongst cultural theorists in and outside Latin America, and that the term has not yet been properly introduced into architectural debates, it is necessary to examine the origin and development of the term itself before further architectural analyses can be developed.

As mentioned above, the term transculturation was coined by the Cuban anthropologist Fernando Ortiz, and was created in order to explore the

---

[2] The term 'minorities', in this case, refers to those sections of the society that do not have easy access to the institutions of power. Consequently, it transpires that the minorities, in Latin America, exceed in numbers the so-called 'majorities'.

cultural dynamics in operation between Cuba and metropolitan centres. Since then the concept has been applied to the whole of Latin America, and latterly, it has also been used as a generic term in order to examine issues relating to the cultural economy between peripheries and centres. Given the complexity of the various processes of cultural formation constantly at work in Latin America, the notion of transculturation is used in order to defy the assumption that cultures develop taxonomically and unidirectionally. Transculturation refers to a multi-directional and endless interactive process between various cultural systems that is in opposition to unidirectional and hierarchical structures determined by the principle of origin that is always associated with claims for cultural authority. Thus, the term 'transculturation' places the theorisation of processes of cultural exchange between peripheries and centres on a more democratic basis. Moreover, transculturation is the antithesis of the notion of acculturation, which implies the supremacy of one cultural system over another, hence the ultimate elimination of non-dominant cultures.

In theory, the term 'acculturation' was supposed to 'comprehend those phenomena which result when groups of individuals having different cultures come into continuous first-hand contact, with subsequent changes in the original cultural patterns of either or both groups' (Spitta 1995: 3). Although it has been defined as a process that connotes a certain mutuality, acculturation, as Ortiz understood it, was rather different: it was a culturally motivated *misunderstanding* of the term in the sense that, for him, acculturation implied the unidirectional imposition of one dominant culture upon another. His interpretation derives from the fact that, in practice, anthropologists generally studied the impact of acculturation on the colonised, and not on the coloniser. Thus, acculturation actually signifies the loss of culture of the subaltern group. In other words, acculturation is seen here to correspond to modern Euro-American cultural and political homogenising agendas, and to be reductive in its approach to cross-cultural encounters, whereas transculturation is offered as a more dynamic theoretical model in keeping with the reality of such encounters. Transculturation is held to overcome the hierarchical implications of the previous term. By 'transculturation', then, Ortiz means that a process of mutual interaction exists between cultures, despite the unequal distribution of power characteristic of transcultural relations (Hernández 2002: 1-15).

In sum, the main theoretical value of the concept of transculturation in Ortiz's work lies in the fact that it creates a new form of cultural dynamics that understands cultural productivity not in binary terms but as a fluid complex operation among differing and contesting cultural sites. In addition, transculturation has a powerful political potential that undermines hegemonic and homogenising claims the aim of which is the ultimate elimination of cultural difference. Transculturation is therefore a primary theoretical tool with which to examine the complex dynamic implicit in the interaction between cultures and the continual redefinition of cultural contexts that it brings about. It follows that transculturation is particularly relevant to discussions of Latin American architecture, for it opens up a whole new area of inquiry about the nature and characteristics of Latin American cities and buildings.

Transculturation and the Development of Andean Cities

The Peruvian ethnographer and novelist José María Arguedas appropriated Ortiz's notion of transculturation in an insightful analysis of the fragmented nature of Peruvian culture (Arguedas 1975). Arguedas pays particular attention to the multiplicity of practices that have allowed indigenous groups to survive, and even to thrive, after years of brutal miscegenation. His examples show how those groups, which kept themselves isolated from the influence of the coloniser, disintegrated with the arrival of a new social order and new technologies. On the other hand, groups that maintained close contact with European cultures after colonisation developed 'antibodies', as he calls them, that allowed their survival and further development. Among these latter groups are the rural indigenes that migrate to the cities. Arguedas maintains that rural immigrants regrouped themselves in the cities according to origin, which permitted them to continue to live similarly to the way they had lived in their original communities although in a displaced space, translated from the rural to the urban. In the cities, the space of mass culture, indigenous groups had nonetheless to reconfigure their identities in order to survive.[3] Instead of being a tool to construct a coherent history, in his account of the development of urban cultures on the coast of Peru, transculturation appears as a non-essentialising and non-foundational term that responds to the multiple and convoluted historical experiences of the people who inhabit Peruvian cities. Through his comparative ethnographic studies Arguedas attempts to prove that sustained close contact between cultures has permitted indigenous groups to survive and to reinforce their cultural identities.

In another aspect of his inquiry, Arguedas sees the configuration of Andean cities as being substantially determined by the various and continuous processes of transculturation that had taken place throughout their history. In what can be seen as an archaeological study of coastal Peruvian cities, Arguedas examines how the colonial city that was conceived as a homogenous symbol of European superiority —a centre of absolute power— mutated dramatically with the arrival of a multiplicity of minority groups.

---

[3] Arguedas (1975: 139) discusses the way Peruvian indigenous peoples have adapted to the urban spaces of the city, carrying with them their traditions and social practices.

Cities became culturally and socially heterogeneous, the urban fabric became fragmented, and the whole image of cities like Lima or Chimbote became 'Andeanised', to use Arguedas's own term. The latter city, Chimbote, was the location for Arguedas posthumous novel *El zorro de arriba y el zorro de abajo*. He was particularly interested in the case of Chimbote due to all the changes it has undergone throughout its history. Initially, Chimbote was an Inca settlement. After colonisation it became a small colonial beach town with strong remnants of the previous indigenous culture. Later, due to the development of the fishing industry, the town grew to become a city of several thousand inhabitants where indigenous groups still coexist with the mestizo population and also with foreigners —fishermen, sailors and tourists. These characteristics, and the emergence of a precarious industrialisation in the early twentieth century, fascinated Arguedas who saw Chimbote as a prime example of transculturation, yet one that confronted him with a dramatic reality that led him away from the optimistic approach of other and previous texts.[4] For, in Chimbote, Arguedas discovered the impossibility for transculturation to be a harmonious fusion, or even coexistence, of differing and antagonistic socio-cultural groups. On the contrary, most processes of transculturation are conflictive, determined by situations of social inequality and imbalances in the distribution of power. Such conditions do not imply, as many critics suggest,[5] that transculturation is altogether unachievable. The problem lies in the fact that in Arguedas's earlier work transculturation was understood as a teleological term, as something that could be accomplished and therefore reach an end. For this reason, it is necessary to reassess the notion of transculturation to overcome Arguedas's theoretical shortcomings. In fact, from an architectural point of view, Chimbote is an interesting case to drive forward this initiative. In Chimbote there are still some remains of Inca architecture and urban infrastructure in dialogue —although not necessarily in harmony— with colonial buildings organised on an orthogonal grid as well as with various modernist buildings. In addition, there is evidence of a major unrealised master plan designed by the firm Town Planning Associates (whose main partners were Josep Lluís Sert and Paul Lester Wiener) in the 1950s, in which the posture of the government of Peru, as well as the homogenising modernist agenda of the planners, with regard to Chimbote's cultural multiplicity appears to be clear: the forceful elimination of differences using architecture as a vehicle. For all these reasons, Chimbote offers plenty of extraordinary potential for an enhanced and continued architectural analysis; that is, the city in relation with the whole range of issues brought forward by Arguedas in his ethnographic studies.

---

[4] See Arguedas (1975) where he talks about a future of harmonious integration between indigenous groups and the *mestizo* elites.
[5] See Moreiras (2001).

Surprisingly, neither architects nor architectural theorists have addressed these questions critically in any of the major theoretical projects produced during the second half of the twentieth century in Latin America. Social heterogeneity and mass migration into the main cities have always been seen negatively from an architectural perspective as they obfuscate architects' and planners' projects to keep cities free from contrasting spatial and aesthetic differences. Yet, from a different perspective, the fact that numerous socio-cultural differences coexist in the urban space of Latin American cities is a condition pregnant with opportunities for architectural exploration.

Arguedas's most important contribution is that he scrutinises the univocal authority of the mestizo elites —the so-called majority— by highlighting the fact that cultural subjectivity and identity have to be 'understood as historical and cultural constructs that are always in flux, split between two or more worlds, cultures, and languages' (Spitta 1995: 8). Arguedas's work, carried out in the 1950s and 1960s, can therefore be taken as a prelude not only to García Canclini's work on Latin American hybrid urban cultures (1995), but also to that of other theorists such as Bhabha (1994) whose work refers to other peripheries.

Like Arguedas, the Uruguayan theorist Angel Rama also elaborated extensively on the notion of transculturation in the Andean region. Although his approach is mainly literary —he uses transculturation in order to analyse Latin American literatures, which, for him, are situated in a liminal space between various ethnicities and different linguistic traditions—, he also studied the effects of transculturation on the development of Latin American cities.

In his posthumous book *La ciudad letrada* [The Lettered City] Rama explores the way in which imbalances of power between the coloniser and the colonised became a decisive factor in the shaping of most Latin American cities. Rama finds a close relationship between the creation of a hierarchically designed urban space, materialised through the use of an orthogonal grid, and the forceful imposition of a hierarchical society. In fact, Rama demonstrates, in a Foucaultian fashion, that colonial cities were created as part of a strategy of control and domination that would soon clash with those pre-existing structures, which did not disappear completely. On the contrary, the antagonistic urban and social structures have coexisted in a conflictive relation that continues today and which also defies foundational and essentialist approaches to both cultural and urban development.

Despite the fact that Rama does not arrive at a critical conclusion with regard to the city as an architectural construct (this was clearly not his intention as he was not an architect) he does engage with important debates that require the attention of architects and architectural theorists in Latin America. In the same way that Rama looks at the constant interaction between various sociocultural groups that stand in different positions of power, architects ought to engage with the whole range of architectural practices that take place in Latin American cities instead of trying to occlude them for the sake of creating a coherent canon. It stands to reason that processes of transculturation have also occurred within architecture giving rise to a kind of 'transarchitecturation' that has affected buildings as well as cities. Therefore, it is clear that the use of the notion of transculturation within architectural debates urges engagement with issues beyond the limits of the merely formal.

In the work of Ortiz, Arguedas and Rama the term 'transculturation' was employed to unveil the interactive reality of cultural relations. Contrary to the concept of acculturation, which implies the imposition of superior cultures over those considered inferior, transculturation makes visible how cultures become mutually affected as a result of their interaction. Thus these theorists attempt to dismantle genealogical and hierarchical structures that underpin the hierarchical claims to cultural authority. However, their work is unable to eliminate such structures completely, perhaps because their criticism remains attached to structural and positivist methods of critique. Ortiz's, Arguedas's and Rama's work on transculturation represents an important breakthrough for Latin American cultural and literary theory in the analysis of the nature of differential cultural identities. Nonetheless, it is necessary to reassess the notion of transculturation not only in order to respond to the new realities of Latin American cultures, but also in order to return to the term the critical and political values that it has lost. In an attempt to carry out this task, I propose to approach the concept of transculturation via the work of Gilles Deleuze and Félix Guattari, paying particular attention to the notion of the rhizome.

Becoming Transcultural: a Post-Structuralist Approach

Contemporary cultural theory finds its most powerful method of critique in the legacy of post-structuralism. Post-structuralism offers ample opportunity to dismantle and transgress structural methods of theoretical analysis for it is understood that natural systems, such as social systems, do not evolve along premeditated orderly lines. On the contrary, they manifest multiple and often unpredictable patterns of becoming. An illuminating way to model those patterns of becoming is to draw on the notion of the rhizome as elaborated by Deleuze and Guattari. The rhizome is a figure appropriated from biology but used within philosophical discourses in opposition to traditional tree-like structures of analysis. The latter are determined by the principle of origin and follow a certain linearity. If the tree represents a foundational, linear and highly hierarchical structure, the rhizome represents a dynamic structure that has no point of origin and is capable of establishing multiple connections with any other kind of system while at the same time avoiding stratification. Thus, the notion of the rhizome serves to place under scrutiny notions like origin, foundation, centralism and hierarchy.

I explained above how the notion of transculturation brings to the fore the dynamism that characterises cultural contacts and how such contacts affect all cultures involved in the process to a similar extent. Transculturation is therefore conceived as a multidirectional phenomenon constantly at work in our globalising culture and not only within colonial situations. For this reason, the notion of the rhizome appears to be appropriate in re-examining the term.

According to Deleuze and Guattari, rhizomes are characterised by certain approximate features. Among those features is the *principle of asignifying rupture* according to which a rhizome cannot be destroyed. Wherever a rhizome is broken or shattered, it starts up again. Its capacity to connect unrestrictedly at any point with other systems allows it to restart every time that it is disrupted. Rhizomes are also characterised by the *principles of cartography and decalcomania,* which imply that, due to their dynamism, there is no way in which it is possible to trace rhizomes. Since rhizomes are anti-genealogical, they can be mapped, but not traced. For 'what distinguishes the map from the tracing is that it is entirely oriented toward an experimentation in contact with the real. [...] The map is open and connectable in all its dimensions; it is detachable, reversible, susceptible to constant modification' (Deleuze and Guattari 1998: 12). In other words, the map differs from the tracing because the latter suggests a linearity of evolution always based upon a number of certainties.

Three features of this argument become central to our inquiry because they help understand the relation between the rhizome and socio-cultural apparatuses. They are the principles of connection, heterogeneity and multiplicity. The first two principles examined by Deleuze and Guattari are *connection* and *heterogeneity*. These two principles imply that rhizomes can be connected to *anything other*, and, in fact, *must be*. Rhizomes are capable of connecting to other systems different from rhizomes; they can change in nature in order to make connections with 'anything other'. In addition, due to their heterogeneity, they are capable of establishing multiple connections simultaneously. Therefore, rhizomes are diametrically different from tree-like or root-like structures. In these latter structures, there is a clear origin that sets the rule for possible future developments. Deleuze and Guattari criticise binary logics not because they are too abstract, but because they are not abstract enough. They affirm that such binary tree-like systems 'do not reach the abstract machine that connects a language to the semantic and pragmatic contents of statements, to collective assemblages of enunciation, to a whole micropolitics of the social field' (Deleuze and Guattari 1998: 7). Here, it is implied that binary logics are not capable of representing the dynamism, heterogeneity and unpredictability with which socio-cultural formations establish connections within themselves and with others. The reason why rhizomes achieve a higher degree of abstraction is because they are alien to any idea of genealogical axiality. Binary logics are abstract, yet they represent an idealised natural order that does not adequately respond to the real complexity of natural systems. In other words, although they are abstract they also reduce the potential to multiple connectability inherent in all living systems. They belong to the order of a totalising macropolitics that is opposite to the differential specificity of rhizomatic micropolitics. The rhizome, for its part, does not fix represented systems to foundational structures, and maintains a dynamic middle point of permanent becoming.

An important political component appears with the *principle of multiplicity*: power. According to this principle, it is argued that unity does not exist and that all we have are multiplicities which remain in permanent transformation. Only a power takeover can disrupt the heterogeneity and connectability of a rhizome in order to impose apparent unity. Otherwise, a rhizome would ceaselessly establish connections between 'semiotic chains, organisations of power, and circumstances relative to arts, sciences and social struggles' (Deleuze and Guattari 1998: 7). Because multiplicity is the primary condition of all systems, unity is only achieved when it is imposed. Deleuze and Guattari maintain that:

> The notion of unity (*unités*) appears only when there is a power takeover in the multiplicity by the signifier or a corresponding subjectification proceeding: this is the case for a pivot-unity forming the basis for a set of bi-univocal relationships between objective elements or points, or for the One that divides following the law of binary logic of differentiation in the subject. Unity always operates in an empty dimension supplementary to that of the system considered (overcoding). (Deleuze and Guattari 1998: 8-9)

Multiplicity, as a principle of the rhizome, is what saves it from overcoding. In other words, a rhizome never becomes overcoded or saturated because it is always being recoded. The above paragraph also reinforces the notion that power influences the connection-making process of all systems, primarily in the case of social systems.

Power is an important component that conditions the notion of rhizomatic becoming. In this sense, it is my contention that cultures have rhizomatic characteristics: they are assemblages of multiplicities that are always in a middle, always in a process of becoming. In their process of becoming, cultures establish simultaneous multiple connections with other cultural formations. As a result, cultures regenerate, change in nature, and recreate themselves constantly. However, these processes are conditioned by institutions of power. Such institutions have a great impact on the way connections are established, and the very notion of unrestricted connectability can be jeopardised by power formations that tend to construct a model of order by stratifying everything. This is what occurs in the majority of transcultural relations: a power takeover disrupts the rhizomatic nature of processes of cultural becoming by stratifying everything within foundational and totalising systems.

Although the notion of the 'rhizome' implies that all cultural systems are connected —and, in fact, always have been— it does not suggest a fusion nor does it deny the existence of differences between interconnected cultures. In other words, despite being rhizomatically connected, cultures may remain and evolve separately. Deleuze and Guattari use an analogy between orchids and wasps whose existence is possible due to their constant interaction yet, at no point, do they cease to exist as separate organisms. Quite the opposite: by means of their rhizomatic relation, they reaffirm their identity as separate beings, and contribute to their individual processes of permanent rhizomatic becoming, because being is not considered a fixed given condition, but a dynamic process of permanent becoming. More importantly, in spite of being independent living organisms, neither the orchid nor the wasp is here seen as a complete system in itself, but as systems existing through interaction with other systems in a process of constant becoming. The model of rhizomatic becoming can, by the same token, be extended to the relation between cultures, which, as living social systems, remain in constant flux, in a process of permanent becoming.[6]

Thus, it is clear that the notion of the rhizome, developed by Deleuze and Guattari, appears to offer ample opportunity to rethink the term transculturation and also to introduce a renewed and, possibly, more effective critical capacity. It is not my contention to replace one term with the other or to equate transculturation with the rhizome for each term belongs to a different sphere. It is clear in the work of Ortiz, for example, that transculturation belongs, and is tightly connected to, a social sphere; that is, the conflictive historical realities of different sociocultural groups which were forcefully brought into contact by the coloniser. On the other hand, Deleuze and Guattari's rhizome is much more abstract in its approach to society and culture. Therefore, by associating the notion of the rhizome with transculturation I am not attempting to jump the abyss between philosophy and sociological/anthropological work and so, misleadingly to correct the theoretical shortcomings found in transculturation. However, the (rhizomatic) connection between these two terms allows us to recast transculturation as an

---

[6] For a more elaborate interpretation of the analogy between the orchid and the wasp and its relation to transcultural architectural debates in Latin America see Hernández (2002).

endless process that is necessary for cultures in order to evolve while being impossible to achieve, at least in teleological terms. The main issue lies in the fact that the notion of rhizome provides an alternative to replace the *finaliseability* found in the term transculturation as used by Ortiz, Arguedas and Rama.[7] In many of the examples used by these theorists there is a tendency to equate transculturation with fusion of elements which, when achieved, implies the end of the process. Thus, by analogy, the rhizome introduces major dynamism thereby removing the limits to processes of cultural connectability. As shown above, the rhizome does not have a clear origin nor does it need to point towards a certain destination. It constantly establishes connections with other systems, even if they are of a different kind. The rhizome also benefits from those connections, and so do the structures to which it is connected. In this way the rhizome constantly regenerates itself but never loses its independent identity. The rhizome is never finished in itself but always in a process of becoming. More importantly, the notion of the rhizome illustrates the way in which different cultures can maintain their separate identities despite existing in a permanent relation with one another. In sum, understanding transculturation as a process of cultural rhizomatic becoming allows us to overcome some of the limitations found in Ortiz, Arguedas and Rama. This is by no means an unproblematic process of mutual interillumination between cultures. On the contrary, this approach brings to the fore the existence of a variety of structures of power —especially economic and technological— that prevent the fluent interaction between cultures from happening harmoniously and on a horizontal ground. Consequently, the notion of transculturation within architecture cannot be understood as an innocuous, exclusively descriptive, term but as a link between architecture and broader, as well as more complex, socio-political issues. Thus, the notion of architectural transculturation would reveal areas of architecture that have never been studied properly, it would also open doors for the study of minority architectural practices that have never received adequate attention and would encourage the continued exploration in search for alternative architectures that respond more appropriately to the socio-political realities of Latin American peoples.

The Transculturation of Architecture

Despite the significance of the notion of transculturation and the impact it has had, and continues to have, amongst scholars who study Latin American

---

[7] See, for example, the analogy with the parents and the child that Ortiz uses to illustrate the process of transculturation in his book *Cuban Counterpoint. Tobacco and Sugar* (Ortiz 1995), 103.

cultures, transculturation has not had a great effect on the development of either architectural theory or its different practices.

The term transculturation alone has been used occasionally in order to describe the coexistence of different socio-cultural groups within the space of the Latin American nations but not in order to theorise the effect that such coexistence has had on cities and architectural practices. It is possible that, due to a lack of rigour in their critical approach, architects and architectural theorists tend to understand notions such as transculturation, hybridisation and other similar terms in a negative way.[8] For this reason, none of the main architectural theories produced in Latin America during the second half of the twentieth century has seriously engaged with these notions as a way to analyse the complex social, cultural or political circumstances that affect the development of its cities and buildings. Neither do they engage with the work of Latin American cultural theorists such as Ortiz, Arguedas or Rama, nor with that of more contemporary scholars such as Román de la Campa, who has explored the impact of Latin American citizens on the main cities of the USA (Davies and de la Campa 2001).

Instead, Latin American architectural history and theory still rely heavily on essentialist and genealogical structures that allow architects to create systems of referentiality with which to judge architectural production. Although, admittedly, the general attitude towards architectural practices is currently changing —and this volume is testimony of that change—, I refer mainly to the work carried out in the twenty years between 1975 and 1995, which had a great deal of impact on the way we analyse Latin American architecture today. Take, for example, the work of Enrique Browne with his theory *La otra arquitectura latinoamericana* or Cristián Fernández Cox with his thesis on *La modernidad apropiada*. Both architects make an exclusive selection of buildings whose main value is found in the fact that their roots can be traced to the buildings produced by some of the great masters of modern architecture while responding to the climatic, telluric and technological conditions of Latin America.

It seems as if architects felt compelled to construct a univocal architectural narrative, which has generally depended only upon the features of a few paradigmatic buildings, those comparable with hegemonic architectural Euro-American models. However, this approach runs the risk of positing the architectural value of the buildings that have been chosen as referents on the basis of their similarity to others. In other words, the values of the so-called 'other Latin American architecture' are not inherent in the buildings themselves and in the relation they establish with the sociocultural context where they exist but in their compliance with pedagogically devised

---

[8] In fact, it seems that in the whole of the Andean region transculturation and hybridisation are understood as negative processes that threaten the homogeneity of the nation and the achievement of modernisation.

architectural narratives. Consequently, this reconstitutes a binary logic that categorises Latin American architectures as an inferior *other*.

Besides, and more importantly, such an approach to Latin American architecture overlooks and, in fact, occludes the numerous architectural practices that do not comply with the system. This is seen, for example, in the way some critics deny the architectural validity of buildings produced by the less privileged members of the society.[9] In a study carried out in the early 1980s about spontaneous settlements in Medellín, Colombia, the Colombian critic Fernando Viviescas found

> considerable expressive potential, which might form the basis for a genuine architectural position. However, the circumstances under which these 'barrios' are established prohibit a reference to architecture. Rather, we are referring to the basic, immediate and desperate need for shelter. [...] The spatial configuration of these barrios responded not so much to any authentic development initiating from within, but rather to an inevitable (given the material conditions) impoverished superimposition of ideological, aesthetic and environmental values originating in other more affluent parts of the city. [...] The result tends inevitably towards a penurious kitsch. (Viviescas in Kellett in this volume: 29)

Viviescas dismisses minority architectural practices with the argument that they are 'derivative'. This assumption confirms my view that architects and theorists tend to produce architectural hegemonic narratives that are detached from the sociocultural realities of the contexts where they exist (Colombia, in this case), thus avoiding engagement with the complex, fragmented nature of Latin American cultures. Here, Viviescas elevates the architectures of higher social classes, or more affluent parts of the city, to use his own words, to the level of originals. Consequently, he tacitly reassembles a genealogical and hierarchical architectural structure that gives authority to the architectures of certain Colombian social classes. Viviescas seems not to realise the risk of attempting to recreate a referential system with which to judge the validity of non-dominant architectures. As a result of the reconstruction of such hierarchical structures, the totality of Colombian architecture could be seen as derivative, hence inferior, with regard to Euro-American architectures that would reappear as *the* originals. This is because the architectures of those more affluent parts of the city, which Viviescas takes as an allegedly homogeneous referent, are also superimpositions of ideological, aesthetic, and environmental values originating in other more affluent sociocultural, and economic, contexts outside the nation. In consequence, the same argument used to disqualify minority practices as

---

[9] See Peter Kellett's essay 'The Construction of Home in the Informal City' included in this volume.

architecture also challenges the authority of the assumed architectural system considered referential. What is more, governmental statistics prove that the number of architectural solutions produced by rural and other migrants in Latin American cities —people who move to the city due to economic fluctuations or those displaced by violence as in the case of Colombia, for example— greatly exceeds those that have been produced by architects. Consequently, the effect that so-called informal architectures have on the image and morphology of Latin American cities is considerably larger than that of main-stream architecture. It thus follows that popular, or informal, architectures are a much representative example of the dynamic realities of Latin American cities.

The notion of architectural transculturation itself does not provide a solution for the dilemmas with which Latin American architecture is now faced. What is important about the use of this term within architectural debates is its enormous potential to connect such debates with other aspects of our cultures that require attention if we are to respond architecturally to the realities of Latin American people in more accurate ways. Due to the great number of different issues with which transculturation is intrinsically connected, it appears a useful tool in order to dismantle the essentialist, genealogical and hierarchical structures with which Latin American architectural practices have been approached. Consequently, the use of the term transculturation within architecture would open up doors to study and understand main-stream architectures in alternative ways while engaging with the whole range of architectural practices that give shape to Latin American cities.

The essays collected in this volume unveil the potential of interdisciplinary collaboration and show alternative, as well as traditional, ways to analyse Latin American architectures, spaces and urban realities transgressing the limits of merely formal analyses of buildings. This volume covers a wide spectrum of issues that range from cultural theory to the materiality of cities and buildings. Some essays engage with issues that have never been fully examined before, or at least not to the same extent as in this book, while others reveal aspects of paradigmatic Latin American architectures that had never been analysed at all. In general, the arguments put forward in this volume are situated at the interface between architecture, history, politics and social and cultural theory.

Essays are organised according to thematic areas of interest. The first section, 'Space, Place and Identity', focuses primarily on the processes through which spaces and places are produced physically and conceived psychologically as a result of people's daily life and experiences. The concept of identity, both individual and collective, is also examined in this section. Here authors engage with a wide range of cultural theories in order to challenge traditional ways of approaching Latin America. Monika Kaup and

Robert Mugerauer, for example, use the extraordinarily suggestive concept of 'fluid hybridity' in order to study processes of identity formation in the Caribbean. Peter Kellett adopts a more sociological approach in his analysis of informal domestic architecture in Colombia. He also uses the concepts of hybridity and hybridisation this time in order to endow the architectures produced by rural migrants in Colombian cities with political and architectural validity. Jane Rendell works on the notion of identity in an intriguing piece that is, at the same time, autobiographical, critical and architectural. Like Kaup and Mugerauer, Rendell elaborates on spaces of liminality and fluidity, understanding identity as identification rather than as something fixed. A similar trend is picked up by Michael Asbury who presents a comprehensive historical and critical account of the development of modern art and architecture in Brazil during the twentieth century. Section two, 'Re-Viewing the City', focuses on the way cities such as Mexico City have been imagined and represented by artists, architects, planners and cultural theorists. It also explores some of the ideologies and hidden political agendas behind the development of significant areas of the city such as El Pedregal in Mexico City. In this section, Luis Carranza revisits the Mexican avant-garde of the early twentieth century and examines critically the way in which members of the *Estridentista* movement envisioned, almost prophetically, the future of the city. Anny Brooksbank-Jones explores the place of visuality in the construction of contemporary cities. In so doing, she connects two different —and, according to many, also antagonistic— methods for the analysis of the way cities are perceived by their inhabitants. She elaborates mainly on the work of Kevin Lynch and Néstor García Canclini so as to reveal the shortcomings that exist in both their approaches. Helen Thomas concludes this section with an essay that compares the radical political connotations of the term *Heimat* in Germany with the homogenising political agenda behind the construction of modern Mexico. Thomas looks at the construction of the 'Ciudad Universitaria de Mexico' in great detail. Her analysis uncovers the historical tensions between socio-cultural groups in Mexico. The final section of this volume, 'Theorising Architectures', presents us with a series of innovative methods to analyse Latin American architectures. This section engages directly with history and cultural theory, and is abundant in linguistic and literary analogies that serve not only to interpret Latin American architectures in different ways but, also, to reveal aspects that have remained understudied for many years. The first essay in this section, for example, uses the notion of translation as a vehicle to bridge the gap between architecture and other aspects of cultural theory. By this means, this essay discloses a range of political questions that need to be addressed by architects and architectural theorists in Latin America. In the second essay, Adrian Forty also uses a linguistic analogy in order to examine the role played by concrete —a material generally linked with universalising aspirations and the elimination of cultural difference— in the formation of Brazil's modern architectural identity. Carlos Comas, for his part, contributes with a sophisticated analysis of Niemeyer's casino at Lake Pampulha. Comas demonstrates that the architectural values of the casino lay not in its similarities with other Euro-American modernist buildings, but in its differences. Sandra Vivanco also elaborates on modern Brazilian architecture and the work of Oscar Niemeyer. However, she prefers to explore the critical potential offered by the notion of the baroque as a postmodern avenue to inquire into modern Latin American architectural production. Finally, at the end of the volume, Mark Millington resumes the debate about the term transculturation opened in this introduction. While his essay does not engage directly with any of the architectural issues explored by other contributors, his thoroughgoing analysis of the concept of transculturation itself proves to be fundamental in order to understand the critical potential inherent in the term. Nonetheless, Millington is keen to emphasise that there exist a series of theoretical shortcomings also inherent in the concept of transculturation. He reminds us that no single term can be expected adequately to deal with the range of cultural processes in play in our contemporary world. Consequently, he recommends caution and warns against the facile appropriation of the term transculturation not only in architecture but also in other disciplinary areas.

Geographically, this volume covers most of Latin America: from Argentina to Mexico, Brazil to Peru and also the Caribbean. The authors whose kind contribution made this volume possible share an interest in Latin America, yet not all of them are Latin American nor do they live or practise in the continent. During the various years that we worked on this project, we communicated in different languages and our communication bridged the gaps between different disciplines and modes of practising architecture as well as between different continents.

In sum, the essays collected in this volume prove that there exist numerous ways to approach, theorise and analyse Latin American architectures. In place of essentialist, genealogical and hierarchical methods of analysis and critique that occlude the realities of Latin American cities and cultures, the contributors to this volume have directed their efforts at revealing those areas of conflict where the very fractures of Latin American cultures can be found, and where diverse and often antagonistic sociocultural groups clash and negotiate their differences. For the contributors to this volume, the complex reality of Latin American cultures is not seen as a negative feature that requires resolution. On the contrary, the articles assembled here show that the complexity of Latin American socio-cultural dynamics is pregnant with opportunities for architectural exploration both in theory and in practice.

Works Cited

Arguedas, José María (1975) *Formación de una cultura nacional indoamericana* (Mexico DF: Siglo Veintiuno Editores).

Bhabha, Homi (1994) *The Location of Culture* (London and New York: Routledge).

Davies, Mike and Román de la Campa (2001) *Magical Urbanism: Latinos Reinvent the US Big City* (New York: Verso).

Deleuze, Gilles, and Félix Guattari (1988) *A Thousand Plateaus: Capitalism and Schizophrenia* (London: Athlone Press).

García Canclini, Néstor (1995 [1989]) *Hybrid Cultures: Strategies for Entering and Leaving Modernity*, trans. Christopher L. Chiappari and Silvia L. López (Minneapolis: University of Minnesota Press).

Hernández, Felipe (2002) 'The Transcultural Phenomenon and the Transculturation of Architecture', in *Journal of Romance Studies* 2.3, 1-15.

Kellet, Peter (2005) 'The Construction of Home in the Informal City', in Felipe Hernández and Mark Millington (eds), *Transculturation: Cities, Sapce and Architecture in Latin America* (Amsterdam and Atlanta: Rodopi).

Moreiras, Alberto (2001) *The Exhaustion of Difference: The Politics of Latin American Cultural Studies* (Durham NC and London: Duke University Press).

Ortiz, Fernando (1995) *Cuban Counterpoint. Tobacco and Sugar*, trans. Harriet de Onís (Durham NC and London: Duke University Press).

Rama, Angel (1996) *The Lettered City*, trans. John Charles Chasteen (Durham NC and London: Duke University Press).

Spitta, Silvia (1995) *Between Two Waters: Narratives of Transculturation in Latin America* (Houston: Rice University Press).

Section One:

Space, Place and Identity

Reconfiguring the Caribbean's Sense of Place: From Fixed Identity to Fluid Hybridity

Monika Kaup and Robert Mugerauer

Abstract

In contrast to the traditional understanding of the Caribbean (and most other places) as having a stable (even if contested) essential identity, current re-theorisations are newly articulating the region in terms of fluid processes and hybrid characteristics. These alternative configurations provide a way to avoid the exclusionary and confrontational emphases typical of the usual contrast of global activities such as tourism and local 'senses of place'; instead, the new perspective shows how the Caribbean's 'marine spaces' provide changing sites of pluralism and exchange.

* * *

Introduction

Understanding the Caribbean's sense of place is especially difficult, not only because of its complex historical constitution from the colonial past and post-colonial struggles, but because of current trends of globalisation and post-structural, post-colonial retheorising of the built environment. The borders within this region and between the Caribbean basin and the rest of the world are especially tensed in the current political and economic situation. Here globalised tourism provides an especially fruitful lens for exploring the dynamics of the forces attempting to maintain or unbind traditional identities. Tourism does offer the possibility of new modes of exchange; but, at the same time, it requires critique because many of its commodifications and objectifications genuinely threaten the Caribbean's distinctive sense of place. In addition, current shifts in theory provide a strategy through which the Caribbean Sea is being reinterpreted as offering a new mode of compromise with and resistance to globalised tourism, actually disrupting the dominant understanding of sense of place —as centred and with a stable identity. This currently dominant view, especially as presented in the phenomenological research literature on 'authentic' places such as the New Mexican Pueblos (Saile 1989), Mediterranean coastal villages (Violich 1989), or Khartoum (Norberg-Schultz 1979), is being contested by post-structuralist, post-colonial approaches that would replace the 'fixed' with fluid spaces, language and architecture that are decentred and hybrid.

Methodologically, this essay will contrast two interpretations of the Caribbean's sense of place by comparing the 'classic' phenomenological approach (Tuan 1977, Relph 1978, Norberg-Schultz 1985) to the alternative, emerging post-structuralist, post-colonial counterpoetics of creolisation developed by Francophone Caribbean writers such as Édouard Glissant (Glissant and Dash 1992 and Glissant 1997) and Patrick Chamoiseau (1997). The planning and architectural evidence shows how globalisation in the form of tourism is double-edged: both threatening the local sense of place and providing the economic basis for local hosts to carry out their own autonomous agendas. The Francophone postcolonial theorists make clear that effective strategies for liberating the oppressed voice of the Caribbean other are to stay where and who they are, not to travel to a better place elsewhere, and to dissolve the solid ground of dominant identity through the central trope of the sea and fluid alterity.

Alternative Senses of Place: A Phenomenology of the Caribbean as Tropical Paradise

Phenomenology provides the dominant approach to sense of place. It has been a major achievement since the 1970s for phenomenologists to turn their attention to the built and natural environments, thus providing a non-arbitrary description and interpretation of person-world patterns. By applying the methodology, especially as developed by Martin Heidegger (1962 and 1971) and Maurice Merleau-Ponty (1962), cultural geographers, anthropologists and sociologists, historians, and planning and architecture critics have begun to explore empirically the ways in which physical, social and often spiritual phenomena form coherent patterns. It appears that when these dimensions exhibit a high degree of 'mutual responsiveness', both inhabitants and visitors experience a strong sense of place; congruently, when the coherence is absent, the environment is experienced as placeless. The character of the particular material, cultural and sometimes sacred features, as well as the distinctive mode of 'gathering together' as Heidegger calls it, amounts to what we call sense of place (Mugerauer 1994 and 1998, Seamon 1979).

Given the variety and complexity of places and the method's stress on the every-day life-world, phenomenologies of place have focused on describing small, especially coherent and often traditional or ordinary places: villages, market places, and houses (Seamon and Norden 1980, Richardson 1982, Mugerauer 1985 and 1992). Because of the difficulties of the project, the inherent focus of phenomenology and the character of the places chosen, the places described are seen and interpreted as relatively stable or timeless. As to the first of these aspects, it is very difficult to describe anything as complex as a natural or built environment, the person-world dynamic that constitutes a place. Not surprisingly, then, the first phenomenologies of place properly engaged a modest range of simple places. Beyond this, of course, it needs to be noted that phenomenology does seek the essential features of the things it would describe. Many phenomenologists, along with most traditional philosophers, understand these essential features to be stable or timeless; others, especially Heidegger (1977), have developed a very sophisticated interpretation of time and history which allows an explanation of both how things have an essential character as they appear within each historical epoch or 'world' and yet how that essential character changes from one major epoch to another.

Further, the essential features of phenomena obviously vary according to the phenomena themselves, where all places may not be the same. In the cases of the Zuni 'cosmic' landscape (Saile 1989) or Irish Holy Wells (Brenneman 1989), for example, it would appear that they have remained substantially as they are for a long time. That is not to deny that traditional environments change, but only to note that they have at least an extraordinary continuity. The most ambitious phenomenologies of place, such as Christian Norberg-Schultz's (1979), do consider places such as Rome, Khartoum or Budapest that have changed over time or as the result of different cultural groups or historical epochs that can be correlated with distinctive built environments in the same location. Frances Violich (1998) elaborated his initial, basic phenomenology of Dalmatian coastal villages into a more comprehensive description of the region's historical identity and changes under political duress. Mugerauer has worked on a continuing series of analyses of the multiple and contested senses of place of Austin, Texas (1988; 1989; 1996; Mugerauer and Branch 1996: 4, 5, 12; Mugerauer and Thorsheim 2004). These projects amount to a more elaborate hermeneutical phenomenology, where the hermeneutical dimension traces changes over varying temporal or spatial horizons, thus complementing the more atemporal phenomenological orientation.

In addition, given the background, experiences and interests of active researchers, it is not surprising that the earlier descriptions emphasised places in Europe, the Mediterranean and North America; more recently, no doubt as part of the trend toward pluralism or diversity of all the environmental disciplines, increased attention has been given to tropical environments, with arguments being developed that hot and humid landscapes constitute a distinctive type and descriptions made of dwelling forms and behaviours (Richardson 1980 and 1982; Devakula 1998; Mugerauer 1995; Mugerauer and Rimby 1994).

In any case, it is clear that a relatively fixed set of 'essential' features of the Caribbean have long been experienced, implicitly and explicitly recognised, and appreciated-exploited by many Europeans and North Americans. Ever since 'Cuba, the pearl of the Antilles, had startled

Christopher Columbus with its lush tropical beauty and sweetly scented air, the Caribbean has been and still is interpreted by explorers, investors, tourists, and researchers alike as a Tropical Paradise' (Schwartz 1997: 42). To note one paradigmatic case or sub-area, Cuba has consistently been seen as 'a paradise on earth' (Gibson, cited in Pérez 1999: 17) or, as Rosalie Schwartz wonderfully documents it, as a 'Pleasure Island' (1997), a description supported by a large body of popular media and academic research literature (Blednick 1988; Judd and Fainstein 1999; Ryan 1997; Pérez 1999).

Figure 1: Tropical Paradise
The Caribbean's Stable Sense of Place and Identity
(Península de Ancón, Cuba)
©Robert Mugerauer & Monika Kaup

Given the Caribbean's identity as a tropical paradise, since that is the dominant sense of place as the phenomenon is currently constructed, two aspects are worth special attention (both of which could be generalised beyond the Caribbean with little effort). First, the stable image of the Caribbean is highly selective given the full range of phenomena that present themselves. Second, the basic, distinctive sense of place is a dimension of the Caribbean's human-natural dynamic that would seemingly be the very opposite of the homogeneity and placelessness of international modernity; yet, simultaneously, this very sense of place is also promoted, utilised and even consumed by global tourism.

As noted, phenomenologists of place and identity often describe traditional environments such as the New Mexican pueblos, Italian hill towns and Mediterranean coastal villages. In the Caribbean, attention is turned to centred and stable features such as the coasts' or islands' white sanded beaches with palm trees and coral reefs; or, in urban settings, to memorable, romantic places such as Cuba's La Habana Vieja or the Malecón. When the Mexican government developed Cancún and nearby sites such as Chichén Itzá, Tulum, Isla Mujeres, Cozumel and Xel-ha, the area was chosen in part because of local economic needs, but largely because of the wonderful long stretch of beaches with brilliant sand (95-97% calcium carbonate, the rest silicates and carbon), 243 days of sun a year, cooling breezes to mitigate the heat, with wonderful water and coral reefs (as well as Nichupté Lagoon) alive with tropical fish, and, finally, Maya ruins (Bosselman 1978, Heirnaux-Nicolas 1999, Wong 1993: 55-65). Similarly, Cuba has 289 beaches as well as a tradition of sport fishing associated with the romantic name of Ernest Hemingway; in addition it has historic sites and a rich Spanish colonial heritage (Barclay 1990). It also is commonly remarked that since the U.S. trade embargo of 1962, which prohibited U.S. citizens from travelling to Cuba, the enticement of the 'forbidden' has enhanced the Island's allure for many. As to individual and social experiences, suffice it to say that tourism in the nineteenth and twentieth centuries has revolved around the perception of the Caribbean as a source of pleasure, an image in which the essential sensual and exotic dimensions have been carefully cultivated (Schwartz 1997; Blednick 1988; Judd and Fainstein 1999; Ryan 1997; Espino 1993).

Against this background, it is not surprising that for the early revolutionary society 'tourism was perceived as too closely associated with capitalist evils of prostitution, drugs, gambling and organised crime' to be encouraged (Espino 1993: 110). Yet, even under Cuban governmental authority today, the 'come-on' remains the same, acknowledging and exploiting the old essential characteristics. Visitors are still lured with the reputation of a permissive paradise. The pitch is low —but effective, effective enough to require the paternalistic protection of the moral character of local residents from the influences of tourists and their preferred activities. As noted by travel writer Pico Iyer, the basic message on Cubatur brochures remains: 'Ven a vivir una tentación!' (Come to live out a temptation!) (Iyer 1997: 380).

Clearly, throughout the Caribbean, the 'hosts' to tourism are neither silent nor passive in relation to global economic forces. In fact, there are usually multiple hosts with differing agendas: national public leaders and population by extension, local government authorities, local residents, immigrating workers and international capital partners. To simplify, it appears that the initial motivation and power for tourism development comes from capital systems and central governments. While the latter explicitly intend to serve tourists in order to benefit local populations, as noted, they also sacrifice some dimensions of the local for the greater regional and national good, which requires a complex series of changes in order to distribute justly the goods and harms at all levels. The Mexican governmental goals, articulated by politicians and institutions (*National Council for Tourism*, 1961; *National Tourism Development Plan*, 1962) include increasing currency flow into Mexico as a whole, generating new jobs outside urban centres, countering patterns of regional inequality and political instability (Hiernaux-Nicolas 1999; Enriquez Savignac 1972; Bosselman 1978). Cuba's leadership has stated similar goals, explicitly dedicating the effort to 'achieve socialist values', through the 'equal distribution of goods, services, opportunities'; to 'enhance visitors' cultural and ideological awareness by [...] convincing them of the superiority of socialism;' and to 'avoid introducing "anti-socialist", "revisionist" or "capitalist" influences to "turn the heads" of the indigenous population working in the tourist industry and coming into contact with foreign tourists' (Hall 1992). National governments, then, obviously promote their own value systems.

That is not to say that the visitors' and hosts' often different interests and ways of life seamlessly blend together in the same spaces. The agreement on the essential identity of the region occurs even while its desirability is contested —while tolerated and exploited for visitors, many dimensions of a permissive paradise are not seen by national governments as good or desirable for local peoples. Given the power of tourists' preferences and desires, the need to preserve, or at least foster, the prospect of an experience of tropical paradise, unspoiled by the realities of actual tourism and current economic and social disparities, may largely be the source of the phenomenon of ghettoisation. 'Much criticism is made of [these] exclusive tourist "bubbles" or "ghettoes", such as [in Jamaica, the Yucatan Peninsula, or] Antigua's Mill Reef [...] on the grounds that they appropriate the choicest sites, exclude non-elite locals (except as menial employees) and fail to contribute to the well-being of adjacent settlements' (Weaver 1988: 319; cf. Weaver 1998; Judd 1999: 35-53; Blednick 1988; Britton 1980; Freitag 1994). Inversely, host powers may act paternalistically to separate locals from tourists as a 'means of protecting the traditional way of life from "contamination" by tourists', as happens in the Maldives (Domroes 1985) and Cuba, where the government's controversial policy intends to protect Cubans from the social-moral harms of tourists by prohibiting those not working at the enclave resorts (especially Varadero and Cayo Largo) and urban facilities (especially in Old Havana) from having access to many beaches, hotels, restaurants, clubs and tourist taxis (Espino 1993: 107; Gebler 1987; Gibson 1987; *GWR* 1990; Hall 1992: 116-18; Iyer 1997; Schwartz 1997: 210; Suckling 1999: 119).

Given these shifts in power and the replacement of local systems with those of international capitalism, it is not surprising that many critics argue that tourism is a new neo-colonialism (Gayle and Goodrich 1993: 11). In the worst cases, it is claimed, tourism amounts to an imperialism that may result in 'the hatred of the rich, the arrogance and the neo-colonialist appearance of the tourists' (Negi 1990; Nash, 1989). Tourism in the Caribbean during the dependency period of the 1970s, complicated by the dominance of tourists from North America and Europe who were served by darker-skinned locals, generated what became known as Black servility theory (Erisman 1983; Pérez 1973-74; Harrigan 1974; Finney and Watson 1975; Weaver 1988; Shivji 1973; Tabb 1988; Lea 1988; Pleumarom 1992; Plog 1987; Nash 1996; Freitag 1994) and attendant local anger (as articulated by Jamaica Kincaid in *A Small Place* [1988]).

The Caribbean's unspoiled islands and waters and its sensuous cities are perceived and experienced by many tourists and others as 'authentic', indeed as persisting despite the pressures to change. But, precisely this aesthetic of the 'authentic' or the 'indigenous' is brought into the service of global tourism, which seeks and promotes exotic realms such as the Caribbean. The natural environments focused upon by the international environmental community as well as global tourism are often uncritically constituted by 'aesthetic' and 'exoticising' filters. The Caribbean's fragile coral reefs, colourful marine life, barrier islands, water exchange systems and tropical forests that form the fantastic image of 'paradise' are important to the westernised consciousness of tourists and researchers alike; but there is little or no touristic concern for the ordinary agricultural land in any of these areas, nor for everyday rural life. Thus, the dominant sense of place, which amounts to a centred and fixed bio-cultural-regional (or local) identity, apparently will not hold against globalisation's reductive processes.

Tourism has emerged as a major circuitry in the global flows of capitalism partly because earlier processes have been refined, making fuller use of the imagery of desire and virtual as well as physical environments in vertically integrated systems that transform historical and newly exotic locations, producing astonishing profits. Clearly, tourists, Caribbean governments, international corporations and local businesses do appropriate features of the environments by using stereotyped concepts and images of the 'tropical' and 'exotic pleasures', with little concern for the existing environmental or cultural traditions. The public-sector partners in these developments sacrifice the sites, severing them from the continuous fabric of everyday life. The tourists visiting these destinations have little interest in connections with the fine-grained natural and social patterns and do indeed colonise them through their aggressive expectations for specific types of accommodations, services and entertainment.

Since the often differing values and agendas of host areas, tourists, and the international systems allow for both mutual self-interested interactions and exploitation, and since the globalised flows of capitalism do appropriate marketable aesthetic factors, it is not surprising that the Caribbean's stable sense of place and identity, which conceptually has been seen as opposite to global homogenisation, is itself used by —is in danger of being co-opted by— tourism.

Of course, a full phenomenology of the Caribbean, complete with variations, remains to be done. The project would involve a detailed discussion of the ways indigenous peoples, successive waves of outsiders (Spanish, French, English, Dutch, German, Chinese, Indian, Muriaco, Loango, Real, Carabali, Arará, Mandinga, Lucumí, North American, to begin a list), and professional practitioners of international modernism and eclectic post-modernism have responded to the various micro-climates and natural features. Responses to light and colour, variable humidity and rainfall, plant, animal and fish life, and diverse building materials need to be registered. Attention would have to be given to the multiple bio-regions that range from the usually emphasised rainforest to the arid areas such as Bonaire or the exposed environments resulting from deforestation; it would have to elaborate the differing cultural built forms, the agricultural, fishing and production practices (from plantations to manufacturing), the religious observations and social customs-behaviour patterns (from clothing, sexuality, music, daily routines to diet and the use of tobacco and rum).

Transcultural dynamics would have to be traced out. Obviously transculturation in the Caribbean is not the same as that for all of Latin America, but the Caribbean does combine aspects of Mediterranean and local cultures in the marketplace, for example, or in the baroque architecture and literature that runs from European origins to the New World Baroque, or in the retention of preferred forms such as dense urban settlements. Then too, there are rich connections from the plantation tradition to the Levant, Asia and Europe. We would expect that such a full phenomenological description would belie the understanding of the Caribbean as having but one identity, much less a fixed one. Whether there might be a deeper set of essential features, perhaps epochally varying, that would adequately describe this complex region over the last five hundred years remains to be seen.

Interpreting the Caribbean's complex sense of place, of course, need not be limited to the phenomenological approach. This is especially important since it turns out that, though many factions agree that the Caribbean has an essential identity and that it largely consists of the place's manifestation as a tropical paradise, their symbiotic relations are paired with what appear to be unavoidable exclusions and oppositions concerning fundamental values and practices. A further question thus presents itself: is there a way in which international and local systems may open up to each other, but in which new, alternative languages and modes of building might articulate a sense of place that is unlike traditional centred sites of fixed identity, and that, by emphasising differences, might better be able to resist globalisation's homogenisation and, perhaps, even its oppositions and exclusions?

The Post-Structuralist Articulation of the Caribbean as Fluid Resistance

Instead of attempting to opt out of the flows of global capital (which is self-defeating in today's globalised economy), or to oppose them through hostile confrontation (which cuts off tourism and exchange, as is seen by the exclusions of Haiti and Cuba from the systems of flow or from Jamaica's difficulty in again becoming a desirable destination after attacks on tourists), more subtle forms of coexistence and resistance appear to be emerging in the Caribbean. In agreement with current trajectories of politicised theory, the Caribbean theorists of creolisation conceptualise an indirect 'dissolution' rather than a direct confrontation or deconstruction. Specifically, this line of force is found in Édouard Glissant and Michel Dash's *Caribbean Discourse* (1992) and *Poetics of Relation* (1997) and Patrick Chamoiseau's novel, *Texaco* (1997). Since the 1960s, postcolonial and feminist intellectuals have become more sceptical about the possibility of radical opposition to the dominant colonial or patriarchal power, as advocated by Negritude and Fanonism, and more perceptive about the ways that such radical opposition actually mimics that which it opposes. Thus, tactics of opposition named by Glissant, in the absence of a 'proper' space and language of resistance, are ruses and detours. Glissant in his theories of creolisation and hybridity and Chamoiseau in his novel *Texaco* outline borderlands between binary opposites, a mode of resistance that is a third term between the absolutes of coloniser and colonised. By halting the escalation of challenge and counter-challenge, these theorists and writers eschew the logic of dominance and authority; originating from 'below' rather than imposing themselves from 'above', this counterpoetics of difference operates by acceptance and inclusion, rather than rejection and exclusion.

These postmodern writers and theorists of Caribbean culture, ranging from Glissant and the creolists from Martinique to Antonio Benítez-Rojo from Cuba, articulate the Caribbean Sea as ex-centric and limitless (Kaup 2004). According to the creole poetics of cross-cultural relations, the Caribbean Sea is a space of encounter, a site of a localised poetics of the between that itself remains unaffected even as it lets the many forms of 'passing through' occur. Those who would interrupt the place that is the Caribbean, on voyages of discovery or conquest —in our case, to visit or profit as part of global tourism— pass by, but neither experience nor inhabit the sea as place. In the words of Luce Irigaray,

> Their passage leaves no permanent trace. Once they are gone, she returns to her rhythm and her measure. Even as the ships cross over her, she remains. The same. Incorruptible. And she laughs as they move onward, seeking the secret of their truth. (Irigaray 1991: 48)

The sea cannot be conquered by linear passage. She cannot be forced to surrender to a quest for knowledge and projections from afar that avoid entering into reciprocal relation between self and other. Instead, the sea as place (rather than passage-to-somewhere or to-something else) is excess, rapture, an inclusive vastness that contains and 'undoes all perspectives' (Irigaray 1991: 47), including those of tourism. Here linear-appropriative passage is negated and the singularity of place affirmed, with a new and positive order immanent in relationships, without fixing its identity in terms of transcendent goals or projects. With the structures of distance and one-directional knowledge cleared away, all parties need to risk abandoning themselves to the closeness and touch required for non-reductive encounters —a border zone of mutual and multi-dimensional exchanges.

Just as outsiders' attempts to 'overcome' the fluid sea by universalising linear passages are resisted and outlasted by the place that is the sea, Glissant and Chamoiseau say that the non-western other is opaque, that creolisation is opposed to Manichean oppositions, and that its language is fluid, in other words, its mode of speaking is orality. The argument of Glissant and Chamoiseau is made at two levels, the level of (Caribbean) space and identity and (creole) language.

Why posit a borderland poetics of cross-cultural relations rather than a doctrine of, say, insurgent and univocal 'blackness'? One answer is that the non-western Other is 'opaque'. Glissant writes, 'We demand the right to opacity'; but, 'The opaque is not the same as the obscure [...]. It is that which cannot be reduced [...]' (Glissant 1997: 189, 191). Directed against the 'requirement for transparency', which Glissant notices is the basis of '"understanding" people and ideas from the perspective of Western thought', opacity affirms the right to difference, and thus a right to not being wholly understood. If Glissant opposes Western universalisation, he is also consistent in opposing non-western modes of nationalist mono-culturalism. Thus, 'the right to opacity [...] is not enclosure within an impenetrable autarchy but subsistence within an irreducible singularity' (Glissant 1997: 190).

Figure 2: Fluidity and Inclusion
Hybrid Encounters and Environments in Cienfuegos, Cuba
©Robert Mugerauer & Monika Kaup

This equation of creolisation with process, inclusion and the rejection of closure is the core of Glissant's disagreement not only with the 'male warrior' doctrine of Negritude, but also with his students, the Creolistes Jean Bernabé, Patrick Chamoiseau and Raphael Confiant, so named for their (in)famous 1989 manifesto, *Eloge de la créolité* (*In Praise of Creoleness*), in which they assert the closure of Creole identity by exclusion: 'Neither Europeans, nor Africans, nor Asians, we proclaim ourselves Creoles' (Bernabé et al. 1989: 13). In *Poetics of Relation*, published a year after the Creoliste manifesto, Glissant clarifies his dissent from Creolity, affirming cross-culturalism as process (not product) and capturing it through the progressive and plural term, 'creolisations'. He argues that 'creolisation, one of the ways of forming a complex mix —and not merely a linguistic result— is only exemplified by its processes and certainty, not by the "contents" on which these operate' (Glissant 1997: 89).

Glissant calls his non-reductive concept of cultural hybridity 'relation-identity', as distinct from the so-called 'root-identity'. Root-identity derives from a single place of origin, for example, Africa or Europe. In contrast, 'relation-identity' cannot construct linear, transoceanic passages between a singular (African) past and a (Caribbean) present and future. The constitution of creole 'relation' works like the marine currents of the Caribbean Sea, connecting diverse places and people in multiple directions. (This move is part of the deployment of a new sense of place as 'always becoming' as Deleuze and Guattari would put it, distinct from what can be seen as a fixed and essential or 'root' identity as described in the phenomenological approach. For the latter, there generally would be agreement that the Caribbean has a fixed essential identity that may be understood in terms of oppositions but disagreement about whether it is 'europeanness' or 'blackness' or some other privileged pole of a binary set that is the positive term matching up with 'place' in the 'place'-'placelessness' pair.

In *Texaco*, a historical novel celebrating the creole Caribbean, Chamoiseau traces the creolisation of Martinique's black majority population, spanning two centuries from slavery to the late twentieth century. Opacity in *Texaco* is operative as black Martinicans, ex-slaves and descendants of slaves, are cut off from their African roots. Neither African nor French, uprooted from their African lineage, black Martinicans had to embark on a trajectory of relation-identity in a cultural no-man's land. This void becomes a fertile interval of creolisation between the French culture of Martinique's white settlers and the lost or opaque cultures and languages of their African ancestors. Creole, the Martinican vernacular, embodies the complex and makeshift nature of the speakers' identity. Originated as a contact language between African slaves and white slave-owners, Creole does not offer blacks a self-enclosing space of autonomy because the creole vernacular is too familiar or 'transparent' to Martinique's white upper classes to engender black separatism. At the same time, its 'openness to otherness' is an asset, enabling the assertion of lived difference.

Texaco recreates the dialogics of the Creole world through a multi-layered narrative voice. Following the convention of testimonial narrative, the story of the shantytown Texaco, as told by its female founder (Marie-Sophie Laborieux) to 'the Christ' (an urban planner), is narrated by two fictional editors (the Haitian Ti-Cirique and the Martinican Oiseau de Cham, called 'The Word Scratcher'). Fictional editors Ti-Cirique and Oiseau de Cham embody the battle over the hybrid vernacular of Martinique. Ti-Cirique, humanistic intellectual and advocate of high culture, wants Caribbean literary French to live up to a universal standard, 'a French more French than the French' (Chamoiseau 1997: 9). Oiseau de Cham, in contrast, believes in creole as a home-made vernacular for a homemade world. His doctrine, 'literature in a place that breathes is to be taken in alive', affirms a living language on the borders of standard French, whose 'excesses should be preserved in literature. Here creole space and creole language are consistent: just as the residents of Texaco are squatting on the fringes of oil giant Texaco's land and the city, Fort-de-France, so the Creole vernacular is squatting on the fringes of the French language. Against the view of the hierarchical powers, the minority of the Word Scratcher, and by extension, Chamoiseau, view the squatting as positive —as a creole poetics of relation.

This returns us to the idea of place as between versus that of passage-through by the rest of the world. The most striking description in *Texaco* of the shantytown as a border site on the creole fringe of the French colonial world comes from the urban planner. Converted from his initial mission of razing the shantytown for urban renewal, the urban planner now writes as the 'saviour' of Texaco, describing the preservation of vernacular architecture in terms of fluid, de-centred differences:

> I understood that Texaco was not what Westerners call a shantytown, but a mangrove swamp, an urban mangrove swamp. The swamp seems initially hostile to life. It's difficult to admit that this anxiety of roots, of mossy shades, of veiled waters, could be such a cradle of life for crabs, fish, crayfish, the marine ecosystem. It seems to belong to neither land nor sea, somewhat like Texaco is neither City nor country. Yet City draws strength from Texaco's urban mangroves, as it does from those of other urban quarters, exactly like the sea repeoples itself with that vital tongue which ties it to the mangroves' chemistry. Swamps need the regular caress of the waves; to reach its potential and its function as renaissance, Texaco needs City to caress it; meaning: it needs consideration.
> (Chamoiseau 1997: 263)

Neither land nor sea, neither the Martiniquan capital city nor the hinterland of historical maroonage, neither French nor African, Texaco yet needs to contact and be nourished by both dimensions. Texaco incarnates Glissant's relation-identity —an intermediate and fertile site. Over the thirty years during which Texaco has been razed and rebuilt countless times, the squatter's collective battle against the city has forged a common creole identity and memory. But the most climactic feat of creolisation is the conversion of the 'Western urban planner'. Whereas formerly he saw 'shantytowns as a tumour on the urban order, [...] [as] a threat', after his creolisation, he comes to believe that 'we must dismiss the West and re-learn to read: learn to reinvent the city. Here the urban planner must think Creole before he even thinks' (Chamoiseau 1997: 269-70).

Figure 3: The Mangrove Manifests Relation-Identity:
A Fertile Site Intermediate between Sea and Land (South Coast of Cuba).
© Robert Mugerauer & Monika Kaup

So, we have in the literature, just as in the physical realm, environments that are characterised by multiple places and multiple languages, side by side, with each one generated out of, sustained by and porous to the others. Here continuing encounter is crucial. Along with global capitalism's company towns (and a few remaining plantations), we have the tourism enclaves that exist as parallel universes to —and co-generators with— local urban and rural backstages. We have emphasised the Caribbean poetics of resistance and hybridity, which clearly plays out as a poetics of fluid, ex-centric space in architecture and urban development. Thus we arrive again at the distinctive character of the Caribbean. The Caribbean sense of place is not one; the myriad forms, including the 'colonial' ones, are not mere representations, but continuously renewed and fruitful hybrid productions.

Given the possibility of a fluid sea that resists globalisation insofar as it is an ex-centric place in itself that allows the passage of the tourist-others across it, without recourse to opposition or hiding, we have the emergence of a new type of place, so that the encounters that occur through tourism in the Caribbean need not be exploitative, though they often are. They may occur, as Deleuze and Guattari would put it, in the almost unavoidable stratified systems of the dominant or major culture, architecture and language (as centred and fixed places in global space); but, they also involve becoming other —continually generated by differences still becoming as minor variations, specifically as Creole languages and the Caribbean's hybrid built environment. In the Caribbean Sea there are apparently two worlds, two symbiotic universes: the spaces of globalised, homogenising international tourism with their fixed sense of place as exotic paradise and the fluid local places that may host, but not succumb to tourism, that manage to elude and resist the globalisation whose structures play across the Caribbean's fluid surfaces. Thus, in addition to the traditional tropical paradise, in the Caribbean Sea we find a submarine and eccentric place, where a new line of force is underway, always becoming minority, always keeping its differences dynamically alive.

Works Cited

Barclay, J. (1990) 'Castro's Revolution of Restoration', in *The Independent*, 12 December, 6-9.

Bernabé, Jean, Patrick Chamoiseau, and Raphael Confiant (1989) *Eloge de la créolité* (Paris: Presses Universitaires Créoles).

Blednick, P. (1988) *Another Day in Paradise? The Real Club Med Story* (Toronto: Macmillan of Canada).

Bosselman, Fred P. (1978) *In the Wake of the Tourist: Managing Special Places in Eight Countries* (Washington DC: Conservation Foundation).

Brenneman, Walter L. Jr. (1989) 'The Circle and the Cross: The Holy Wells of Ireland', in David Seamon and Robert Mugerauer (eds), *Dwelling, Place, Environment* (New York: Columbia University Press), 137-58.

Britton, S. (1980) 'The Spatial Organisation of Tourism in a Neo-colonial Economy: A Fiji Case Study', in *Pacific Viewpoint* 21: 144-65.

Chamoiseau, Patrick (1997) *Texaco* (New York: Vintage Books).

Devakula, Piyalada (1998) *A Tradition Rediscovered: An Interpretive Study of Meanings and Experiences of the Traditional Thai House* (Ann Arbor: University of Michigan, Dissertation).

Domroes, M. (1985) 'Tourism Resources and Their Development in the Maldive Islands', in *Geojournal* 10, 119-26.

Enriquez Savignac, Antonio (1972) 'The Computer Planning and Coordination of Cancun Island, Mexico: A New Resort Complex', in *The Values of Travel Research: Planning, Techniques, Applications* (Wheaton, CO: The Travel Research Association), 107-16.

Erisman, H. (1983) 'Tourism and Cultural Dependency in the West Indies', in *Annals of Tourism Research* 10, 337-61.

Espino, Maria Dolores (1993) 'Tourism in Socialist Cuba', in Dennis J. Gayle and Jonathan N. Goodrich (eds), *Tourism Marketing and Management in the Caribbean* (New York: Routledge), 101-10.

Finney, B. and Watson K. (eds.) (1975) *A New Kind of Sugar: Tourism in the Pacific* (Honolulu: East-West Center).

Freitag, T.G. (1994) 'Enclave Tourism Development: For Whom the Benefits Roll?', in *Annals of Tourism Research* 21, 538-54.

Gayle, Dennis J. and Jonathan N. Goodrich (eds) (1993) *Tourism Marketing and Management in the Caribbean* (New York: Routledge).

18 *Monika Kaup and Robert Mugerauer*

Gebler, Carlo (1987) 'At the Beach, Santa Maria and Varadero', in Alan Ryan (ed), *The Reader's Companion to Cuba* (New York: Harcourt Brace & Company), 319-44.

Gibson, Graeme (1987) 'Santiago and Beyond', in Alan Ryan (ed), *The Reader's Companion to Cuba* (New York: Harcourt Brace & Company), 304-18.

Glissant, Édouard and Michel Dash (1992) *Caribbean Discourse* (Charlottesville: University of Virginia Press).

Glissant, Édouard (1997) *Poetics of Relation* (Ann Arbor: University of Michigan Press).

GWR (Granma Weekly Review) (22 July 1990).

Hall, Derek R. (1992) 'Tourism Development in Cuba', in D. Harrison (ed), *Tourism and the Less Developed Countries* (London: Belhaven Press), 102-20.

Harrigan, N. (1974) 'The Legacy of Caribbean History and Tourism', in *Annals of Tourism Research* 2, 13-25.

Heidegger, Martin (1962) *Being and Time* (New York: Harper and Row).
——— (1971) *Poetry, Language, Thought* (New York: Harper and Row).
——— (1977) *The Question Concerning Technology* (New York: Harper and Row).

Hiernaux-Nicolas, Daniel (1999) 'Cancún Bliss', in Dennis R. Judd and Susan S. Fainstein (eds), *The Tourist City* (New Haven: Yale University Press), 124-38.

Irigaray, Luce (1991) *Marine Lover of Friedrich Nietzsche* (New York: Columbia University Press).

Iyer, Pico (1997) 'Holguin, Santiago, Havana, the Beach — 1987-1992', in Alan Ryan (ed), *The Reader's Companion to Cuba* (New York: Harcourt Brace & Company), 372-89.

Judd, Dennis R. and Susan Fainstein (eds) (1999) *The Tourist City* (New Haven: Yale University Press).

Kaup, Monika (2004) 'The Sea That Is Not One: Fluid Hybridity in Caribbean Discourse' presented at 'Hybrid Americas', the Bielefeld Symposium (2002, Germany) and translated into Spanish in AMEC (Asociación Mexicana de Estudios Caribeños), UNAM, Mexico, forthcoming (2004).

Kincaid, Jamaica (1988) *A Small Place* (London: Virago Press).

Lea, J. (1988) *Tourism and Development in the Third World* (New York: Routledge).

Merleau-Ponty, Maurice (1962) *A Phenomenology of Perception* (New York: Humanities Press)

Mugerauer, Robert (1985) 'Midwestern Yards', in *Places* 2:2, 31-38.

———— (1988) 'Austin as Gathering Place: Images and the Emergence of Urban Environment', presented at Spirit of Place Conference, University of California at Davis, unpublished.

———— (1989) 'Images of Austin', in *Community and Regional Planning Program Working Paper Series* (Austin: University of Texas' CRP Program).

———— (1992) 'Toward an Architectural Vocabulary: The Porch as Between', in David Seamon (ed), *Dwelling, Seeing, and Designing: Toward a Phenomenological Ecology* (Albany, NY: SUNY Press), 103-28.

———— (1994) *Interpretations on Behalf of Place* (Albany, NY: SUNY Press).

———— (1995) 'Body, Settlement, Landscape: A Comparison of Hot and Cool Humid Patterns', in *Traditional Dwellings and Settlements Review* VII: 1, 25-32

———— (1996) 'Austin's Contested Identity and the Symbolic Analysts', in Dennis Crow (ed), *Geography and Identity: Exploring and Living the Geopolitics of Identity* (Washington, DC: Mainsonneuve Press), 307-36.

———— (1998) 'Phenomenology and Vernacular Architecture', in Paul Oliver (ed), *Encyclopedia of Vernacular Architecture of the World* (London: Basil Blackwell).

———— (2003) 'Toward a Phenomenology of Hot and Humid Landscapes', in Wayne Attoe (ed), *Architecture and Planning for Hot and Humid Climate* (Baton Rouge: Louisiana State University) (forthcoming).

Mugerauer, Robert and Branch, Shelly (1996) 'High-Technology Landscapes and the Quality of Life', in *Platform*, 4.5, 4, 5, 12.

Mugerauer, Robert and Rimby, Grant (1994) 'Learning from Maya Architecture: Cosmography > Humanistic Concerns > Style', in Andrew Seidel (ed), *Banking on Design* (College Station, TX: Texas A&M), 112-24.

Mugerauer, Robert and Thorsheim, K. (2004) 'Go-Back: Contested Land in Transition', submitted to *Landscape*.

Nash. D. (1989) 'Tourism as a Form of Imperialism', in V. Smith (ed) *Hosts and Guests: the Anthropology of Tourism*, 2nd ed. (Philadelphia: University of Pennsylvania Press), 37-54.

———— (1996) *Anthropology of Tourism* (London: Pergamon).

Negi, Jagmohan (1990) *Tourism Development and Resource Conservation* (New Delhi: Metropolitan).

Norberg-Schulz, Christian (1979) *Genius Loci* (New York: Rizzoli).

———— (1985) *The Concept of Dwelling* (New York: Rizzoli).

Pérez, L.A. (1973-74) 'Aspects of Underdevelopment: Tourism in the West Indies', in *Science and Society* 37.4, 473-80.

Pérez, Louis Jr. (1999) *On Becoming Cuban: Identity, Nationality, and Culture* (Chapel Hill: The University of North Carolina Press).

Pleumarom, A. (1992) 'The Political Economy of Tourism', in *Ecologist* 24, 142-48.

Plog, S. (1987) 'Understanding Psychographics in Tourism Research', in J.R.B. Ritchie and C. R. Goeldner (eds), *Travel, Tourism, and Hospitality Research: A Handbook for Managers and Researchers* (New York: John Wiley and Sons), 302-13.

Relph, Edward (1978) *Place and Placelessness* (London: Pion).

Richardson, Miles (1980) 'Culture and the Urban Stage', in I. Altman et al. (eds), *Human Behavior and Environment* (New York: Plenum Press), 209-42.

―――― (1982) 'Being-in-the-Market Versus Being-in-the-Plaza: Material Culture and the Construction of Social Reality in Spanish America', in *American Ethnologist* 9, 421-36.

Ryan, Alan (ed) (1997) *The Reader's Companion to Cuba* (New York: Harcourt Brace & Company).

Saile, David (1989) 'Many Dwellings: Views of a Pueblo World', in David Seamon and Robert Mugerauer (eds), *Dwelling, Place, Environment* (New York: Columbia University Press), 159-82.

Schwartz, Rosalie (1997) *Pleasure Island: Tourism and Temptation in Cuba* (Lincoln: University of Nebraska Press).

Seamon, David (1979) *A Geography of the Lifeworld* (London: Croom Helm).

Seamon, David and Christine Norden (1980) 'Marketplace as Place Ballet', in *Landscape* 24, 35-41.

Shivji, J. (1973) *Tourism and Socialist Development* (Dar es Salaam: Tanzania Publishing House).

Suckling, James (1999) 'Your Home in Havana', in *Cigar Aficionado* (June), 116-28

Tabb, W. (1988) 'The Economics of Tourism: Who Benefits'?, in *Economic Issues of Tourism, Consultation IV* (Stoney Point, NY: NACRT), 7-12.

Tuan, Yi-Fu (1977) *Space and Place* (Minneapolis: University of Minnesota Press).

Violich, Frances (1989) 'Toward Revealing the Sense of Place', in David Seamon and Robert Mugerauer (eds), *Dwelling, Place, Environment* (New York: Columbia University Press), 113-36.

―――― (1998) *The Bridge to Dalmatia: A Search for the Meaning of Place* (Baltimore: The Johns Hopkins University Press).

Weaver, D.B. (1988) 'The Evolution of a "Plantation" Tourism Landscape on the Caribbean Island of Antigua', in *Tijdschrift voor Economische en Sociale Geografie* 79, 311-22.

———— (1998) *Ecotourism in the Less Developed World* (New York: Center for Agriculture and Biosciences International).

Wong, P.P. (1993) *Tourism vs. Environment: The Case for Coastal Areas* (Boston: Kluwer Academic Publishers).

The Construction of Home in the Informal City[1]

Peter Kellett

Abstract

The cities of Latin America are expanding rapidly largely through the energy and efforts of ordinary people who are creating their own dwelling environments in informal settlements with varying degrees of support or condemnation from municipal authorities. Although there is considerable diversity between settlements, most share three key characteristics. Firstly, these environments are conceived and constructed by the occupants themselves independently of external controls or professional advice; secondly, occupation and construction frequently take place simultaneously; and thirdly, such places are usually in a process of dynamic change and demonstrate considerable ingenuity and creativity within limited resource constraints. To explore these process of informal place-making and the resulting environments this chapter draws on data from a study of squatter settlements in northern Colombia. Through analysis of the processes of making, both collectively and at household level, we will gain insights into the multiple influences on the decision-making processes involved. Far from the common image of inadequate, chaotically organised places it will be argued that these environments respond to clear, culturally embedded ideas about how cities and dwellings should be configured.

* * *

> Houses are both concrete embodiments and imaginary representations of people's relations to their conditions of existence. (Holston 1991: 456)

Introduction: Beyond Shelter

There is an implicit assumption underlying much academic writing on low-income housing that poverty and the struggle for survival will mean that the dwellings of the urban poor, especially those which they have created for themselves, respond essentially and only to the basic need for shelter. Such a reductionist view of poor people's needs as predominantly material and

---

[1] We would like to thank the editors of the *Journal of Romance Studies* for permission to reproduce 'The Construction of Home in the Informal City' which was originally published in: *Journal of Romance Studies* 2.3, 17-31.

predetermined is now being challenged and is leading to more holistic analyses that include non-economic dimensions. This discussion has been informed by studies that have examined the similarities between informal contemporary Third-World housing and vernacular settlements (Rapoport 1988; Kellett and Napier 1995). Such studies have attempted to shift the discussion away from superficial interpretations of visual images towards analysis of underlying processes and cultural patterns, to conclude that informal settlements offer a potentially fruitful arena in which to study aspects of the complex interrelationships between dwellers and their dwelling places. This is partly because informal settlements generally develop without the plethora of official controls, regulations and rules which undoubtedly impact on more 'conventional' environments. In addition such user-created environments are worthy of our attention because they are accommodating increasing proportions of the urban poor, who, through their low economic and political status, are denied access to both formal private and public housing markets.

Visually such informal environments may well appear disordered, chaotic and unplanned, especially in the early stages of their development. However, this article suggests that they do in fact respond to purposeful decisions and actions which are based on culturally constructed images of what dwellings and settlements should be like. Indeed the process of incremental growth and the improvement evident in many such environments are focused towards 'imagined futures' (Holston 1991). Despite formidable economic constraints such images and meanings play a fundamental role in influencing the behaviour of low-income residents and the dwelling environments which they create. Central to this discussion is an understanding of the meaning of 'home', and how such meanings are created through the processes of settlement and consolidation of the dwelling.

The literature on contemporary low-income housing in Third-World cities has focused almost exclusively on the more pragmatic issue of shelter and has largely ignored the concept of housing as home (Huttman 1993: 464), and conceptual studies of home have been biased towards middle-class households in northern countries (Despres 1991: 102). However, within this literature there are fundamental issues concerning the complex relationship between dwellers and their dwelling environment which may in fact be more identifiable and visible in informal settlements precisely because of the absence of external actors and the need to optimise the limited resources. More recent studies are attempting to combine socio-economic analyses with cultural issues and concepts of meaning (Pugh 2000). Through the use of field-work data at the micro-level this paper attempts to shed light on how individuals within such settlements articulate their own value systems through construction of their dwelling environments.

A Case Study: Santa Marta, Colombia

The Caribbean coastal city of Santa Marta is a regional capital with an urban population of over 210,000. The majority live in settlements which begin as organised, illegal (sometimes violent) invasions of land, the first of which date from early in the twentieth century. Land invasions appear to be tolerated, and at times encouraged, because powerful interest groups in the city benefit through unequal client-patronage relationships with the low-income settler populations (Kellett 1997). Land subdivision is carried out by the settlers who aim to create plots of equal dimensions within a conventional gridiron layout. Land invasion and layout are collective activities, but dwelling construction and consolidation are largely done at household level. Over time most dwellers are able to change their temporary shelters into well-built, substantial houses: a change from small, single-room, unserviced dwellings towards multi-room, larger, fully-serviced houses in permanent materials.[2] Such changes occur at varying speeds, with numerous factors impacting on the process, including cultural background and complex patterns of residential mobility which mean that different households may occupy (and build) at different stages in the life of the dwelling (Kellett 1992, 1999). It is clear that the majority continue to improve the dwelling well beyond the resolution of basic shelter needs. Besides the addition of rooms, the upgrading of finishes and the improvement of services, they introduce furniture, pictures, painting, trees and flowers. Such actions may be described as home-creating processes. Within the constraints of their context, people are attempting to create dwelling environments which respond to their individual and collective understanding of the components, attributes and images which together give meaning to the idea of home.[3]

Home has many attributes and levels of meaning, but at its centre is a 'highly complex system of ordered relations with place, an order that orientates us in space, in time, and in society' (Dovey 1985: 39). At one level it is concerned with the domestic spaces and activities of everyday life, and simultaneously it has broader dimensions which relate to issues of identity, economic and social positions —in short a person's place in society. There is

---

[2] The author lived with a family in one of the settlements for extended periods to observe and document the process of house and settlement consolidation. The main method of data collection was the recording of oral testimonies to explore the residents' housing histories, their experiences and motivations for joining the land invasions and their aspirations for the future (Kellett 2000). A central focus was an examination of decision-making related to resource allocation and space configuration, and the use values and meanings associated with particular spaces and furnishings within the house. Forty households from five settlements were documented in detail over a six-year period (1986–91), and three other were surveyed in less detail, with follow-up visits in 1996 and 1998.

[3] Rapoport (1995) has demonstrated deficiencies in the use of the term 'home', but in this study it proved to be a most useful conceptual tool.

a complex interrelationship between these two scales: the microcosm of the dwelling and the macrocosm of the world in which individuals and groups must define their place. In this paper we will explore some of these relations in order to demonstrate how home creating processes are integrally linked to the position of informal dwellers within society.

Memory and Meaning

In conventional, formal housing systems the dweller will normally enter the process when the dwelling is completed and most decisions about the physical form have been made. This means exclusion from much of the process of creation and construction. In contrast, informal settlers, especially those who have endured the hardships and dangers of the land invasion, inevitably have a different experience of and relationship with both the site and the dwelling. For many this is a long, slow process of construction and change which is closely intertwined with other fundamental aspects of life (birth, death, household formation and separation), economic position (through income-generating activities in the dwelling), as well as apparently small details of everyday existence. The plot is not merely a demarcated piece of land, nor is the house only 'bricks and mortar': they are both full of memory and meaning. We can see this echoed in this extract of an account by interviewee Doña Carmen describing her plot in the early years when the dwelling and her seven children were small and she was recently widowed:

> all that area over there was open, we used to sit here, and there where the kitchen is now there used to be a large almond tree and we would rest below it. Just beyond the almond tree was the place for washing clothes. I used to wash there in peace and quiet. That was when the children were young.

In this example we can see how the speaker relates to different parts of the dwelling through memories of what was there before, and of the activities which took place in particular places. However, rather than evoking affective responses of nostalgia, the recollection of deprivations and minimal living conditions in the past emphasises present achievements as well as giving strength to hopes for the future. The focus is forwards, with little evidence of nostalgia for the past, either for earlier phases in the settlement or for previous places of residence.

Most new settlers are couples in their twenties or thirties with young families who had previously been living for several years with parents or in-laws in cramped, overcrowded houses in older squatter areas, where they had little space, privacy or autonomy. Others are escaping high rents in poor-quality accommodation. Most have limited experience of rural areas but even in the accounts of migrants to the city there are very few examples of respondents painting an idyllic picture of rural life, and the dominant view is one of identification with urban life, despite the manifest problems.[4]

Distance from the Natural World

Beliefs and attitudes relating to the natural world vary considerably between cultures, and to a lesser extent between individuals within the same broad cultural groupings. In Latin America the dominant image of rural life is negative (Rapoport 1982: 144; 1985: 270). In an early study of a small town in Colombia, Richardson (1974: 35-51) demonstrates how a polarised series of beliefs towards the natural and man-made world can help explain the form of the town and the social behaviour of its residents. In common with many societies, 'nature' is conceptualised as the opposite of 'culture' (Eagleton 2000): the natural, rural, negative world *(monte)* is contrasted with the positive, progressive urban world of *cultura*, and the two worlds should be clearly demarcated and bounded:

> The house, with its wattle walls, dirt floors and thatched roofs, is another source of psychic discomfort. The construction materials of this type resemble too closely the unhumanised products of the 'monte' [...]; they do not sufficiently testify to the occupants' departure from nature. The town fights a continual battle against the grass that periodically springs up along the sides of the dirt streets. The streets, even if they are unpaved, are part of man's 'cultura', and the grass is the 'monte', which constantly and insidiously tries to invade the human domain. The grass and trees in the park, however, receive careful attention, because they —like the flowers that the housewife tends in her patio— have subdued themselves to man and have become parts of his 'cultura'. (Richardson 1974: 44)

The dwelling consolidation process in informal settlements can be interpreted as a move away from the temporary materials and typologies of the natural, rural world *(monte)* towards the ordered, permanent constructions which represent the world of *cultura*. In addition, this duality helps explain the permanence of the traditional rectilinear urban layouts throughout Latin America, for in addition to their equivalence with conventional urban form, such clearly man-made, geometric patterns symbolise in a very concrete way

---

[4] Only 15.7 per cent of migrant household-heads in the five settlements surveyed expressed a wish to return to their place of origin.

the dominance of 'man' over the haphazard, curved, natural forms of the natural world.[5]

Figure 1: Temporary Dwelling
© Peter Kellett

Natural World, Man-Made World: A Tale of Father and Son

Strong preference for the ordered rectilinear approach is manifest in the relative merits of the location and shape of plots. In the Santa Marta study there were a few areas where the regular street layouts were thwarted by topography or human error, leading to a scattering of irregularly shaped plots which are clearly regarded as 'sub-standard' and less desirable by the majority. Fausto Varela chose to live on such an irregularly shaped and steeply sloping corner plot and is one of a minority of settlers who have made little attempt to follow the dominant urban-oriented lifestyle. As you enter a small opening between the large overgrown trees and bushes which form a green barrier between his house and the street, you are crossing a threshold into another world which in appearance and function is like a small piece of rural Colombia transposed into the city. Fausto built the two-room dwelling himself from bricks which he fired on the plot. As in rural areas the small kitchen is separate from the house, and the family cooks exclusively with firewood that Fausto collects with his donkey from the hills beyond the settlement. There are a variety of other animals and birds and everywhere are

---

[5] See Kostoff (1991) on the history and meaning of the urban grid.

plants, bushes and trees which have been planted specifically for food consumption or medicinal purposes. Fausto is a *curandero* (healer) who uses traditional knowledge of the medicinal properties of plants. He charges a small amount for each consultation, and supplements his income through his ingenious ability to recycle found objects, thereby gaining sustenance from the plot.

In clear contrast is the house built next door by one of Fausto's sons, Rigoberto, on a part of the original plot given to him by his father. Rigoberto lives with his wife and young sons in a small but typically urban-style house, with an eye-catching entrance. Although Rigoberto has had more cash resources at his disposal (from his time working at a mine) the dramatic contrast in the form and image of the two adjacent houses reflects more fundamental differences in world-view. To quote Rapoport (1969: 47): 'what finally decides the form of a dwelling, and moulds the spaces and their relationships, is the vision that people have of the ideal life'. For Fausto the place to be is the countryside, where he feels life is comfortable. Hence his house in the city is formed to reflect this: he has created a rural oasis full of sights, sounds and smells with which he can identify. He appreciates the uneven and steep nature of his plot from where he gets a direct view of the hills, and, in clear weather, of the mountains beyond. In contrast Rigoberto, although born in the countryside, has spent his formative years in the city. He is building a house which consists of only two rooms at present, but he confidently expects to extend to at least five with all the finishes, furnishings and services of an urban lifestyle. Already he has invested in the entrance which confidently and proudly announces to neighbours and passers-by that this is the house of an upwardly mobile urbanite. The front of the dwelling is clearly visible at the top of the steps surrounded by controlled and subjugated vegetation to demonstrate the dominance of the man-made world over that of the natural world. Next door, his father's house cannot be seen from the street, and the entrance could be easily missed: instead a wall of exuberant vegetation proclaims that Fausto remains resolutely within the world of *monte*.

Urban and Rural Values and Images

In many ways Fausto is an exception. He has consciously adopted a lifestyle that is more typical of rural areas. For others in the settlement who live in houses of temporary materials of rural origin this is intended to be merely a phase from which they will 'progress'. Such progression between contrasting value systems was examined in Ecuador by Klaufus (2000) who based her analysis on Miller's (1994) concept of dual values. *Transient* values are associated with the present time, the short-term, expressiveness and change;

whereas *transcendent* values relate to long-term memory, continuity and moral values handed down through the generations. She goes on to show how 'residential architecture helps determine social stratification [and how] an individual household can profile itself within the group through the competitive application of taste and originality in architecture and consumption' (Klaufus 2000: 343).

Figure 2: Consolidating Dwelling
© Peter Kellett

In Santa Marta we can interpret aspects of the visual appearance of the dwellings through an understanding of the imagery associated with rural and urban values combined with an appreciation of transient and transcendent values. The pitched roof is strongly symbolic of the rural house and it is noticeable how much effort and expense are devoted to disguising its presence. Many consolidated dwellings appear to have flat roofs which are associated with the urban houses of the rich. This illusion of flatness is achieved by erecting a low parapet or fascia at the front eaves which is commonly extended over the entrance to provide an overhang, sometimes with features made of the water outlets or supporting columns. These fascias require skill to execute and are invariably contracted out to the more skilled builders in the settlement. Such 'modern' exteriors reflect transient, changing values and are designed to demonstrate prestige and link the occupiers with urban based ideas of affluence and progress.

Burgess (1990: 204), Gough (1992: 105) and Mosquera (1983: 322) in their studies of low-income housing in Pereira and Cali also report on the importance attached to the public side of the dwelling and give several examples of dwellings with horizontal parapets disguising pitched roofs. In all these cases we also find examples of relatively small dwellings at the early stages of consolidation, where resources and effort have been expended on addressing issues of image rather than resolving more practical questions of space and quality. This apparent inversion of 'rational' priorities underlines the importance of understanding less tangible but no less significant issues of meaning in housing. Turner provides a good example of this: 'On one occasion in Peru, I well remember criticising the local habit of building a more or less finished street facade even while the owners lived in a shack behind it, and receiving a highly articulate lecture from Señora Romero, the homely lady I was speaking to, about the sense and economy of doing just that: how the preview of the street of finished homes confirms the faith of the builders and stimulates the realisation of their expectations' (Turner 1974: 15).

Modern Urban Futures

Despite daily hardships and injustices, the world is seen as a place of opportunity where effort and initiative can be rewarded. It is a world view in which change and modernity are welcomed. Such attitudes are reflected in the way people build: 'The aesthetics of building [are] shaped [...] by a view of the world as changing, as offering opportunities for individual progress, as being a place in which one looked beyond the neighbourhood in space and away from the past in time for models of success' (Peattie 1992: 28).

The settlers do not need to look far. The models of success are nearby in the low density, middle-class areas of the city. Despite contrasting pedigrees and modes of production, these low-rise formal houses share numerous design features with the squatter dwellings: both have recessed, stepped entrances which are centrally positioned with verandas; both have rendered walls painted in pastel colours; front areas are sharply demarcated by low walls with a distinctive semi-circular motif, sometimes with decorative security railings. Curved plastic forms sometimes link the walls with the facade, and both types of dwelling include trees and shrubs as integral parts of the front of the dwelling. Shared aesthetic ideas may also be reinforced by proximity. Squatter builders will be familiar with their external appearance, and some women will have been inside (as domestic workers). Some men also will have been employed as gardeners and odd-job men but will have had a less intimate contact with the interiors.

But are the dwellings of the more affluent necessarily the role models for those of the poor? There is undoubtedly a wide range of possible influences both from within the country and abroad: many residents are migrants from other parts of the country, others have travelled, especially to neighbouring Venezuela; and Colombian television, which is accessible to all, shows many films and shows from abroad (mostly the USA), as well as commercials, and 'soap operas' made in Colombia, all of which provide examples of different domestic settings and lifestyles. Such images are as important for the values portrayed as the forms illustrated.

Figure 3: Middle-Class Dwelling in a Nearby Formal Settlement
© Peter Kellett

There are significant differences in dwellings throughout the country, but in Santa Marta the similarity between well-consolidated, popular dwellings and middle-class houses suggests that local role models are significant in influencing the design vocabulary. In his study of Barranquilla, Foster (1975: 180) interprets the type of dwelling constructed by the poor as 'an economical copy of a more wealthy man's house'. But it is much more than a simple copy. In a study from Brazil, Holston (1991: 461) also identifies similar sources, but argues that low-income dwellers are not attempting to imitate, but rather to develop 'original copies' which display both their origin as well as demonstrating sufficient uniqueness. Through this complex translation process new hybrid forms are being produced which make reference to different sources of ideas and levels of meaning. Hybridisation is a dynamic and unfinalisable process rooted in specific post-colonial contexts and 'embraces a whole spectrum of cultural practices' (Hernández 2002: 84).

Some critics deny the architectural validity of such hybrid forms. In a study of spontaneous settlements in Medellín, Viviescas (1985, 1989) found 'considerable expressive potential' which might form the basis for a 'genuine architectural position'. However:

> the circumstances under which these 'barrios' are established prohibits a reference to architecture. Rather, we are referring to the basic, immediate and desperate need for shelter. [...] the spatial configuration of these barrios responded not so much to any authentic development initiating from within, but rather to an inevitable (given the material conditions) impoverished superimposition of ideological, aesthetic and environmental values originating in other more affluent parts of the city. [...] The result tends inevitably towards a penurious kitsch. (Viviescas 1985: 45)

This echoes Bourdieu's (1989) assertion that the relatively disadvantaged in terms of power or resources are inarticulate in terms of taste, style or refinement, as they must concentrate instead on the most necessary and functional aspects of life. However, a number of studies (Colloredo-Mansfeld 1994; Klaufus 2000) provide compelling evidence of lower-class residents participating with a rich palette of ideas and creativity to produce culturally authentic hybrid forms. Such popular processes have much in common with more traditional vernacular architecture (Kellett and Napier 1995).

The Front Facade: A Controlled Composition

The front facades of consolidated dwellings demonstrate an identifiable design language. The dominant image is of order and symmetry achieved through strong horizontal elements, particularly the apparently flat roof which is suggestive of a more 'advanced' technology of reinforced concrete. The hard horizontal lines are often complemented by semi-circular elements which are sometimes reinforced with changes of texture and colour. Another key component is the metal work: although ostensibly fulfilling a security function, the wrought iron is frequently employed in a highly decorative way, with the interplay of lines and shadows complementing the solidity of the walls.

The facade is a controlled composition using several different elements to produce a visually coherent image which communicates aspiration and modern purpose in a direct and apparently unambiguous way. Few examples of completed houses were found which diverged significantly from the 'rules' or patterns described here. In common with the dwelling plan types, we are seeing the utilisation of a single model with variations that conform to a consistent underlying rule system. The more developed the dwellings and settlements the more they resemble their desired models and the less distinguishable they become from formal, legal, more affluent parts of the city.

In most dwellings there is a dramatic contrast between the public face at the front and private space at the back. This illustrates the importance of presenting an urban, modern, progressive face to others at the front of the house, while at the same time living a lifestyle towards the rear which in many respects is closer to aspects of rural living. This duality partly reflects a gradient from the controlled, ordered and presentable public face towards the more intimate, private and family-oriented back. It also frequently reflects in physical terms the range of levels of consolidation from fully consolidated formal front to unconsolidated informal rear.

Peattie attributes the contrast between the front and back of comparable dwellings in Venezuela as reflecting the importance of demonstrating modern aspirations. Greater effort is made towards the front, but:

> by the time we got to the rear of the house, the public-presentation aspects were much weaker, and in the back yard one would find dish-washing going on in an enamel basin on a deal table, and perhaps a coop of chickens. But this gradient from front to back, from the modern and commercial to the more traditional, was thought of by the barrio people as a gradient also from better to inferior. (Peattie 1992: 29)

Does such duality simply reflect limitations of resources or are we witnessing a transitional stage between urban and rural life for many dwellers? Stea and Turan (1990: 117) believe that much apparent disorder reflects transition from one mode of production to another, as well as transition between different sets of values. The transitional nature both of society and much of the built environment during the consolidation process inevitably leads to the juxtaposition of apparently incongruent elements. The built environment and the objects within it are vehicles for the transmission of meaning, and it is common to mix codes (Oliver, Davis and Bentley 1981: 189). Therefore the dwellings are communicating a range of meanings, some of them contrasting and contradictory.[6] Such hybridisation of built form suggests that in this context hybridity is an aspirational concept through which dwellers aspire to achieve the architectural forms of the dominant classes. However, for most it is an unachievable aspiration which remains only partially fulfilled, suggestive of a state of in-betweenness: no longer rural but not entirely urban either.

---

[6] Ontiveros (1989: 133) reports similar responses in Caracas. In one respondent she observed 'an ambiguity between the acceptance and nostalgia of the spaces (of the rural way of life) and their compulsive rejection implied in the pro-progress concept'.

Figure 4: Completed Informal Dwelling
©Peter Kellett

There is insufficient space here to examine internal space arrangements, furnishings and household objects, which are all part of the same 'modernising project' to which most households subscribe, although Klaufus (2000) argues that the private interior spaces are where transcendent, long-term values are more in evidence. Similarly Lara (2001: 10) identifies a 'dichotomy between the novelty of the facades and the conservatism of the interior'. However, through the furnishing and decoration of their dwellings urban residents are drawn increasingly into habits of consumption dependent on the money economy. This happens partly through the purchase of goods on credit which ties people more tightly into patterns of mass consumption and indebtedness. Holston (1991: 456) argues that such conventionally defined behaviour is strongly in the interest of the ruling elites and undermines much of the radical potential within popular settlements. Private home-building (despite its frequent illegality) is a fundamental tenet of conservative capitalist ideology based on property ownership.

We will now bring together and expand on the range of meanings that have been brought up during the discussion. It is vital, however, to be reminded that the range of circumstances between informal settlements vary dramatically and are constantly changing. Similarly within settlements and households there are differences between groups and individuals, partly related to variations in age, gender, income, ethnicity, etc., and therefore it is unwise to attempt to generalise from specific cases. There are multiple layers of meaning which are continually being constructed and reconstructed as situations and circumstances change.

Home as a Place of Sustenance: Production and Reproduction

A dimension of low-income environments that has until recently received little attention is the integration of economic activities within and around the dwelling. In Santa Marta at least twenty per cent of households[7] generate income in the home through a range of informal sector enterprises including shops, workshops and even nursery schools. Many others reduce expenditure through growing vegetables, tending fruit trees and keeping chickens. Some of these activities appear to have little impact on the domestic activities of the household and the role of the dwelling, but in other cases the spatial configuration is changed and the dwelling is as much a place of production as domestic reproduction (Kellett and Tipple 2000; Gough and Kellett 2001). This has the potential to add to our conceptual understanding of the meaning of home and challenge over-simplistic ideas of the home as an essentially sacred, female, private, domestic space. Thresholds and boundaries are complex and fluid, changing both spatially and temporarily as households, dwellings and enterprises grow and evolve. The dwelling plays a key role in structuring both social and economic interactions, and through patterns of production and consumption links the micro domestic economy to broader macro-economic developments. Therefore the home plays a role as a provider not only of physical security and safety, but also of fundamental economic sustenance, without which the household would perish. The home thereby becomes not merely a container of human life but an essential shelter for those life-sustaining activities. It is clear that the house not only structures social and economic interactions but also acts as a source of core symbols that constitute those interactions. In a study of the domestic economy in Colombia, Gudeman and Rivera (1990: 2) describe how 'all material practices are organised through the house, and the lexicon for them comes from the vocabulary for the physical dwelling: the house as shelter is metaphor for the house as economy'.

Home as an Expression of Moral Order

It is very noticeable that most dwellings, particularly temporary ones, are kept in immaculate condition. Despite the frustrations and difficulties of

---

[7] This is from a sample of 374 households in five informal settlements surveyed in 1991. In older settlements the figure was higher, rising to 24.2 per cent in a twelve-year-old settlement.

achieving order within relatively confined spaces, with large numbers of people, absence of storage space, and often with earth floors and a dusty environment, the dwellings which are not well kept are exceptions rather than the rule. It is clearly important to demonstrate cleanliness and tidiness 'and thus bear witness that the inhabitants are decent people. The achievement of this cleanliness is the work of women' (Gullestad 1993: 148). Judgements are made about the inhabitants by observing and interpreting the dwelling, hence a clear objective is to avoid a negative assessment.[8] This is of course more difficult in a small temporary dwelling. In such circumstances people do not wish be equated with the inadequate physical state of the dwelling, but rather we are encouraged to admire how well-kept the tiny dwelling is, both inside and out. This means that the beds are clean and carefully made; the earth floor must be swept; the plates and cups must be neatly stacked; and the metal cooking pots must be polished, despite becoming black immediately they are placed over the wood fire. This attention to the aesthetics of order and tidiness are vital because 'the connotations of "a good home" are moral, while the connotations of the expression of "a nice home" are of an aesthetic kind. However, through aesthetics a vision of a moral order is created and expressed' (Gullestad 1993: 147).

Home as an Expression of Respectability and Conventionality

Earlier we mentioned how great efforts are made to achieve a standard settlement layout, sometimes overriding the logic of topography. The most vital aspect of the grid layout is that it will be read as conventional, and have the potential to develop and become the same as other parts of the city. Similarly, but perhaps less forcefully, the design of the dwellings themselves echoes the same underlying values. Clearly established patterns of development are followed at different speeds, and the end products all fall well within a relatively narrow band of culturally prescribed characteristics. This echoes the conclusion of an earlier study of popular settlements in Barranquilla where the 'homogeneity of the house form and layout in these barrios [...] can be explained in terms of an adherence by [the] builders to a common set of general principles and approved alternatives' (Foster 1975: 180). Taken together, these principles mean that the dwellers are attempting within the constraints of their resources to create urban form and housing areas that are as close as possible to the dominant conventions. The informal

---

[8] The gender dimension of home is not explored here but is crucially important. In most societies judgements about the condition of the home fall unequally on the shoulders of women. Darke (1994) discusses how this can lead to both negative and positive feelings among women towards their homes.

dwellings can therefore be read as symbols of formal respectability and conventionality.

Home as an Expression of Individuality and Status

It is certainly true that the grid layout has an inherent egalitarian logic: each street, urban block and plot should be of equal dimensions. This might suggest that such principles would be manifest in built form and social interactions. However, despite many inspiring examples of collective action, Colombian society is dominated by strong individualism: a belief that individuals must look after themselves and that the rewards of such efforts are deserved. No shame is attached to those who express material success as conspicuous consumption.[9] In housing this is manifest in the efforts both to demonstrate relative levels of affluence as well as to distinguish between individuals through obvious visual differences in the dwellings themselves. The scale and vocabulary of difference are, however, constrained by attempts to demonstrate conformity to the social order. Individual expression through the 'competitive application of taste and originality in architecture and consumption' (Klaufus 2000: 343) is most visible towards the front of the dwelling, and the facade in particular can be read as a crude barometer of the social standing and economic health of the occupants.

The Home as Symbol of Independence and Achievement

Heidegger explained that 'one's capacity to live on this earth —to "dwell" in the phenomenological sense— is an essentially architectural experience. The very Being of being is linked to one's situatedness in the world' (Leach 2002: 88). Similarly, Turner (1968) has emphasised the existential dimension of self-made environments and believes that in home-building and local improvements a person can find 'the creative dialogue essential for self-discovery and growth' (Turner 1968: 357). He continues:

> The man who would be free must build his own life. The existential value of the barriada is the product of three freedoms: the freedom of community self-selection; the freedom to budget

---

[9] In other societies the reverse is the case. Duncan (1985: 146) describes how in Sri Lanka collectivist ideals predominate over individualism. Changes to the dwelling and the acquisition of private objects can be interpreted as undermining the social order. Klaufus (2000: 343) reports how conspicuous consumption 'appears to be an ambivalent process, whereby efforts are not necessarily rewarded by the appreciation of the neighbourhood'.

one's own resources and the freedom to shape one's own environment.[10]

There is little doubt that the absence of official control and regulation may be able to release creative action and energy which in other contexts can be severely inhibited, but it is vital not to play down the issue of resource scarcity and constraint: most informal dwellers construct their homes through necessity, not choice. However, this article provides some substantiation for these claims, not least for the depth of meaning which even the humblest of dwellings can contain, and the sense of purpose among many dweller-builders.

This is in sharp contrast to the despair and hopelessness frequently experienced by relatively disadvantaged groups in more affluent parts of the world. For example, Alba, a single mother of two was involved in a violent land invasion and managed to obtain a plot and begin constructing a small dwelling:

> My situation has improved because now I have what I didn't have before —a house of my own. [Although] the work situation has got worse, I must thank God that I've got enough to eat. I came here to have something of my own. I feel very content here in my little house. You can live well in a house of wooden boards especially if it's nicely kept, and I'm always doing something. I'm really so happy here: people ask me when am I going to rest from knocking in nails and things, but I am so delighted to be here: I've never had a house before!

Her optimism about the future is clear and she is relishing the independence and opportunity offered by having a home of her own. She had lived for many years in a difficult relationship with the father of her children, followed by a time living with her sister and family. Despite the minimal physical attributes of her current home, she keeps it in pristine condition: it is a tangible symbol of her independence and achievement.

Conclusion

The social position of individuals in society plays a vital role in determining their actions. Squatters are highly conscious of their low social status and how their physical conditions reflect this low status. Their efforts can be

---

[10] There is an increasing recognition by people in 'developed' parts of the world of the validity of such ideas, but for most the building of their own home would be considered a luxury. The paradox is that 'it is a luxury that almost all poor people in the so-called underdeveloped world enjoy' (Rybczynski, cited in Peattie 1992: 29).

interpreted as a striving for dignity and respect. From her personal experience of living in a squatter settlement in Venezuela, the anthropologist Lisa Peattie concluded that:

> the construction characteristics and the service deficiencies [...] have a common attribute; they represent attributes which are devalued and devaluing. People who live in this way are thought of as people to be looked down on. That is why the energy that goes into housing improvement [...] is as much a drive for respect as it is for comfort. (Peattie 1992: 29)

Such energy and values are manifest in the aesthetics of the built environment where:

> the underclasses are constructing images and identities to counter those that subjugate. Not only are they transforming themselves as citizens but they are also changing the images of disrespect that bind them to a denigrated sense of their own persons. They are replacing these images with new ones of competence and knowledge in the production and consumption of what modern society considers important. (Holston 1991: 462)

Informal settlement processes are now the dominant form of housing production in the rapidly expanding cities of Latin America. These cities are the sum of the continuing actions of low-income households each attempting to construct in physical terms their vision of the life and values to which they aspire. As we have seen, such visions are ambitious and require the commitment of prodigious energy and creativity, leading in turn to a hybrid domestic architecture rich in meaning. Exploration of these self-made environments can offer insights into the critical role of domestic architecture in consolidating and transforming economic relations and cultural identity.

Works Cited

Bourdieu, Pierre (1989) *Distinction: A Social Critique of the Judgement of Taste* (London: Routledge).

Burgess, Rod (1990) 'The State and Self-help Building in Pereira, Colombia' (PhD thesis, University College London).

Colloredo-Mansfeld, R. (1994) 'Architectural Conspicuous Consumption and Economic Change in the Andes', in *American Anthropologist* 96.4, 845-65.

Darke, Jane (1994) 'Women and the Meaning of Home', in R. Gilroy and R. Woods (eds), *Housing Women* (London: Routledge), 11-30.

Despres, Carole (1991) 'The Meaning of Home: Literature Review and Directions for Future Research and Theoretical Development', in *Journal of Architectural and Planning Research* 8.2, 96-115.

Dovey, Kimberley (1985) 'Home and Homelessness', in I. Altman and C. M. Werner (eds), *Home Environments* (New York and London: Plenum Press), 33-64.

Duncan, James S. (1985) 'The House as Symbol of Social Structure: Notes on the Language of Objects among Collectivistic Groups', in I. Altman and C. M. Werner (eds), *Home Environments* (New York and London: Plenum Press), 133-51.

Eagleton, Terry (2000) *The Idea of Culture* (London: Blackwell).

Foster, David W. (1975) 'Survival Strategies of Low-income Households in a Colombian City' (PhD thesis, University of Illinois).

Gough, Katherine (1992) 'From Bamboo to Bricks: Self-help Housing and the Building Materials Industry in Urban Colombia' (PhD thesis, University College London).

Gough, Katherine and Peter Kellett (2001) 'Housing Consolidation and Home-based Income Generation: Evidence from Self-help Settlements in Two Colombian cities', in *Cities: International Journal of Urban Policy and Planning* 18.4, 235-47.

Gudeman, Stephen and Rivera, Alberto (1990) *Conversations in Colombia: The Domestic Economy in Life and Text* (Cambridge: Cambridge University Press).

Gullestad, Marianne (1993) 'Home Decoration as Popular Culture: Constructing Homes, Genders and Classes in Norway', in T. del Valle (ed), *Gendered Anthropology* (London: Routledge), 128-61.

Hernández, Felipe (2002) 'On the Notion of Architectural Hybridisation in Latin America', in *The Journal of Architecture* 7, 77-86.

Holston, James (1991) 'Autoconstruction in Working-class Brazil', in *Cultural Anthropology* 6.4, 447-65.

Huttman, Elizabeth (1993) 'The Homeless and "Doubled-up" Households', in E. G. Arias (ed), *The Meaning and Use of Housing: International*

Perspectives, Approaches and Applications, (Aldershot: Avebury), 457-78.

Kellett, Peter (1992) 'Residential Mobility and Consolidation Processes in Spontaneous Settlements: The Case of Santa Marta, Colombia', in *Third World Planning Review* 14.4, 355-69.

—— (1997) 'City Profile: Santa Marta, Colombia', in *Cities: International Journal of Urban Policy and Planning* 14.6, 393-402.

—— (1999) 'Cultural Values and Housing Behaviour in Spontaneous Settlements', in *Journal of Architectural and Planning Research* 16.3, 205-24.

—— (2000) 'Voices from the Barrio: Oral Testimony and Informal Housing Processes in Latin America', in *Third World Planning Review* 22.2, 189-205.

Kellett, Peter and M. Napier (1995) 'Squatter Architecture: A Critical Examination of Vernacular Theory and Spontaneous Settlement with Reference to South America and South Africa', in *Traditional Dwellings and Settlements Review* 6.2, 7-24.

Kellett, Peter and A. Graham Tipple (2000) 'The Home as Workplace: A Study of Income Generating Activities within the Domestic Setting', in *Environment and Urbanization* 12.1, 203-13.

Klaufus, Christien (2000) 'Dwelling as Representation: Values of Architecture in an Ecuadorian Squatter Settlement', in *Journal of Housing and the Built Environment* 15.4, 341-65.

Kostoff, Spiro (1991) *The City Shaped: Urban Patterns and Meanings through History* (London: Thames and Hudson).

Lara, Fernando (2001) 'Brazilian Middle-class Appropriations of Modernist Vocabulary' (paper presented at the conference of Transcultural Architecture, London, November 2001).

Leach, Neil (2002) 'The Dark Side of the Domus', in A. Ballantyne (ed), *What is Architecture?* (London: Routledge), 88-101.

Miller, Daniel (1994) *Modernity: An Ethnographic Approach: Dualism and Mass Consumption in Trinidad* (Oxford: Berg).

Mosquera, Gilberta (1983) *Morfología, desarrollo y autoconstrucción en Cali: diagnóstico preliminar* (Medellín: Programa de Estudios de Vivienda en America Latina [PEVAL]).

Oliver, Paul, Iann Davis and Ian Bentley (1981) *Dunroamin: The Suburban Semi and Its Enemies* (London: Barrie and Jenkins).

Ontiveros, Teresa (1989) *La casa de barrio: aproximación socioantropológica a la memoria espacial urbana* (Caracas: Sección de Estudios Urbanos, Universidad Central de Venezuela).

Peattie, Lisa (1992) 'Aesthetic Politics: Shantytown Architecture or New Vernacular?', in *Traditional Dwellings and Settlements Review* 3.2, 23–32.

Pugh, Cedric (2000) 'Squatter Settlements: Their Sustainability, Architectural Contributions and Socio-economic Roles', in *Cities: International Journal of Urban Policy and Planning* 17.5, 325-37.

Rapoport, Amos (1969) *House Form and Culture* (Englewood Cliffs: Prentice-Hall).

——— (1982) *The Meaning of the Built Environment: A Non-Verbal Communication Approach* (London: Sage).

——— (1985) 'Thinking about Home Environments: A Conceptual Framework', in I. Altman and C. M. Werner (eds), *Home Environments* (New York and London: Plenum Press), 255-86.

——— (1988) 'Spontaneous Settlements as Vernacular Design', in C. V. Patton (ed), *Spontaneous Shelter: International Perspectives and Prospects* (Philadelphia: Temple University Press), 51-77.

——— (1995) 'A Critical Look at the Concept "Home"', in D. Benjamin (ed), *The Home: Words, Interpretations, Meanings and Environments* (Aldershot: Avebury), 25-52.

Richardson, M. (1974) 'The Spanish American (Colombian) Settlement Pattern as a Societal Expression and as a Behavioural Cause', in H. J. Walker and W. G. Haag (eds), *Man and Cultural Heritage* (Baton Rouge: Louisiana State University).

Stea, David and Mete Turan (1990) 'A Statement on Placemaking', in Mete Turan (ed), *Vernacular Architecture: Paradigms of Environmental Response* (Aldershot: Avebury), 102-21.

Turner, John F. C. (1968) 'The Squatter Settlement: An Architecture that Works', in *Architectural Design* 38.8, 355–60.

——— (1974) 'The Fits and Misfits of People's Housing', in *RIBA Journal* 81.2, 14-21.

Viviescas, Fernando (1985) 'Myth of Self-build as Popular Architecture: The Case of Low-income Housing in Colombian Cities', in *Open House International* 4, 44-8.

——— (1989) *Urbanización y ciudad en Colombia: una cultura por construir en Colombia* (Bogotá: Foro Nacional por Colombia).

From Austin, Texas to Santiago Atitlán, Guatemala and Back Again[1]

Jane Rendell

Abstract

This paper examines places of cultural exchange in relation to architecture and language. It does so with reference to three particular moments that took place on a journey from the United States of America to Guatemala, and back again. Each encounter concerns a misunderstanding that occurred as a result of the author's desire to communicate. These three moments hold in common the creation of unforeseen trajectories, involving displacement, slippage and unpredictable actions. In each encounter, the desire to understand through dialogue and conversation turned out, through a combination of assumption, translation and imagination, to produce unexpected results. Each transcultural exchange is located within a specific architectural space and speculative connections are made between the spatial configuration and social meaning of these physical sites and their linguistic, material and physic equivalents. The paper argues that misunderstandings might be the starting point for cultural encounters that return the subject to him/herself through transformation rather than repetition.

* * *

> For the rest of her life, Isabelle would remain severely dependent on narcotics and on alcohol; in North Africa, she would function for days without sustenance, as long as she had enough kif and arak to stun herself with. Every last borrowed franc was spent on these habits, for she had the makings of a hardened addict —the loss of all will power, of all sense of reality and self-respect (Kabbani 1987: vi).

---

[1] We would like to thank the editors of the *Journal of Romance Studies* for permission to reproduce 'From Austin, Texas to Santiago Atitlán, Guatemala and Back Again' which was originally published in: *Journal of Romance Studies* 2.3, 89-100.

Jane Rendell

Introduction

In 1989, on the way from Austin, Texas to Santiago Atitlán, Guatemala, I met a Chicano artist, who gave me a book, *The Passionate Nomad*. The book was the diary of Isabelle Eberhardt, a young woman from an affluent French family who spent the later part of her short life disguised as an Arab man wandering the deserts of northern Africa. She died aged twenty-eight on 21 October 1904, in a flash flood at Ain-Sefra. Her diary is one of my favourite books. I too have had addictive relationships with travel.

I was born in Al Mahktoum Hospital, Dubai in the Middle East. As a girl I lived in Sudan, Afghanistan and Ethiopia. My movements followed the pattern of my dad's work. Unlike many children in similar situations, I was not put into a boarding school at the age of eleven, but came back to live in England with my mum and sister. I say, 'came back'. The phrase implies that I was coming back to somewhere I had already been. But I had never lived in England before. It was my parents' country of origin, but not mine. I have never felt at home back (t)here. But then I have never felt at home anywhere.

Moving is not strange to me; both physically and emotionally, I am most comfortable in motion. For me, being in motion itself provides a sense of stability, having left but not-yet-being-there. This has a familiar feel to me, and it seems I am not alone. Postmodern feminism is full of stories of travel: of women who have moved out of their place. Their writing speaks of displacement. There is much at stake in moving, moving out of your place. Movements vary in their political dimensions. Not all journeying is to be celebrated (Rendell 2002).

Recent work in philosophy, cultural studies and human geography has increasingly focused on issues of identity, difference and subjectivity. The language of these texts is highly spatialised, with words such as 'mapping', 'locating', 'situating', 'positioning' and 'boundaries' appearing frequently. Academics 'explain' this new emphasis on space as typical of postmodern discourse. Searches for new ways of knowing and being are currently framed in spatial terms. For those concerned with issues of identity —race, gender, sexuality and ethnicity— spatial metaphors constitute powerful political devices which can be employed as critical tools for examining the relationship between the construction of identities and the politics of location. In such on-going theoretical disputes as the essentialism/constructionism debate, positionality provides a way of understanding knowledge and essence as contingent and strategic —where I am makes a difference to what I can know and who I can be.[2]

---

[2] The most commonly cited examples of such writings include: Anzaldúa (1999), Braidotti (1994), hooks (1989), Kaplan (1996), and Minh-Ha (1991).

My early childhood made me into a traveller. For years I travelled physically all the time. Recently I have been moving frequently too, giving lectures, delivering papers, but choosing to place my voice in a position of authority. I have been travelling in new ways. Through writing, reading, teaching, researching. I lose myself in other people's heads. Sitting still with students coming through the door in an endless stream I am on the move. Students tell me their stories and I tell them mine too. I do so to try to shift the power dynamic between us, to make a space of trust. By telling them stories of difficulty —'I've been there too'— I also reveal weaknesses, aspects of myself that disempower me.

We all like to tell stories. Many of our stories are about journeys — travelogues and autobiographies. They describe where we have come from, where we are going and what it is like along the way. Personal stories can be a microcosm of a greater whole, a detail of a larger pattern. Telling a story is one way of trying to communicate across difference. At one point in her book *Mappings*, Susan Stanford Friedman summarises the modes in which post-colonial theory discusses cross-cultural encounter. She outlines a number of tendencies: the use of stories of intercultural contact that focus on movement; the syncretist blending and clashing of difference; mimetic forms of cultural borrowing, assimilation, appropriation and parody; bonds of connection and disconnection as well as reciprocal agencies in subject/subject encounters (Friedman 1998: 143).

In 2001 I attended 'Transcultural Architecture in Latin America', a conference held at the Institute of Romance Studies, University of London, organised by Felipe Hernández, Mark Millington and Iain Borden. While I was listening to the papers, some stories came back to me concerning encounters that took place while I was travelling in Guatemala in 1989. These are not stories I am now going to tell in order to illustrate a previously held theoretical position. (Somehow I wish this were the case, for this kind of research would hold a more certain academic status.) It is rather the reverse. Having sketched out each event or story as I remember them, I have then discovered the kinds of resonances that occur with the narratives of cross-cultural encounter that Friedman describes:

> These patterns of interaction, I would further suggest, arise out of a dialectical or dialogic oscillation between sameness and difference in the ethnographic encounter. Travel —a form of movement through space— brings about an engagement with the other or others in a liminal space materially, psychologically or culturally in between. (Friedman 1998: 143)

Encounter 1: Speaking in Tongues

I spend several hours in the church in the Guatemalan village of Chichicastenango. I am fascinated by how the colonised Mayans have appropriated the iconology of the Catholic church enforced upon them through subtle but repetitive day-to-day rituals. An elderly lady approaches me. I engage her in conversation by pointing at a wooden image of a saint surrounded by fruit, flowers, incense and candles. I have previously been told that the Mayans believe that sickness can be transferred from people to other animals, such as dogs, via eggs. A number of eggs are being 'blessed' this way in the church. I gesture towards this.

My new companion responds by taking me outside the church and then some way outside the village, to a hill-top grove, where she shows me a site of special stones marked with honey, flowers and candles. On the way we talk in broken Spanish. Following her instructions, keen to learn more about Mayan religious rituals, I set off to find some friends of hers in an isolated town well off the travellers' trail. I catch a series of buses, but end up at the wrong end of a dead-end street. I never reach my intended destination. Did it only exist in my imagination? Were we really talking in Spanish? I later discover that many Mayans speak only their own language. But my desire to communicate with her was real, real enough to take me well out of my way.

For his inaugural lecture at the University of Nottingham in 2000, 'Speaking in Tongues', Christopher Johnson talked about language and difference. He made reference to three 'scenes' concerned with language. The first is the scene of Pentecost, when those present are able to speak new languages and understand one another, what Johnson calls 'the gift of foreign languages' (Johnson 2000). The second is a scene taken from *Salammbô*, a historical novel by Gustave Flaubert (1931), published in 1862, but set in the period after the first Punic War. Here the story-line is concerned with the 'unifying effect of the gift of tongues', but Johnson's interest is in the technical problems of translation. How can Flaubert speak like a third-century Carthaginian? Using indirect speech, Flaubert acts like a translator, assimilating the distance or difference of the other culture, an act that Johnson compares to the contemporary dubber of foreign-language films. The third scene is taken from a chapter in Claude Lévi-Strauss's autobiographical book, *Tristes Tropiques* (1955). At one point Lévi-Strauss recounts a scene from fieldwork conducted in Brazil. He has been working with the Nimbikwara tribe, who do not write, but to whom he has given pencils and paper as an experiment. When they go on a visit to a neighbouring village inhabited by a different tribe, the initial encounter is managed by the Nimbikwara chief, who reads out a text that he has 'written' using the pencils and papers given to him by Lévi-Strauss. In Johnson's view, the chief is performing an act of writing, indicating that he has at least understood the function of language —'to control and to manipulate'. Here Johnson bemoans the lack of translation, which would at least have given us a glimpse into the mind of the chief.

So first Johnson stresses the importance of speaking foreign languages in allowing us to communicate. Next he demonstrates the dangers of assimilation and appropriation if the act of translation replaces the original tongue. Finally he emphasises the need for translation, not as a replacement, but as an addition. By making a plea for subtitles rather than dubbing, Johnson is arguing for a situation where two languages can exist side by side. Rather like Walter Benjamin's essay, 'The Task of the Translator', where the act of translation is considered to be the creation of something new, rather than the production of a copy, Johnson suggests that instead of using translation to replace the original, both original and copy must run alongside (Benjamin 1992). Retaining the spoken text alongside the translated subtitle maintains difference.

But what does my story tell us in the light of these comments? If we follow Johnson's suggestion that we need both the original and the translation, then would I have been better off learning the Mayan language if I was to travel in the highlands of Guatemala? Or should my Mayan friend have learnt the Spanish language of her coloniser? If we had been able to communicate in words, then perhaps she would never have needed to take me up the mountain to show me the ritual site; words would have stood in for the existence of another place?

Or should we focus instead on the moment of misunderstanding itself? Let's turn for a moment to the tenets of deconstruction. Jacques Derrida's position could be crudely described as a defence of writing against speech: where speech has been prioritised, at the expense of writing, for being closer to the presence of meaning. For Mladen Dolar, Derrida's critique of 'phonocentricism':

> consisted in the simple and seemingly self-evident assumption that the voice is indeed the basic element of language, its natural embodiment, and is consubstantial with it, whereas writing presents its derivative, auxiliary, and parasitic supplement, at the same time secondary and dangerous. (Dolar 1996: 11)

It is in writing that Derrida finds a distance from presence and so a potential for slippages in meaning to occur. Mieke Bal summarises Derrida's position as outlined in *Dissemination* (Derrida 1993):

> Dissemination is based on three tenets related to the interplay of contemporary semiotics and deconstruction that challenge art history's pursuit of origins; intertextuality, entailing the dispersal

of origins; polysemy, entailing the undecidability of meaning; and
the shifting location of meaning, entailing the dispersal of agency.
(Bal 2001: 67)

It is this uncertainty of meaning Derrida finds in writing that I wish to
bring back to the realm of speech, so that the identities of each —writing and
speech— can question each other. Rather than focus on the misreadings
possible through writing, what about the misunderstandings possible in
speech? What about the inability of the speaker to say what s/he 'really
means', an issue well covered in psychoanalytic theory. Dolar has critiqued
Derrida for depriving the voice of ambiguity, by 'reducing it to the ground'
of illusory presence. As Dolar has commented, the voice is not only the voice
of self-presence but also that voice that one cannot control (Dolar 1996: 15).
There is also the question of memory in story-telling. Bal points out that the
story a person remembers is not identical to the one that happened, but that it
is the 'discrepancy' itself that becomes the dramatic act: '"Memory" is an act
of "vision" of the past, but as an act it is situated in the memory's present. It
is often a narrative act: loose elements come together and cohere into a story
so that they can be remembered and eventually told' (Bal 2001: 47-48).
      And   then   there   is   the   question   of   the   listener   and   the
misunderstandings possible though listening. In *The Location of Culture*,
Homi Bhabha draws an important distinction between cultural diversity and
cultural difference. In his opinion, cultural diversity is the 'recognition of pre-
given cultural contents and customs', connected to liberal notions of
multiculturalism, whereas the concept of cultural difference is more radical
and allows new positions to arise. Bhabha notes how 'the problem of cultural
interaction emerges only at the significatory boundaries of cultures, where
meanings and values are misread or signs are misappropriated' (Bhabha
1994: 34). Does misunderstanding itself indicate, as Bhabha suggests, the
problems of cultural interaction? If so, how can we understand the shades of
difference in the misunderstandings possible in speaking and writing, in
reading and listening, and in repetition and story-telling? An emphasis on
misunderstanding suggests that even if we had 'spoken' the same language
and I had reached my destination, I would still not have understood, since the
whole notion of 'getting there' sidesteps the impossibilities inherent in
cultural translation. Are linguistic skills adequate tools for negotiating
cultural difference? Perhaps understanding is not the point.
      As Nikos Papastergiadis has pointed out: 'The positive feature of
hybridity is that it invariably acknowledges that identity is constructed
through a negotiation of difference and that the presence of fissures, gaps and
contradictions is not necessarily a sign of failure' (Papastergiadis 1997: 279).
I am interested in locating misunderstanding as a place of possibility for
change, not perhaps in Bhabha's manner, for to me, his is not a redemptive

position. But following Gilles Deleuze and Félix Guattari, I would prefer to see things this way: 'there is no language in itself, nor are there any linguistic universals, only a throng of dialects, patois, slangs, and specialised languages. There is no ideal speaker-listener, any more than there is a homogeneous linguistic community' (Deleuze and Guattari 1988: 7).

Encounter 2: The Mimetic Faculty

Tired of the tourist trail, I hide on board a tiny ferry crossing Lake Panajachel. I find a place to stay: a small garden with a shed housing a platform to sleep on. In the garden there are a stone basin and a stand-pipe. There is little to do in Santiago Atitlán except sit in the garden and write. Sometimes I go to the market and buy tortillas —two instead of twenty. I get giggled at. I have sent most of my clothes back home by sea and prefer to wear a piece of Guatemalan fabric, wrapped around me like a skirt, in the way my Guatemalan Spanish-language teacher, Rosa, has shown me. I develop the idea that I am partly indigenous. But with my western T-shirt and trainers I am more boy than girl. All the indigenous women here wear traditional costume. The weave of the fabric, the colours, and, in particular, the specific motifs in the embroidered patterns, indicate the village the women come from. But the boys are more hybrid, they wear Pepsi Cola T-shirts and Nike trainers with skirts woven out of traditional fabric.

I meet a man from California who has settled here, having married a woman from Santiago Atitlán. I learn that this place is not as sleepy as it appears. Santiago Atitlán has seen a lot of trouble, past and present. There have been a number of disappearances and executions. Father Stanley Rother, a Catholic priest who served in the parish from 1968 to 1981, sympathised with the Indians and made his views against the redistribution of land well known. Rother was assassinated by a parliamentary death squad. His heart was removed and buried in the church. No one wants to talk about it. Santiago Atitlán is also unique in being the first village in the country to expel the armed forces. Extensive guerrilla activity to the north of the village gave the government a reason to establish a military base and raise accusations concerning the villagers' allegiances with the rebels. Throughout the 1980s almost 300 villagers were killed over eleven years. No one wants to talk about this either. Instead the American guy wants to sell me his wife's clothes. He can make a lot of money that way. And I'll look more like a woman.

Today, there certainly seems to be a fascination with critical debate around modes of movement, from flânerie to nomadology. From the spy to the skateboarder, we seem increasingly obsessed by figures that move

Jane Rendell

through space. A central motif in recent debates concerning urban experience is the literary flâneur. This city stroller, who appears in Charles Baudelaire's poems of 1850s Paris, has featured most famously, at least in academic circles, in the work of Walter Benjamin. For Benjamin, writing in the 1920s and 1930s, as well as for surrealists such as André Breton and Louis Aragon, and now for writers such as Iain Sinclair and Patrick Wright and film-makers like Patrick Keiller, urban roaming defines a particular approach to creative practice.[3]

There is a kind of thinking that corresponds to moving: one that follows a general thematic, keeps up a certain pace, but is in constant motion. From one thing to another, engaging only in passing, the external world operates as a series of prompts for more philosophical musings. These journeys —actual and imagined— are story-telling in motion. In some cases, the work takes the form of a narrative unfolding through space, in others the events discovered on the way are enough to create the story. The spatial element of story-telling is stressed in Michel de Certeau's notion of 'spatial stories' (de Certeau 1984:115-30). Stories take place, asserts Certeau. The 'spatial story' is a device that allows connections to be made between people and places. Through the journey, these connections are continually made and re-made, physically and conceptually over time and through space. Public concerns and private fantasies, past events and future imaginings are brought into the here and now, into a relationship that is both sequential and simultaneous.

Between departure and arrival, we are in motion. The journey is as important as the destination or the sites stopped at en route. The fleetingness of travel, of being 'nowhere' for some time, has been celebrated theoretically, in allowing us to occupy a limbo position. The feminist philosopher Rosi Braidotti's interest in nomadism does not so much describe the nomadic subject, the person who moves from place to place; rather, she is inspired by nomadism as a way of knowing that refuses to be pinned down by existing conditions (Braidotti 1994: 4-5). For those concerned with issues of identity and the oppression of minorities, the kind of thinking engendered through walking is important for emancipatory politics since it provides a way of imagining a beyond, an 'as if ' (Braidotti 1994: 5-8).

A corresponding interest in transformation through travel is also apparent in more theoretical discussions about the traveller and the tourist. Kaja Silverman has posited two modes of identification: 'heteropathic' identification where the subject aims to go outside the self, to identify with something, someone, somewhere different, and 'cannibalistic' identification

---

[3] See, for example, Aragon (1994), Baudelaire (1997), Benjamin (1997), Breton (1987). Patrick Keiller's films *London* (1995) and *Robinson in Space* (1997) are good examples of contemporary flânerie.

where the subject brings something other into the self to make it the same (Silverman 1996: 22-27). These two modes of identification operate often through 'styles' or 'rhetorics' of consumption —through what we say, wear, eat; through where we have been and where we are going. This two-way street —with its parallel movements towards difference and sameness— is interesting to consider in relation to food and travel. I tend to see the traveller in the 'heteropathic' mode, desiring of difference, and the tourist in the 'cannibalistic' mode, desiring of the same.

The metaphor of the cannibal is also used by the Brazilian Movement founded by Oswaldo de Andrade called 'Antropofagia' (Vieira 1999). Here, though, the cannibal is the colonised subject, the one who is able to appropriate and transform the coloniser by eating part of him or her. In this context cannibalism is an act to be celebrated: eating like a cannibal is an act of positive transformation rather than an act of assimilation. So the potential of the metaphor of the cannibal alters depending on the specifics of the eating encounter. 'Eating to make the same' can be a way of refusing the kind of difference that has the potential to destroy, but then again, 'eating to make the same' can also be a way of assimilating difference by equating it with the self. It is not that particular acts hold within them the seeds of oppression or the promise of liberation —that, for example, writing is more transformative than speaking— but rather that the potential of any act is characterised by the distribution of power that occurs at that specific moment of encounter.

So when we travel are we aiming for difference, to transform ourselves by becoming other, or for more of the same, to remain intact by incorporating external things and places? Or is it that we seek to blend in by adopting aspects of the other we encounter? For Michael Taussig, the mimetic faculty is based on imitative play or the representational performance of the other (Taussig 1993: 19). In wearing a piece of fabric like a Guatemalan skirt, am I trying to become Guatemalan or aiming to show I understand what it means to be a Guatemalan? I don't fold my cloth in exactly the right way, but that's because I haven't perfected the art of wrapping yet, and my cloth is a bit too thick. I choose to wear my skirt with a T-shirt and trainers. Is this mimicry then rather than mimesis, a copy that knows itself to be a copy rather than an original?

But do we not need to be more precise about the relationship between the traveller and those whom he or she encounters? Gayatri Spivak casts the emphasis not on the traveller, the 'me' in my story, but on those that 'I' travel to meet. Spivak (1993) has argued that the 'subaltern cannot speak', that there can be no representation of subaltern consciousness, that the act of representation is always accompanied by an appropriation, and that alienation is the price of every representation (Papastergiadis 1997: 276). As Papastergiadis points out, Spivak advises against the possibly benign identification with the subaltern, the well-meaning gesture of solidarity. For

Jane Rendell

her, subalternity is not a condition to be desired. Spivak 'warns against the presumption that subaltern experiences are texts that are available for translation' (Papastergiadis 1997: 276) and instead focuses attention on what the work 'cannot say'. This insight takes us back to Benjamin, and to his observation that no translation offers an exact correspondence between different languages.

For Bhabha, in the moment of encounter, elements transform each other. Hybridity works two ways. There is the mimicry of the colonised and the mimicry of the coloniser. How do they intersect? What is the difference between a girl from England and a boy from Guatemala wearing a Guatemalan skirt with a T-shirt and trainers? Note that my T-shirt and trainers are anonymous and his are Pepsi Cola and Nike. He shows he knows about brands, I show I know about indigenous culture. Bhabha suggests that 'interdisciplinarity is the acknowledgement of the emergent sign of cultural difference produced in the ambivalent movement between pedagogical and performative address' (Bhabha 1994: 163). The boy and I show how 'terms of cultural engagement, whether antagonistic or affiliative, are produced performatively' (21). He and I perform each other, but for each of us this means something very different. In this story, as in many others, a certain equation is made between travel and colonisation: here the traveller is equated with the coloniser, while the person who is 'travelled to' is one of a colonised group. How would things be if he travelled to me? As Bhabha points out, the question of hybridity is both routine and transgressive, but it depends on place and history (Friedman 1998: 86). We would both be understood differently if I were him and he were me, or indeed if we were in London, or New York, or La Paz.

Encounter 3: Bridge

On the last day of my trip, heading back through Mexico towards Texas, I am in the border town of Nuevo Laredo. I have accumulated a lot of things. As well as my rucksack, I am carrying a string bag bought in Guatemala, clinking with heavy bottles of Tequila. A clean-shaven middle-aged Latino approaches me and asks if he can help me by carrying a bag. It is easier to say yes than no. We head through town towards the border control point on the bridge. On the way we make conversation —my homebound journey to the US, my family in the UK; his kids in Laredo, on the Mexican side, his brother, a hairdresser, in Laredo, on the US side. He is keen to introduce me to his brother, very keen.

At the checkpoint, I show my US visa and UK passport. No problem. The border police nod towards my companion. They ask him some questions. He explains he is with me. No problem. Then he says something else, again in

Spanish, but this time very fast, so fast I cannot quite follow. I know that he has said something that concerns the exact nature of our relationship. I keep quiet. I am keen to keep moving. They let us through. I expect now to be invited to visit the brother at the hairdressing salon. But I am mistaken. Once over the bridge, my companion is gone. I never meet up with his brother, the hairdresser. Nor, I suspect, does he.

In a piece of work entitled 'Bridge', the conceptual artist Victor Burgin has photographed the Golden Gate bridge in San Francisco with a woman lying below. As with much of Burgin's work, a deceptively simple image reveals, under careful scrutiny, a wealth of ideas. The artist's interest in bridges encompasses not only the usage of the word in everyday speech, to talk of exchange between two as well as the transition between states, but also the powerful metaphoric role that bridges play. For Burgin, the relationship between the bridge and the water that flows beneath is gendered; the bridge is a metaphor for masculinity and the water stands for femininity (Catalogue 2001). The suggestion is that the bridge is static and the water flowing beneath is in flux. It is interesting how it was my mobility, my ability to move across the border because of my nationality, that gave my Mexican companion access to a new place. But it is also interesting how, at the same time, it was my gender that gave him access to my nationality. Would he ever have approached a gringo rather than a gringa and offered to carry his string bag? And it was my lack of linguistic agility that gave him physical and cultural mobility.

In dreams, bridges may refer to the linking role of the penis in sexual intercourse, as well as the transitional states of birth and death. There are many who would claim the existence of architectural archetypes. The psychoanalyst Carl Jung, for example, believed in a collective unconscious where there lay buried a language of symbolic forms that all could relate to and understand (Storr 1973: 39-61). My intellectual and rational side tells me that there is no such thing as a universal symbol —surely the meaning that certain objects are capable of communicating must depend on historical period and cultural background? Why is it then that certain architectural forms —like doors and bridges— hold such potency the world over? Perhaps it is because they hold physical resemblances to certain kinds of psychological states. Bridges speak of meetings and separations between people. The bridge is a metaphor for connection or movement between two sides. If the act of translation presupposes some kind of imbalance, demanding that one side be understood in terms of the other, dialogue signifies the desire to communicate by both participants. In this sense we can understand the bridge as built dialogues and, in the context of this discussion, the bridge represents hope and the possibility of a two-way conversation.

The French philosopher Michel Serres is very interested in communication, mediation and transformation as a result of exchange between people. Serres even suggests that certain places of transition or interchange, such as airports, other places of mass transit and sites of new technologies, are 'a passing-place of angels' (Serres 1995: 224). According to Serres, it is in such spaces that messages from angels increase in number and intensity. But perhaps the most interesting thing Serres has to say about angels is that they are the personification of prepositions. Prepositions — those small words like 'on', 'in' and 'at'— make connections between people, objects and places. Some prepositions emphasise position, others focus on relationships and yet others indicate the directional nature of these connections.

Bridges operate much like prepositions —they make links between two locations. As places of mediation, of encounter and crossing, bridges are for me very much connected with angels. Within religious scripture angels are spirits or heavenly beings who mediate between human and divine realms. Put simply, angels are messengers, like Hermes, the Greek god with winged feet. Messengers are also agents of transformation: the messages they bear can change things. Because of their fluid, ever-changing status as both spirit and matter, angels challenge tradition and offer opportunities to think about the world differently (Rendell 2001).

This might seem rather unrelated to bridges, but if you stand still at the centre point of any bridge, half-way between one side and the other, you'll understand what I mean. The feeling you get is one of disconnection and separation. To look at a bridge may bring to mind unity, since to travel across a bridge is an act of connection, but to be halfway across is to be held apart. Being in the middle of a bridge places us, like angels, in between, offering us a moment for contemplation and self-reflection. It is interesting to think of bridges this way, as places that intensify the feeling of 'being in the moment', in terms of unpredictability, when we are still undecided what will happen next. For me, there is a close relationship between this position and what Diane Elam has called 'the politics of undecidability', her understanding of the political imperative of deconstruction (Elam 1994). It is within this context that I am interested in locating misunderstandings. Even dialogues composed of miscommunication are important forms of exchange, for they allow us to focus on the problems that arise when we try to avoid the cultural and linguistic asymmetries usually prioritised in the ways in which we 'understand'.

Crossroads and Meetings

> As narrator she is narrated as well. And in a way she is already
> told, and what she herself is telling will not undo that somewhere
> else she is *told* (Bhabha 1994: 150).[4]

I have always considered autobiographical writing to be confessional, part of a process of revelation, one that uncovers the truth beneath. For me, uncovering is an act of bravery that allows the writer to feel alive and involved in the telling. But I have found that once a story is repeated the fear goes and one is no longer being brave in the telling or testing the edge of oneself but is simply performing an act that confirms one's presence. I have come to realise that a 'confessing' is not a revealing of what lies underneath, but rather a constructing of myself in relation to another, to my reader or my listener. To 'tell about myself' with all the dangers a confessional can bring, to be aware of the encounter, I must make myself differently every time I write or I speak.

Speaking and writing (the traces of telling) are architectural. Certain forms of architecture and patterns of space, the view from a hilltop, the two-way traffic on a bridge, the clutter and colour of a market square, offer the story-teller physical and material forms, as well as the social possibilities, for certain kinds of encounter to occur. Places loaded with cultural and historical significance, as well as those considered archetypal, such as tables, doorways, windows or rooftops, often allow certain kinds of stories to unfold and psychological transformation to take place. Architecture is often used metaphorically in literature, but writing is also a place in its own right. The way I position myself in my writing is architectural and has implications for the way in which I meet my reader. I tell stories about myself to make a place of encounter. Certain forms of communication make walls, others create bridges, while others are crossroads for ongoing traffic. Some stories close down possibilities for discussion, others invite participation, and yet in each case the voice of the story-teller is only present for a brief moment of time, soon to be replaced by the person who has just heard the story. The architecture of a confessional construction is less about me, less about how differently I may tell each time; it is not the teller who is the architect. Regardless of what I tell, I will always be told again, elsewhere, in ways that I will never know. It is the listener who makes architecture.

I am telling you. But what will you tell of me?

---

[4] Interestingly this quote comes not from Bhabha himself but from Bhabha quoting Lyotard and Thébaud (1985: 41). The emphasis is Bhabha's.

Bhabha talks of performative time, arguing that the subject is only graspable in the time between telling and being told. This emphasises the temporal element in 'telling'; but there is also a spatial aspect, the time between telling and being told is also the place between here and somewhere else. This is a double scene, Bhabha says, a scene which demonstrates that the very condition of cultural knowledge is the alienation of the subject (Bhabha 1994: 150). Importance shifts for Bhabha from the one who is telling, or 'articulating', and to where this articulation is taking place. Bhabha's phrase for this is the 'topos of enunciation' (Bhabha 1994: 162). This is architecture of the encounter, of the confessional construction.

Los Encuentros

The suggestion that the listener will tell again, somewhere else, interests me, for it shifts the focus from one point of telling, even if a contingent one, to multiple tellings. These tellings can be defined spatially, but such a mapping is not certain; rather it can only be defined through undecidability, through difference and deferral. Multiple tellings in many places at once emphasise difference through simultaneity; re-tellings over time highlight slippage through deferral.

When did you tell and where did you tell it? What did you tell about me?

Los Encuentros and Los Cuatro Caminos were my favourite points along the Carretera InterAmericana, the main highway that runs through Guatemala from Mexico to Honduras. These names marked the places where I got off one bus and decided which one to flag down next.

Los Cuatro Caminos. North, south, east, west. From Austin, Texas to Santiago Atitlán, Guatemala and back again.

Works Cited

Anzaldúa, Gloria (1999) *Borderlands/La Frontera: The New Mestiza*, 2nd edition (San Francisco: Lute Books).

Aragon, Louis (1994) *Paris Peasant* (Boston: Exact Change).

Bal, Mieke (2001) *Looking In: The Art of Viewing* (Amsterdam: G and B Arts International).

Baudelaire, Charles (1997) *The Parisian Prowler* (London: The University of Georgia Press).

Benjamin, Walter (1992) [1955] 'The Task of the Translator', in *Illuminations* (London: Fontana Press), 70-82.

———— (1997) *Charles Baudelaire: A Lyric Poet in the Era of High Capitalism* (London: Verso).

Bhabha, Homi K. (1994) *The Location of Culture* (London: Routledge).

Braidotti, Rosi (1994) *Nomadic Subjects* (New York: Columbia University Press).

Breton, André (1987) *Mad Love* (London: University of Nebraska Press).

Catalogue (2001) *Victor Burgin* (Barcelona: Fundació Antoni Tàpies).

de Certeau, Michel (1984) 'Walking in the City' and 'Spatial Stories', in *The Practice of Everyday Life* (Berkeley: University of California Press), 91-110; 115-30.

Deleuze, Gilles and Félix Guattari (1988) *A Thousand Plateaus: Capitalism and Schizophrenia* (London: Athlone Press).

Derrida, Jacques (1981) [1972] *Dissemination* (London: Athlone Press).

Dolar, Mladen (1996) 'The Object Voice', in Renata Salecl and Slavoj Žižek (eds), *Gaze and Voice as Love Objects: SIC 1* (London and Durham: Duke University Press), 7-31.

Elam, Diane (1994) *Feminism and Deconstruction: Ms. En Abyme* (London: Routledge).

Flaubert, Gustave (1931) [1862] *Salammbô* (London: Everyman's Library).

Friedman, Susan Stanford (1998) *Mappings: Feminism and the Cultural Geographies of Encounter* (Princeton: Princeton University Press).

hooks, bell (1989) *Yearnings: Race, Gender, and Cultural Politics* (London: Turnaround Press).

Johnson, Christopher (2000) 'Speaking in Tongues', Inaugural Lecture, University of Nottingham (unpublished).

Kabbani, Rana (1987) *The Passionate Nomad: The Diary of Isabelle Eberhardt* (Boston: Beacon Press).

Kaplan, Caren (1996) *Questions of Travel: Postmodern Discourses of Displacement* (Durham NC: Duke University Press).

Keiller, Patrick (dir.) (1995) *London*.

———— (dir.) (1997) *Robinson in Space*.

Lévi-Strauss, Claude (1955) *Tristes Tropiques* (Paris: Librairie Plon).

Lyotard, Jean-François and Jean-Loup Thébaud (1985) *Just Gaming*, tr
    Wlad Godzich (Manchester: Manchester University Press).
Minh-Ha, Trinh T. (1991) *When The Moon Waxes Red: Representati*
    Gender and Cultural Politics (London: Routledge).
Papastergiadis, Nikos (1997) 'Tracing Hybridity in Theory', in Pn
    Werbner and Tariq Modood (eds), *Debating Cultural Hybrid*
    Multi-cultural Identities and the Politics of Anti-Racis
    Postcolonial Encounters Series (London: Zed Books), 257-81.
Rendell, Jane (2001) 'Imagination is the Root of all Change', in *Bridges*
    book accompanying three films on bridges by Lucy Blakstad
    (London: August Publications), 30-37.
———— (2002) 'Travelling the Distance/Encountering the Other', in Davic
    Blamey (ed), *Here, There, Elsewhere: Dialogues of Location an*
    Mobility (London: Open Editions), 43-54.
Serres, Michel (1995) *Angels: A Modern Myth* (Paris: Flammarion).
Silverman, Kaja (1996) *The Threshold of the Visible World* (London:
    Routledge).
Spivak, Gayatri Chakravorti (1993) 'Can the Subaltern Speak?', in Patrick
    Williams and Laura Chrisman (eds), *Colonial Discourse and*
    Postcolonial Theory: A Reader (Hemel Hemsptead: Harvester
    Wheatsheaf), 66-111.
Storr, Anthony (1973) *Jung* (London: Fontana).
Taussig, Michael (1993) *Mimesis and Alterity: A Particular History of the*
    Senses (London: Routledge).
Vieira, Else (1999) 'Liberating Calibans: Readings of Antropofagia and
    Haroldo de Campos's Poetics of Transcreation', in Susan Bassnett
    and Harish Trivedi (eds), *Postcolonial Translation: Theory and*
    Practice (London and New York: Routledge).

Changing Perceptions of National Identity in Brazilian Art and Modern Architecture

Michael Asbury

Abstract

This essay focuses on various issues around the development of Brazilian art and architecture during the twentieth century and, especially, on their relationship with various trends of European Modernism. The notion of 'purity', which appears to be inherent in European Modernism, will be central to the discussion. Contrary to what many people think, it will be argued throughout this essay that the transcultural operations that arose from the mediation between perceptions of local traditions and notions of purity were always present within European Modernism and did not pertain to the peripheries alone. In fact, this essay will attempt to demonstrate that the antagonism between centres and peripheries was taken as an advantage by non-European Modernists in order to develop syncretic identity: being entirely Modern while developing specifically national aesthetic languages.

* * *

Introduction

Art historians have in the past interpreted the preoccupation with the representation of national identity as an obstacle in the path towards the development of an autonomous, emancipated or 'universal' avant-garde. More recently, the mediation between national culture and formal concerns which appeared to be more explicit in non-canonical instances of Modernism has been re-evaluated as hybrid in nature and posited as an example of a possible Postmodernism *avant la lettre*. However, interpretations such as these do not seem entirely satisfactory, since they ignore the specific conditions of cultural production at different historical moments and worryingly reinforce the fixity of the notion of national identity.

The notion of hybridity in the context of Latin American art has become inescapably associated to the work of Néstor García Canclini. In *Hybrid Cultures: Strategies for Entering and Leaving Modernity* (1995 [1989]), García Canclini places hybridisation within the politics of subaltern struggles and rejects the claim that Modernism in Latin America did not attain the level of cultural purity present in Europe and the United States due to the late or incomplete Modernisation of the continent. He argues instead that Latin American Modernity did not replace pre-Modern culture but coexisted with the traditional. Within such coexistence, the subaltern, through the process of hybridisation, opens a space of negotiation with the dominant culture, while maintaining a sense of identity through the preservation of local traditions.

In effect, Canclini acknowledged operations present within the history of the continent since its colonial experience, placing them in the specific context of more recent relations and negotiations with Modernism and Modernisation. However, the apparent a-historical presence of hybrid cultural processes, coupled with the term's etymology —the sterile product of two pure entities— seems insufficient to capture the fluid nature of cultural production. Although hybridity has been increasingly associated with mediating processes between centre and periphery, its meaning is not restricted to the domain of cultural mediation. Contemporary art, for instance, has also used the term broadly to define any activity that cuts across different domains of specialisation such as art and technology. The term transculturation could perhaps describe more appropriately the fluid nature within mediations and translations of different cultural traditions.[1]

This essay will discuss the development of art and architecture in Brazil during the twentieth century and their relationship with European Modernist ideals such as 'purity'. It will argue that the transcultural operations arising from the mediation between perceptions of local traditions and notions of purity, rather than pertaining to Modernism in the periphery, were already present within early European Modernism. Indeed, the existence of such antagonisms was appropriated by non-European Modernists in order to develop syncretic modes of operation: being entirely Modern while developing specifically national aesthetic languages.[2]

According to the British architectural and design historian Peter Reyner Banham, the inheritance left by Modern design was one of deception. Banham remarked that none of the major architects of the 1920s could be considered a pure Functionalist, that is, an architect who designs without aesthetic intentions (Banham 1960: 162). While modern architecture's functional purpose concealed its aesthetics, modernist painting's associated rhetoric of aesthetic purity, concealed its inevitable contamination. Banham's argument that different trends in European Modernist architecture developed through often contradictory cultural references, is perhaps a useful reference for the historian of Latin American art and architecture as a means of investigating issues of difference within transcultural processes. Banham's formative years as a cultural activist were informed by his engagement within

---

[1] For a parallel history on the specific theme of hybridity in painting and its relation to Brazilian modern art see Asbury (2003).
[2] For a distinction between the terms syncretism and hybridity, see Bécquer and Gatti (1991), 65-81.

the Independent Group. In the post WW2 period, this loose gathering of artists, critics and architects re-assessed the legacy of Modernism and its mediation with contemporaneous developments in science, mass media, industrial design and so on. Banham utilised such wide cultural references to question the rhetoric and symbolism of the Modern architectural tradition. His writing is transculturally referred to here as a means of gauging Western architectural thought at a time when Brasilia was being constructed and major articulations were occurring in Brazilian art between the emergence of mass culture and the re-evaluation of national popular culture. In effect, Banham re-evaluated the legacy of Futurism at a moment in which Brasilia, the heroic Futurist city, was being built as the embodiment of a nation's faith in its Modern destiny.

There is a sense of inadequacy that fuels the pendulous movement in non-central cultural production between concerns relating to the so-called 'local' and those relating to the ideal of 'universality'. If we are to argue that such oscillations also took place within the cultural centre, the inadequacy felt by cultural producers in the periphery is to be further politicised, since it becomes increasingly apparent that such production is submitted to a circuit of dissemination which pertains to the domain of geo-politics rather than pure aesthetics.

Such a vision is of course very distant from Banham's own position. Instead, he argued, that the widening adoption of Modernist ideas, particularly that of functionalism, had entailed a dilution of architecture's symbolic quality (Banham 1960: 320-21). The context in which Modern art and architecture developed in Brazil, contradicts such ideas of dilution through dissemination. This becomes evident when considering the symbolic power of a city such as Brasilia, whose inauguration in 1960, coincided with Banham's publication of *Theory and Design in the First Machine Age*, an extensive survey of the origins of Modern architecture. The coincidence, inconsequential as it may be, serves as the pretext for the collision of the historical narratives discussed below.

The Development of a National Modernism

Modernism in Brazil arose out of a desire for renewal and from an explicit project of asserting the nation's identity. From the Modern Art Week in São Paulo in 1922 to the 1924 *Pau-Brasil*[3] and the 1928 *Manifesto Antropófago*[4],

---

[3] The Manifesto's title *Poesia Pau-Brasil* (Brazil Wood Poetry) written by Oswald de Andrade makes reference to the commodity that gave Brazil its name: Portugal's first interest in its newly discovered territory. For an English translation see Ades (1989), 310-11.
[4] The *Manifesto Antropófago* (Anthropophagous Manifesto) also written by Oswald de Andrade, suggested that cultural producers should emulate the original Brazilians in their rituals of

Modernismo developed strategies for the creation of a specifically Brazilian rhetoric and aesthetic that concurrently displayed a contemporaneity with Europe. Throughout the twentieth century the concerns expressed in Brazilian cultural production oscillated between national/popular culture and metropolitan ideals of Modernity.

Modern architecture could be said to have been a part of that project: in its relation to the ideal of national identity and its shared references to contemporary French culture. However, to analyse the relationship established between architecture and the visual arts, particularly with respect to their association with ideals of national identity, entails an investigation into certain shifts that occurred in the often conflictual tendencies contained within the field of symbolic production from *Modernismo* to the post WW2 period.[5]

Although *Modernismo* in the fine arts is generally assumed to have been a local adaptation of Cubism, it could be more accurately described as an aesthetic which drew upon a desire to create a Brazilian imagery through the adaptation of a variety of European styles, varying according to individual artists. Purism —the post-Cubist interpretation proposed by Ozenfant and Jeanneret (Le Corbusier)— received considerable attention in Brazil.[6]

The French Purist movement was itself embedded in the ideal of nationalism which had emerged following WW1: it promoted, through the journal *L'Esprit Nouveau*,[7] the idea of a *Rappel à l'Ordre* (Call to Order), which considered French culture as the rightful inheritor of the Classical tradition.[8] It therefore proposed a re-evaluation of Cubism, through the sobriety of Classical art, as a means of eradicating all forms of irrational and romantic connotation which were seen as intrinsically Germanic in character. In Brazil, painters such as Tarsila do Amaral would have been exposed to ideas associated with the *Rappel à l'Ordre* as a student of André Lhote, Albert Gleizes and later Fernand Léger. In literature, Mário de Andrade

---

cannibalism whereby through the devouring of one's enemy their power and strength is transformed into one's own. A form of critical appropriation of European culture as an essentially Brazilian activity, Anthropophagy was a cunning strategy for the affirmation of a national identity while concurrently maintaining a correspondence with respect to European culture.

[5] *Modernismo* is used here to define a period in Brazilian art covering the 1920s and leading on into the 1930s. It is a term that describes a movement rather than the wide cultural and aesthetic connotations of the term modernism.

[6] The painting of Tarsila do Amaral is perhaps the most obvious example, but writers such as Mário de Andrade possessed the entire run of the Purist journal *Les Temps Modernes*.

[7] Research has shown that other central figures of Brazilian modernism had intimate knowledge of this section of the Parisian artistic circles, such as in Graça Aranha's use of the term *Espiritonovismo* and Mário de Andrade's collection of the entire run of the journal *L'Esprit Nouveau*. See Teles (1997), 25-35.

[8] For more about the *Call to Order* in Brazilian *Modernismo*, see Fabris (2000-2001), 533-39.

owned the entire run of the Journal *L'Esprit Nouveau*, and in architecture, Le Corbusier became the inevitable reference for young architects following his visits to Brazil in 1929 and in 1936.

Beyond the domain of painting Le Corbusier also expressed a certain affinity with post-Cubist ideals in *Vers une Architecture* and his town planning theories. These became key references for young Brazilian architects. However, rather than a pure and national (French) Classical tradition, the ideals expressed in Le Corbusier's writing and aesthetics already contained a diversity of influences. Indeed, critics such as Banham (1960: 202-13) questioned the inherited influences of Rationalism (through Choisy) and Academicism (through Guadet) amongst those French architects, and Le Corbusier in particular, who would make a large contribution towards the International Style of the 1920s. Instead, Banham suggested that their choice of an architectural idiom was affected by the Parisian system of patronage, the influence of the Cubist tradition —in particular the 'intellectual wing', the *Groupe de Puteaux*— combined with Futurist notions of machined objects. He argued that the latter entered the domain of architecture through Duchamp's ready-mades, such as the 'Bicycle Wheel' and the 'Bottle-Rack', whose subsequent interpretation in terms of Platonic forms became part of the repertoire of *Le Rappel à l'Ordre*.

In Ozenfant's and Jeanneret's (Le Corbusier) *Après le Cubisme*, Cubist painting and contemporaneous trends in architecture were merged, leading to the concept of the *objet-type*, or *objet-standard*. According to Banham it also 'represented a fairly thoroughgoing fusion of the Futurist, Cubist and classicising themes' (Banham 1960: 209). The apparent confirmation of these notions of ideal Platonic geometry and standard forms were concurrent with a period of stagnation in design, following WW1. Banham argued that, during that period, design could still be related to these theories, but, in the following decades, technological advances would increasingly distance the rhetoric of design from its non-architectural practice.

Banham saw Le Corbusier as 'erudite' rather than 'inventive'. In other words, Le Corbusier possessed a vast visual/architectural knowledge, which he *digested* and reapplied when the opportunity presented itself. This was then seen as an inheritance of the French *Beaux-Arts* tradition. However, while Guadet referred exclusively to French architectural history, Le Corbusier made use of 'ready-mades' from Mediterranean architecture, aeronautics, nautics, peasantry, ancient remains, and even from the creations of his own followers. Like the Brazilian appropriative strategy of 'Anthropophagy', Le Corbusier's genius resided on his ability to appropriate such disparate elements into his visual repertoire, transposing them into different contexts.

In fact, the notion of Anthropophagy also has a somewhat perverse relation to the *Rappel à l'Ordre*. Although Oswald de Andrade, the author of the 'Anthropophagite Manifesto', shared his rebellious character with the contemporaneous activities of Dada and Surrealism, the idea of adopting an appropriative strategy based on the attitude of an original Brazilian □ the cannibal□ displayed a similar concern with Purism: the affirmation of a cultural origin or tradition, even if this entailed inventing it. While the Purists searched for a Modern national identity based on Classical tenets, Brazilians searched for a national Modernism based on the nation's primitive origins. The latter was itself an appropriation of the Parisian fascination with the primitive and exotic combined with the Western notion of Arcadia.

In Modern Brazilian architecture, affirmations of cultural origins were less dramatic. However, due to the relative stability of its rhetoric, it was allowed more time to develop within its local context, eventually becoming acknowledged as representative of the nation's Modernity. It began with the pioneering efforts of Flávio de Carvalho and Gregori Ilitch Warchavchik. The latter, in 1925, published a manifesto entitled *Acerca da Arquitetura Moderna* (Concerning Modern Architecture). The date is pertinent since it brings the origins of Modern architecture in Brazil within close proximity to the polemics and manifestos of the Modernist group in São Paulo during the 1920s. Carvalho had produced designs for Modern buildings as early as 1927 and Warchavchik constructed his first Modernist building — his own house— three years after publishing his manifesto. Indeed, it was the reaction to Warchavchik's first Modern house by a conservative establishment that attracted the attention of the Modernist circle in São Paulo. The presence of Warchavchik's Modern house contributes towards an understanding of the enthusiasm for Le Corbusier's ideas amongst the young generation of Brazilian architects during his first visit to Brazil in 1929. At the time, Warchavchik was already constructing his second house, which:

> Opened to the public in March and April of 1930 as the *Exposição de uma Casa Moderna* [Modern house Exhibition]. Presenting the 'tropical garden' designed by [Warchavchik's] wife Mina Klabin Segall, furniture and lighting by the architect, works by leading Modernist artists, a small bronze by Lipchitz, cushions by Sonia Delaunay and carpets by the Bauhaus, as well as soirées with the experiments of Modernist literature, the *Casa da Rua Itápolis* [House on Itápolis Street] achieved the objective of promoting awareness among the general public and also the hoped   for incorporation of Modern architecture with the efforts of the Brazilian avant-garde. (Martins 2000: 579)

Modernism, Nationalism and Populist Politics

In the 1930s, Brazilian Modernism was quite distinct from the non-institutional and somewhat aristocratic nature of *Modernismo* in the 1920s. As a result of the economic crisis of 1929, the nature of the Modern movement during the 1930s would reflect the country's political and economical transition. Until then, politicians, complicit with the rural oligarchies, claimed that Brazil was, and should remain, a country with an essentially agricultural vocation. The 1930s paved the way for the possibility of Brazil's seeing itself as 'a country condemned to Modernity' (Pedrosa 1981b: 304). The 'revolution', or more precisely the *coup d'état*, that placed Getúlio Vargas in power in 1930 was at the centre of the shift in power from the rural oligarchies towards the nationalist middle class that was particularly favourable to industrial development. The effect that such a political shift had on Modernism was diverse and paradoxical, particularly on the relation between architecture and the fine arts.

In the 1930s, Modern architecture gained considerable government support, the most striking example of which was the Ministry of Education and Health in Rio de Janeiro commissioned in 1936. Its design team was led by Lúcio Costa (a former partner of Warchavchik) and included the architect Oscar Niemeyer and the landscape designer Burle Marx. Le Corbusier, the project's consultant, also played a central role in the design's conception and is often attributed the 'authorship' of the building. Furthermore, the Ministry included murals by Cândido Portinari, and it therefore could be seen as another instance in which art and architecture were brought together as a seemingly coherent whole: a synthesis of the arts.

Influenced by the communist party line, Modernist painting during the 1930s became overwhelmingly concerned with the representation of the Brazilian people. The initial concern with creating an art that reflected a national identity during the 1920s, which drew on the mythological imagery of the natives, moved towards themes that could be seen as approaching Socialist Realism. Ironically, such concerns were also useful to a right-wing populist government eager to promote images that demonstrated its proximity to 'real' Brazilians, while affirming its affinity with Modernity. Cândido Portinari, the most prominent Brazilian Modernist painter in the 1930s, thus became, involuntarily perhaps, complicit with government rhetoric. In the words of the artist and art historian Carlos Zilio, Portinari, without being an 'official artist,' managed to receive unanimous approval from both the left and those who were in power:

> Portinari's style embraced the assimilation of various sources, each being predominant at different moments over one another. The formalisation, however, that he lent to this group of influences was perfectly adjusted to the level of acceptance possible for the

Brazilian visual culture of the time, that is, an art that being Modern was not 'unintelligible'. Concurrently he achieved the perfect register of the historical necessities of such culture. He allowed himself to be part of the rhetoric of a political discourse that was capable of embracing the denunciatory platform of the left, with 'social' preoccupations and also the modernising populism of the Getulist dictatorship. (Zilio 1982: 16-17)

Similar political ambivalences existed in the field of architecture. From the early twentieth century, various layers of urban planning had been projected on to the city of Rio de Janeiro. During Le Corbusier's first visit to the country in 1929, an extensive urban plan was being devised (between 1927 and 1930) by the French urban planner Donald Alfred Agache. Although never fully implemented, the Agache project was based on a clearly European model. Le Corbusier's spontaneous response to the landscape of Rio gave rise to a number of sketches suggesting a radical transformation of the city's plan. Although utterly unrealistic, it could be argued that these wild plans had a greater impact on future architectural projects than Agache's careful, albeit outdated, considerations. Le Corbusier's designs comprised a single long multi-storey building raised on pilotis with a motorway running along its top. The concept was later referred to by architects such as Affonso Eduardo Reidy who designed a number of enlightened projects for social housing. Constructed between 1947 and 1958, Reidy's *Pedregulho* housing complex contained a gymnasium, swimming pool, health centre, market, and laundry. Its actual housing quarters evoked the sinuous long building suggested by Le Corbusier's sketch: it followed the slope and curve of the hill, elegantly overlooking the rest of the complex.[9] However, such projects represented isolated examples for a possible future. Although antagonistic towards the dominant ideology, the national popular project, with which the Modern painters and architects identified themselves, legitimised the very object of its criticism. The art critic Mário Pedrosa interpreted the situation as follows:

> The rapidity with which the new architecture developed in the feverish years that preceded the last war [WW2] did not allow a more natural type of growth. Dictatorship is the total liberty of the state and the almost total oppression of the citizens. The one in Brazil, not constituting an exception to the rule, conceived of laws based above all on the day to day concerns of its propaganda, searching as such, in its totalitarian tendency, to attract towards itself the young architects whose ideas and concepts were, however, of totally opposite inspiration. They worked in effect for

---

[9] For further details on this and other projects, see Bonduki (2000), 83-103.

the dictatorship but without renouncing their ideas. (Pedrosa 1981a: 258-59)

Pedrosa saw the nature of the pre-WW2 architecture, and in particular the Ministry of Education and Health, as well as Niemeyer's *Pampulha* complex,[10] as tending towards a grandeur and luxury that were not fundamental characteristics of Modernist architecture itself, but that pertained to the impositions made by its specific form of patronage. Pedrosa, who had spent considerable time in Germany, was perhaps contrasting these to the government-sponsored housing projects such as those carried out by Ernst May.[11] However, paradigmatic Modernist buildings, such as the *Barcelona Pavillion* by Mies van der Rohe and Le Corbusier's *Villa Savoye*, can hardly be described as social housing projects. Both had relied on luxury, expensive materials and a symbolism that purported to be related to the mechanised world. However, as Banham (1960: 320) argued, they did not fully use the potential of contemporaneous technological advances.

For a country such as Brazil that was not yet fully modernised, the symbolism associated with Modern architecture was convenient in portraying an image of an industrial society. It corresponded nevertheless, to a desire of the nation to be Modern rather than being symptomatic of the achievement of full Modernisation. Unlike the implied backwardness of the field of painting by its association with the national character, architecture's affirmation of a Modern Brazil did not raise such unease. An exception, perhaps, was the perceived inconsistency between the Modern architectural form of the Ministry of Education and the figurative nature of Portinari's murals that adorned it, which received severe criticism by the Swiss artist and designer Max Bill (Morais 1994: 223). Lúcio Costa, in defence of Portinari's murals, argued that they referred to the colonial tradition of Portuguese painted titles and therefore reflected the adaptation to the Modern idiom within a country whose architecture had originated in the Baroque tradition. However, appeals to the national tradition seemed increasingly distant from the desires of the post-WW2 generation. Positions of total rupture with the past such as those proposed by Max Bill became increasingly seductive for many post-War artists and Brazil was no exception.

---

[10] A complex of buildings surrounding a lake in the outskirts of Belo Horizonte comprising a casino, a church and a yacht club.

[11] For a discussion on such developments, see Banham (1960), 272.

Modernism, Modernisation and the Re-evaluation of the National Character

The end of WW2 brought with it a positivism that entailed, particularly during the 1950s, a period of incredible growth both in terms of creativity and the development of the institutional structures for culture as a whole: art, architecture, literature, music, and cinema. The 'Developmentalist Nationalist' rhetoric of Juscelino Kubitschek's government, which held power from 1956 to 1961, claimed that Brazilians could no longer accept destiny as a negative entity. In a mood of unprecedented optimism, it set itself the task of transforming Brazil into an industrial nation. Modern architecture's role as the symbol of the drive towards Modernisation became increasingly evident.

Within the field of the fine arts, the context of enthusiasm for Modernity opened the way for the Constructivist/Concretist tendency. This is generally assumed to have its origin in Max Bill's winning the prize for sculpture at the first São Paulo Biennial in 1951 with the work *Tripartite Unity*: as Bill himself claimed (quoted in Vergez 2000: 22-23), his art resulted from the direct application of mathematical theorems.

Concrete art became adopted by artists in São Paulo and Rio de Janeiro, and for much of the 1950s its rhetoric was seen as entirely coherent with the new architecture. This faction of the avant-garde, architecture, and ultimately industry, seemed to possess an unprecedented coherency, leading to the belief that Modernism and Modernisation had finally become synchronous occurrences. This could be interpreted as a crucial shift, whereby art and architecture had transformed themselves from tools for affirming notions of national identity into instruments for affirming the nation's Modernity. The issue of representing the national character which had dominated the art of the previous decades gave way to an art that aspired to a state of equality with that of the developed nations. The association between art, design and architecture became crucial within the perceived function of cultural production within society at large. This function was predominantly seen as the dissemination of good taste through the production of good design. Concrete art and poetry became increasingly involved with graphic design and the emergent culture of advertising. However, very few actual connections were established between art and architecture. This only occurred in 1959 following the formation of the Rio de Janeiro splinter Neo-concrete group (Brito 1985). The latter, although not strictly architectural in nature, was influenced by existentialism and phenomenology and tended to perceive the object of art in direct relation to its surroundings. This in turn led artists to an increasing preoccupation with spatial concerns, and would inform the architectural character of much of Hélio Oiticica's subsequent work.

The Neo-concrete group's brief existence coincided with the peak and rupture[12] of the 'Developmentalist' ideology of the Juscelino Kubitschek government, the administration responsible for the construction of Brasilia. The new capital, a monumental city charged with symbolic significance, displays an urban plan that is reminiscent of the spirit of conquest of the colonisers. Placed as it is in the centre of the country, it resembles the first sign that the European discoverers installed in the new land —the cross.[13] It conveniently also recalls the more Modern form of an aircraft. Other than the ambivalent references to the Modern and the colonial, evident in much of Brazilian Modernism, Brasilia was without a doubt a consequence of a nation demonstrating its power, control, and the imposition of Modernity over its territory.

Returning to Banham's Britain, the 'Festival of Britain' in 1951 has been described as 'a political allegory of the rebirth and restructuring of England and the post-War economy after the devastation of World War II' (Barry 1988: 44-45). However, both Brasilia and the Festival, proved to be profoundly disappointing after the enthusiasm over the ideal of a Modern nation. The ideal proposed by the Festival seemed increasingly incongruous with the continued rationing of certain products into the 1950s in addition to the realisation that the British Empire was coming to a close:

> By the early Fifties [Britain] was no longer broke, but strangely it had lost its confidence. Control of the future no longer seemed so certain. Partly this had to do with the realisation that the days of the Empire were over, partly it had to do with the realisation that with the atom bomb firmly in place there was now a real possibility of there being no future at all. (Lawson 1988: 20-23)

In Brazil, the dissolution of the utopian dream, following the construction of Brasilia, came from the realisation of the precarious reality of the surroundings: underdevelopment and the living conditions of the masses could no longer be overshadowed by such positivist dreams.

---

[12] Ronaldo Brito described the neo-concrete movement in Rio de Janeiro as representing both the peak and the first instance of rupture in the constructive project in Brazil. Neo-concretism held two distinct tendencies: a rationalist humanism which, like concrete art, tended to inform industrial design qualitatively, while preserving the specificity and aura of the work of art; and the other more disruptive, distancing itself from the constructive tradition through a dramatic transformation of art's function and *raison d'être*. See Brito (1985).

[13] The association between Brasilia and the form of the cross is expressed in Martins (2000).

Pop and the Legacy of Constructivism

Following the disillusionment with grand architectural gestures which had
attempted to inscribe upon the nation an identity based upon positivist ideals,
a number of artists incorporated within their work an architectural approach
to form. This was generally seen as a means of further intensifying the
apprehension of the work of art by the spectator, and in some cases, it
became entwined with an articulation of the emergent mass-media. Often,
these three-dimensional environments were the direct result, or logical
development, of transcendental ideas hitherto associated with the field of
painting. Richard Hamilton's and Victor Pasmore's 'An Exhibit' of 1957,
together with Hélio Oiticica's '*Grande Núcleo*' of 1960, are examples of the
respective initial steps towards such a shift in Britain and Brazil. They also
indicate an approach towards a more subjective, individual apprehension of
space. Therefore, a seemingly paradoxical situation subsequently arose
whereby the highly subjectified experience of space, through a process that
took painting beyond its two-dimensional characteristic, collided with artists'
response to the developing mass-media.

In Britain, the 1956 exhibition 'This is Tomorrow' at the
Whitechapel Gallery in London is generally known as a precursor of Pop Art.
However, its significance was far greater. Banham reviewed the exhibition as
resolving the practicalities that the Modern movement's recurring theme —
the synthesis of the arts— tended to overlook.[14] The exhibition was formed
by a number of 'installations' produced by groups which included architects,
artists and critics. Banham saw these environments as operating at different
levels: contributing towards 'smashing all boundaries between the arts';
treating everything as 'modes of communicating experience'; and embracing
'all the available channels of human perception' (Banham 1956: 186-88).
Underlying the exhibition's conception was the legacy of Constructivism,
having been initially devised by the French-based *Groupe Espace*. Although
their proposal was rejected as too rationalist and dogmatic, the exhibition
included individuals who were still involved in the evaluation of abstract
geometrical art.[15]

An exception in Banham's generally favourable review of 'This is
Tomorrow' was the installation by Group 6 (Smithson-Henderson-Paolozzi)
entitled 'Patio and Pavilion'. Accused of being traditionalist for not tending

---

[14] In very different contexts Ferreira Gullar's (1959) 'Theory of the Non-Object' had also argued
that neo-concrete art tended to overcome traditional categories such as painting and sculpture
and later, in 1965, Donald Judd would also argue that it was the case for *Minimalism in Specific
Objects* first published in *Arts Yearbook* (Judd 1965).
[15] Alloway had published an important survey of abstract art in which he discussed the influence
of the ideals of Concrete art expressed by Max Bill in relation to British artists. See Alloway
(1954). For a brief history of the exhibition's organisation see Graham Whitham (1988), 35-39.

towards a synthesis of the arts (Banham 1956: 186-88), Group 6 constructed instead a space that through its roughness reflected a particular view predominant at that moment. Indeed, the Cold War angst expressed in Group 6's 'Patio and Pavilion', whereby civilisation was under the threat of Modernity itself, marked a shift from the notion of Modernity embraced by the Festival of Britain. In this sense, it is possible to compare it to Hélio Oiticica's *Tropicália* installation which recalled the condition of underdevelopment in the aftermath of the 'Developmentalist' era which had created Brasilia.[16] Like *Tropicália*, which was exhibited for the first time in 1967 amongst works by artists with very different approaches, 'Patio and Pavilion' should not be seen in isolation from the exhibition as a whole. In both cases, there was the presentation of a number of re-evaluations of the relationships between art, architecture and society at large. The respective exhibitions also marked the collision of art historical tendencies consensually seen to be irreconcilable such as Dada, Constructivism, Pop, and contemporaneous French notions such as Art Brut.[17]

In Brazil, as the Sixties progressed, and particularly following the arrival of Pop Art, there were attempts at a synthesis between the iconography of mass culture and the experience of popular Brazilian culture which in the case of artists such as Oiticica, incorporated the legacy of the Constructivist aesthetic. Former orthodox Concrete artists such as Waldemar Cordeiro developed a hybrid approach between Pop and Concrete art, which became known as *Popcreto*. Interestingly, the hybridity of Cordeiro's *Popcreto* work does not relate in any way to Canclini's definition of the term. Cordeiro was one of the first artists to make use of a computer in Brazil, merging imagery of popular icons with the serialisation of words and/or numbers (Oiticica 1992: 110). Beyond the preoccupation with form and its mathematical basis of composition, Concrete art possessed an innate openness to new scientific processes and indeed fantasies, communication theories and their consequences or applications (mass advertising or publicity methods and language). It is perhaps not coincidental that many of the artists and poets involved in Concrete aesthetics in Brazil became variously engaged in publicity and advertising.

Neo-concrete artists, such as Hélio Oiticica, Lygia Clark and Lygia Pape, on the other hand, attempted to reconcile their previous Constructivist experimentation with art's exteriority: the social, psychological, political,

---

[16] The art critic Guy Brett, remembering Oiticica's 1969 Whitechapel 'experiment' has indeed suggested that there are connections to be made between these quite independent exhibitions. Brett claimed that 'This is Tomorrow in 1956, which brought together artists like Richard Hamilton and architects like Alison and Peter Smithson, was the product of a different epoch, whose vision of the "future" would make an interesting comparison with Oiticica's' (Brett 2001: 78).

[17] For an analysis of the association between Constructivism and Dada see Ades (1984), 33-45.

ethical, etc. This was pursued through a return to notions proposed by the early Brazilian Modernists such as that of Anthropophagy which re-emerged during the 1960s as a means of dealing with the legacy of Modernity, the unavoidable issue of Brazilian popular culture, and its mediation with the emergent, and predominantly North American, mass culture.

Hélio Oiticica offered a spatial matrix for lived experiences proposing a vision of art as symbolic architecture which was opposed to an architectural monument loaded with symbolism. His work became increasingly associated with popular traditions such as carnival and the notion of marginalisation. The latter related to both a position of Brazilian art with respect to the Canon and referred to the social condition of disenfranchised sectors of Brazilian society. However, Oiticica's art was not a product of popular traditions, nor did it attempt to create a hybrid or synthesis of high and low cultures.

Both Brasilia and Oiticica's *Tropicália* installation are related through the ideal of a national 'Constructive Will', yet they stand respectively on each side of the abyss that irrevocably annihilated the possibility of imagining a Brazilian utopia: the military coup of 1964. Addressing the history of representation in Brazilian Modernism, Oiticica proposed a view of a reality that encompassed the extremes of the Constructivist inheritance and the anarchic aesthetic of underdevelopment. As far as Brasilia is concerned, its formal purity excluded those who had participated in its construction: their temporary accommodation was transformed into permanent shanty-towns circumscribing the Modern city. Claiming that purity is a myth, Oiticica brought the shanty-town aesthetic within the confines of Modern art. It is in this sense that Oiticica's installation, *Tropicália*, has become an important reference of Brazilian cultural production in the 1960s. *Tropicália* functioned in this manner as an anti-monument. It acknowledged national identity as underdevelopment rather than the Arcadian ideal of an original Brazilian identity expressed in the imagery of *Modernismo* or the notion of an absolutely Modern nation in the positivism of Concrete art and the 'Developmentalist' ideology. In its affirmation of one's own identity, *Tropicália* was therefore more real than anything that went before it. Oiticica's work rather than a search for a synthesis of the popular and fine art, placed both categories within a relationship of productive tension. *Tropicália* referred to architectural space as an integral element of its conception as a work of art. Oiticica's great achievement was to manage to develop an autonomous aesthetic trajectory: a formal development which acknowledged the wider context from which it arose.

The relation between Modernism and nationalism in Brazil posits the inauguration of Brasilia as a moment of profound cultural transition. It affirms the impossibility of analysing cultural production within the dualistic frame of local versus universal. In this sense, the associations with contemporaneous British history/theory and practice raised here should not be seen as examples of precedents, but as a means of questioning the essential 'hybrid' condition of Latin American cultural production. In both contexts, there was a re-evaluation of the seeming inadequacy of past national traditions, the heterogeneous character of contemporany aesthetic positions and the struggle for imagining a possible future from a position of present adversity.

Works Cited

Ades, Dawn (1984) 'Dada-Constructivism: The Janus Face of the Twenties', exhibition catalogue, Annely Juda Fine Art, 26 September-15 December (London), 33-45.

——— (1989) *Art in Latin America: The Modern Era, 1820-1980* (New Haven and London: Yale University Press).

Alloway, Lawrence (1954) *Nine Abstract Artists: Their Work and Theory* (London: Alec Tiranti Ltd.).

Asbury, Michael (2003) 'Tracing Hybrid Strategies in Brazilian Modern Art', in Jonathan Harris (ed), *Critical Perspectives on Contemporary Painting: Hybridity, Hegemony, Historicism*, Tate Liverpool Critical Forum, Volume 6 (Liverpool University Press and Tate Liverpool), 139-70.

Banham, Peter Reyner (1956) 'This is Tomorrow', in *Architectural Review* (August—September), 186-88.

——— (1960) *Theory and Design in the First Machine Age* (London and Cambridge: MIT Press).

Barry, Judith (1988) 'Design Aesthetic: Exhibition Design and the Independent Group', in Brian Wallis et al. (eds), *Modern Dreams: The Rise and Fall and Rise of Pop* (New York: MIT Press), 41-45.

Bécquer, Marcos and Gatti, José (1991) 'Elements of Vogue', in *Third Text* 16/17, 65-81.

Bonduki, Nabil (ed) (2000) *Reidy, Affonso Eduardo*, Arquitetos Brasileiros/Brazilian Architects (Lisbon: Instituto Lina Bo e P. M. Bardi).

Brett, Guy (2001) 'Hélio Oiticica's "Whitechapel Experiment"', in *Whitechapel Art Gallery Centenary Review* (London), 76-78.

Brito, Ronaldo (1985) 'Neoconcretismo: vértige e ruptura do projeto construtivo brasileiro', in *Temas e Debates* 4 (Rio de Janeiro: FUNARTE), 91-114.

Fabris, Annateresa (2000-2001) 'Forms of (Possible) Modernity', in *Brasil: 1920-1950, de la Antropofagia a Brasilia*, exhibition catalogue (Valencia: IVAM), 533-39.

García Canclini, Néstor (1995 [1989]) *Hybrid Cultures: Strategies for Entering and Leaving Modernity*, trans. C. L. Chiappari and S. L. López (Minneapolis and London: University of Minnesota Press).

Gullar, Ferreira (1959) 'Teoria do Não Objeto', in *Jornal do Brasil* (December), 19-20.

Judd, Donald (1965) 'Specific Objects', *Arts Yearbook* 8 (New York), 74-82.

Lawson, Thomas (1988) 'Bunk: Eduardo Paolozzi and the Legacy of the Independent Group', in Brian Wallis et al. (eds), *Modern Dreams: The Rise and Fall and Rise of Pop* (New York: MIT Press), 18-29.

Martins, Carlos A. Ferreira (2000) 'Building Architecture, Building a Country', in *Brasil 1920-1950: de la Antropofagia a Brasilia*, exhibition catalogue, (Valencia: IVAM), 578-85.

Morais, Frederico (1994) *Cronologia das Artes Plásticas no Rio de Janeiro: da Missão Francesa à Geração 90* (Rio de Janeiro: Top Books Editora Distribuidora).

Oiticica, Hélio (1992), 'General Scheme of the New Objectivity', reprinted and translated in *Hélio Oiticica*, exhibition catalogue (Rotterdam: Witte With Center for Contemporary Art,/Paris: Galerie Nationale du Jeu de Paume/Barcelona: Fundació Antoni Tàpies/Lisboa: Fundação Calouste Gulbenkian/Minneapolis: Walker Art Center), 110-20. (Originally published as 'Esquema Geral da Nova Objetividade', in *Nova Objetividade*, exhibition catalogue [Rio de Janeiro: Museu de Arte Moderna, 1967].)

Pedrosa, Mário (1981a) 'A Arquitetura Moderna no Brasil', reprinted and translated in Aracy do Amaral (ed) *Mário Pedrosa: Dos Murais de Portinari aos Espaços de Brasilia* (São Paulo: Editora Pespectiva), 255-64. (Originally published in *Architecture d'aujourd'hui* [December 1953].)

———— (1981b) 'Reflexões em Torno da Nova Capital', reprinted in Aracy do Amaral (ed) *Mário Pedrosa: Dos Murais de Portinari aos Espaços de Brasilia* (São Paulo: Editora Pespectiva), 303-16. (Originally published in *Brasil, Arquitetura Contemporânea* 10 [1957].)

Teles, Gilberto Mendonça (1997 13th edition [1972]) *Vanguarda Européia e Modernismo Brasileiro* (Petrópolis: Editora Vozes).

Vergez, Valerie (2000) 'L'Art Concret de sa Formation au Début des Années Quarante', in *Art Concret*, exhibition catalogue (Espace de l'Art Concret, Mouans-Sartoux), 15-23. (Max Bill's quoted statement originally published in *Pevsner, Vantoogerloo, Bill*, exhibition catalogue [Zurich: Kunsthaus, 1947].)

Whitham, Graham (1988) 'This is Tomorrow: Genesis of an Exhibition', in Brian Wallis et al. (eds), *Modern Dreams: The Rise and Fall and Rise of Pop* (New York: MIT Press), 34-39.

Zilio, Carlos (1982) 'Da Antropofagia à Tropicália', in Zilio et al. (eds), *O Nacional e o Popular na Cultural Brasileira* (São Paulo: Editora Brasiliense), 11-56.

Section Two:

Re-Viewing the City

Chopin to the Electric Chair!: The Mexican Avant-Garde and the Revolutionised City

Luis Carranza

Abstract

The Estridentistas, a Mexican avant-gardist group (1921-1927), proposed a radical rereading of the contemporary Latin American metropolis. The group translated the elements of the modern city and its European perception (understood through publications, theories, manifestoes, etc.) into a new reality. In short, they invented (or, in their terms, 'falsified') their ideal modern city and expressed its character and effects through their manifestos, poems, novels, and plastic art. Through this work, the members of the group literally attempted to recreate synthetically the *estridentista* concepts of the city. In the end, their ideal city was 'Estridentopolis' (a modern metropolis seen in the future of 1975) which responded to the needs of creating anew through the use of modern production techniques adapted to the Mexican context and social demands.

* * *

There is something odd, perhaps disturbing, in seeing the projected 1975 view of *Estridentópolis*. Created in 1925 by the painter Germán Cueto, this image of a city, in fact, presented a modern metropolis as it would appear fifty years after its initial conception. According to its main advocate, Germán List Arzubide

> *Estridentópolis* was the realisation of the Estridentista truth: the absurd city, disconnected from everyday reality, correcting the straight lines of the monotone by unfolding the landscape. Erased by the fog, it becomes more distant in the evening and it returns routinely at dawn; worn down by the key of the rain, suns affirm it in the calendars of the new days; its windows rotate towards the landscapes that Ramón Alva de la Canal and Leopoldo Méndez decorated with fullness; the streets fragment, contorted by inaugural anxieties; travellers move through the sidewalks held captive by time; its architectures have been built with brave lines that announce existence; dawn lifts it everyday to be taller and more rigid, it floats over the uncontrolled moment of noon among the anonymous clamor of traffic that spills into the avenue; in the afternoon, it is pompous, made up of solemn skies. Anchored in the abandonment of its buildings whose electric lights announce the advance of night, the absurd city falls gradually silent; it

widens its avenues and it annihilates its passers-by so that in the formal solitude of the hours, abandoned to the elevatory motifs, the founders can sow their aviational words. (List Arzubide 1927: 93-95)

Figure 1: Estridentopolis
© Germán Cueto

In *Estridentópolis*, a mixture of artistic and literary techniques was used. The conceptualisation and artistic expression of this city responded to the new visions of modern life. The way in which the metropolis and its architecture were aesthetically represented gave rise to an abstract and rational sensibility, which was a force with collective influence. Its peculiarity lies in the fact that by imagining an exaggerated form of the metropolis in Mexico, the author (a non-architect) accurately predicts the

Luis Carranza

morphological development of a typical city in the second half of the twentieth century. And, despite his architectural limitations, its form never materialised into the romantic utopias of people like Hugh Ferris, Le Corbusier, or, even, Ludwig Hilberseimer.

In Mexico, the urban environment, particularly the metropolis, became the principal fixation of artistic production since it was an environment inhabited by new modes of production, consumption, and representation; thus, the city exhibited new sensory stimuli. It is well known that a large contingent of the historical avant-garde aesthetically articulated their awareness of the effects of the metropolis on the individual. Their understanding of these effects was similar to that articulated by the German sociologist Georg Simmel in his seminal essay 'The Metropolis and Mental Life' (1903), where the urban subject suffered from a *blasé* attitude caused by the intensification of nervous energy and the predominance of an (anonymous) monetary economy that suppressed individuality (Simmel 1971).[1] Characterised by a lack of individuality, anonymity and alienation caused by the means of production and by new forms of interpersonal relations, the negativity of the metropolis was, according to Manfredo Tafuri, what the formal, ornamental and experimental programmes of the avant-gardes were trying to counteract.[2] For Tafuri, what was central to their problem was: '[h]ow to shake off the anxiety provoked by the loss of centre, by the solitude of the individual immersed in revolt, [...] how to convert that anxiety into action so as not to remain forever dumb in the face of it' (Tafuri 1976: 105). The historical avant-garde, in absorbing the logic of the metropolis, was presented with at least two possibilities. Both involved presenting an exacerbated, completely reified experience of the metropolitan condition as a way of working through its own negativity. The first possibility saw that human action, reduced to mechanical reactions to the city as a result of the blasé attitude, could only be countered by shock —the shock that is captured, for instance, in the acerbic language of Marinetti's Futurist Manifesto or Dadaist chaos. The second possibility assumed that the metropolitan individual was an intellectualised city-dweller capable of a higher degree of comprehension (attributed precisely to the intellectualisation of emotions and relations determined, according to Simmel, by the monetary economy); this intellectualisation is captured by the process of abstraction undergone, for example, by De Stijl. There was a third choice —a middle ground— presented to and taken up by Mexican avant-gardist producers. This entailed accepting the logic of the metropolis and the metropolitan condition —including both its order and chaos, its mass reproducibility and

---

[1] For the relationship between the theories of Simmel and the avant-garde, see Tafuri (1987), 219-20, and Tafuri and Dal Co (1976), 90, 162.
[2] See Tafuri (1987).

its systems of production and consumption— while, at the same time, searching for a comprehensible system that contributed towards a broader legibility of space, place and time and that, ultimately, responded to the post-revolutionary context of modern Mexico.

This mediating proposal should be read as an effect of transculturation. This process, explored by the literary critic Angel Rama, described much of Latin American modern cultural production. For Rama, '[Latin America] has had to select the rejected elements of the European and American systems produced in the metropolis, peeling them away from their context and making them their own in a risky, abstract way' (Rama 1982: 39). Transculturation outlined a critical and selective process through which Latin American cultural producers took certain elements (or structures) from an admired or colonising culture and substituted them for their own. Many times, the process combined these foreign elements with selective aspects (or structures) of its own given culture in new and inventive ways —not always as expected or as proposed by the originating culture.

In most cases, this operation was enacted as a response to questions engendered by the seemingly unmediated (and at times, imposed) application of European traditions during colonisation and later, especially in the second half of the nineteenth century. In Mexico, this was manifested through the obsession, for example, with Paris, the proverbial capital of the nineteenth century, its architecture, urbanism and forms, and through the use of positivism and naturalism by the governing Porfirian elite. The Latin American avant-garde, however, in disputing those European traditions (as morally and formally bankrupt) set up for itself the issues of identity formation, class and race consciousness, and the role of art in the praxis of life. Additionally, this avant-garde enacted a semantic re-articulation of the ideas, forms, and traditions of the historical European avant-garde. This re-articulation was based not only on the changing historical and geographic contexts but also on the different audiences and the different intentions of the authors themselves. Finally, working primarily in environments whose modernisation has been described as 'incomplete', producers were also compelled to call into question the role of new technologies as well as the role of form (giving particular emphasis to the dispute between abstraction and representation).

The 'falsified city' of the Mexican avant-garde group, the Estridentistas (literally, the Stridentists), is an appropriate place to begin to understand this mediation. Given an all-inclusive relationship between art and literature, the Estridentistas established themselves as part of the historical artistic avant-garde of the 1920s, and developed an art that, in a similar fashion to that of Russian productivism, was destined to transform art's very definition to one that rejected bourgeois artistic styles and was therefore accessible to the new post-revolutionary Mexican proletarian masses.

The Estridentista movement, an influential artistic and plastic avant-garde, began in Mexico with the publication and distribution of the manifesto *Actual No. 1* in December 1921. However, the existence of this group was short-lived, ending in 1927 (Schneider 1970: 35, 205). *Actual No. 1*, and three other manifestos that were published and collectively distributed, formulated the strategy of 'beginning a caustic and iconoclastic diatribe against all that was established: academism, solemnity, religion, national heroes, the literary patriarchs of the Nation' (Verani 1986: 13). *Actual No. 1*, written by Manuel Maples Arce, the leader and spokesperson of the group, was influenced by various avant-garde currents of the time, in particular by the Italian Futurism of Marinetti; the Spanish 'Ultraismo' of Guillermo de la Torre and Lasso de la Vega; the 'Creacionismo' of Vicente Huidobro; Cubism; and estrangement techniques common to other literary avant-gardes. These estranging devices —such as the introduction of the absurd, the irrational, the fragmentary and so on— appeared under different guises throughout Estridentista manifestos, publications and plastic arts. In short, their attempt was nothing less than the creation of a new cultural environment.

Their first manifesto (*Actual No. 1*) described the problems of contemporary literature and its possible solutions. The principal tenet of Estridentismo was articulated in most of its points: an urgent and total change in literature and Mexican poetry based on the social and economic transformations brought about by modernity. The change included the necessity of artistic and communicative techniques to translate, communicate and fill the spiritual function of the present —in the plastic arts, this was through the incitement of artists and illustrators to draw placards, geometric posters, suggest movement and other elements which signified the present modern reality. The manifesto also put forth an urgent call for the cosmopolitanism required by modernity —this would be manifested through the elimination of past cultures and a self-determination in the present, quixotically expressed through Maples Arce's self-established 'trademark': 'Chopin to the electric chair!'. In short, the locus of Estridentista imagery was the socially, politically and, equally important, formally revolutionised urban environment.

Besides using the images of contemporary modernity, the Estridentistas used the effects and qualities that this modernity produced. The Estridentistas, according to the literary historian Luís Mario Schneider, mimicked the images and qualities of 'the structure of the metropolis, the trepidation of its machines, the phonetic manifestations that these produced; [forcing] the modern inhabitant aesthetically to reproduce these new conditions' (Schneider 1970: 95). What the work of the Estridentistas managed to recreate through literary texts was the lived experience of the metropolitan condition. In Walter Benjamin's terms, they attempted to reproduce artificially the knowledge [*Erlebnis*] of the authentic experience [*Erfahrung*] of the metropolis (Benjamin 1970).[3]

Maples Arce's poem *Urbe* (1924) established and defined the position through which the Mexican avant-garde group could be located in terms of their relation to the modern metropolis. In this poem, three significant aspects of the Estridentista manifesto were developed: the first was an impetus for social change which characterised the Mexican Revolution, understood as the motivating force of the poem; the second was an attack on older forms of literary expression, in particular realism and *modernismo*; and lastly, a focus on the city and cosmopolitanism which was based on Futurist notions of machinery and technology but which maintained, in accordance with the manifesto, a strict relationship to the present.

The complete title and its dedication to the Mexican workers gives us a first insight into its intention: *Urbe: Super-Poema Bolchevique en 5 Cantos de Manuel Maples Arce*. Through the poem's title and content, Maples Arce established a clear parallel between the Russian and the Mexican Revolutions. He also linked the ideology of social revolutions to literary changes and innovations; insinuating the allegiance of new literatures —new ways of thinking and producing artistic products— with social change:

> The lungs of Russia
> blow towards us
> the wind of the social revolution.
> The literary fly looters
> won't comprehend a thing
> of this sweaty new beauty
> of the century. (Maples Arce 1985: 191)

The poem also made references to social classes and to the problems traditionally associated with the bourgeoisie, referred to as the pilferers of the people. On the other hand, the proletariat, referred to as the masses, was shown to be content due to the social success of the Revolution and to the immense possibilities of the large metropolis.

Within his descriptions of new cities and new industrial technologies, an attack against previous literary forms was also waged. In the poem, Maples Arce redeployed Huidobro's creationism as a way to forge an imaginary conception of the world that would not be grounded in

---

[3] 'This is the nature of something lived through (*Erlebnis*) to which Baudelaire has given the weight of an experience (*Erfahrung*)' (Benjamin 1970: 190).

descriptive or anecdotal elements. The influence of ultraism, as defined by Jorge Luis Borges, was also visible in descriptions composed through 'a series of metaphors, each of which has its own suggestive potential and which comprises an un-edited vision of some fragment of life' (Borges 1986: 51). Beyond this reconceptualisation of the role of the metaphor, Maples Arce mobilised his metaphors throughout *Urbe* to dissolve any possible effect of the real. In realist prose, according to Roland Barthes, the 'reality effect' was constructed through descriptions that gave the appearance of a direct, unmediated reference to reality (Barthes 1986: 147-48). The Estridentistas subverted this strategy by exacerbating the alienated condition of the real which, for them, was manifested through a manipulation of a heightened use of metaphor, the propositions of a new imaginary 'reality' and the complete fragmentation of the text in a non-linear or coherent fashion. This last form was similar to a cubist collage, where ideas were juxtaposed without the sense of a linear narrative structure, forcing relationships between objects or technologies which did not have any common properties. The focus of Estridentista poetry shifted from the naturalisation of traditional and sublimated bourgeois social and individual experiences and environments to the glorification of the masses and their appropriation of the new metropolis.

Within the poem, the city was glorified and aestheticised. The necessity of cosmopolitanism was self-evident in the use of terminology and descriptions that, simultaneously, were to connote the transformation of the means of production, the dissemination of products and ideas and their influence on other fields. At the same moment that the poem re-conceptualised the city into the nucleus of a new sense of modernity, the modern and industrial technologies acquired from and imparted to the metropolis a futurist quality.

> Oh city all tense
> of cables and of efforts
> all resonant
> of motors and wings
>
> Simultaneous explosion
> of the new theories…

Here is my poem:

> Oh strong city
> and multiple
> all made of iron and steel.

The docks. The inner harbors.
The cranes.

And the sexual fever
of the factories.

Clearly, the techniques that Maples Arce used throughout his poem to describe the new technological qualities or environments were not invented or implausible, but rather those which were common to industrial and modern architectures. In addition, the metropolitan experience of fragmentation was represented through the typographic layout of the poem reflecting Stéphane Mallarmé's typographical experiments in 'Un Coup de Dés' (1897) which attempted to reproduce synthetically the real roll of a dice. Finally, it should be obvious that the metropolis described in Maples Arce's poem was an invention designed to demonstrate the vitality of the modern city and its ability to transform the public realm. However, it was also a utopian ideal in which the reifying conditions and effects of industry and modernity no longer existed. The machines and the city were animated by generative social forces and by the interaction between humans and machines. Despite the fact that Maples Arce used an informal address to the city and distinguished it from the poem through 'ode-like' allusions,[4] his poem dematerialised and united the descriptions of the city, technology and the masses into one. Within the poem, in other words, the fragmented sense of the interactions that occurred between them was lost; inducing an organic relation and totality between the poet, the inhabitants of the city, the city itself and the industrial machinery that countered the effects of the division of labour, art and life. These new relationships were seen as part of the universal aspiration toward utopia. Maples Arce's poem and all of the Estridentistas' literary production would become necessary and ready weapons in the struggle for a social, ideological and physical change of society.

Early in the life of the movement, the literary members of the Estridentista group allied themselves with members of the plastic arts. This alliance should not be seen as the union of two disparate groups with different ideas and goals, but rather as a marriage of two groups with similar ideas that would work together to expand the definition of the movement. By using each other's techniques, the members of both groups expanded their theories and ideas to make them manifest. For example, the graphic representations of its artistic members gave life to their literary notions and theories of the city. Similar to the historic European avant-gardes, this Mexican group set itself the aggressive task of transforming the space of the modern into a radical, subversive and dissident weapon that served not only to attack the literature and artistic production of the past, but also to reject the bourgeois socio-economic system of advanced capitalism. According to Schneider, art for the Estridentistas 'became the principal action of human

---

[4] The use, for example, of phrases such as, 'He aquí mi poema' ('Here is my poem').

life and it [was] believed in, not so much as liberty in the creative process but also as the only liberating system for the human race through which norms, moral prejudices, and dogmas [could] be destroyed' (Schneider 1985: 35).

The principal artists of the group included the muralist Diego Rivera; the sculptor Germán Cueto; the painters and engravers Jean Charlot, Fermín Revueltas, Leopoldo Méndez and Ramón Alva de la Canal; the photographers Tina Modotti and Edward Weston; and the composer Silvestre Revueltas. As members of the Estridentista group, they only exhibited collectively once: on April 12, 1924.

Their work responded directly to the Estridentista manifestos which had carefully defined the function of the plastic arts within this new metropolitan reality, and was intended to represent and materialise certain concerns of their political, historical and economic context. The Second Manifesto, for example, determined the direction of their new plastic arts through its opposition to the contemporary art situation (particularly *modernismo* and realism):

> The possibility of a new art, young, enthusiastic and alive, structured in nine dimensions, superimposing our loud spiritual unease upon the regressive force of the coordinated madhouses with police rules, Parisian importations and hand crank pianos at dawn. ('Manifesto Estridentista Número 2' 1985: 49)

Contemporary art practices were described as totalitarian and oppressive. Instead, similar to the strategy employed by the movement's writers, Estridentista artists separated themselves from techniques and styles of the past by using images of a reality which, technically and aesthetically, represented a heightened modernity in order to separate their art from bourgeois art. They also used forms of collective dissemination, following the lead of Maples Arce's printed broadsheet manifesto, to direct their art towards the urban, proletarian masses instead of the bourgeois individual.

Estridentista writers also incorporated graphic vignettes into their poetry and narratives in order to illustrate and articulate poetic ideas about the Estridentista metropolitan world. We see this, for example, in the book covers and pages of Maples Arce's *Urbe* (with a cover and illustrations by Jean Charlot), List Arzubide's *Esquina* (illustrated with woodcuts by Jean Charlot), and the magazines of the group, *Irradiador* and *Horizonte* (filled with illustrations, photographs and woodcuts by Leopoldo Méndez, Tina Modotti, Alva de la Canal, Fermín Revueltas and others).

The Estridentistas also mobilised a language of forms and techniques which, because of their pervasiveness throughout Mexico, were considered autochthonous. This included, for instance, the use of the broadsheet and of woodcuts which were based on the tradition of social and political critique exemplified by the late nineteenth and early twentieth-century work of José

Guadalupe Posada and his editor Venegas Arroyo. Through mass-produced techniques of engraving, photography and printing, their art could reach a massive audience through clear and legible pictorial means. The Estridentistas also appropriated as their own the artistic practice of public murals and public artistic or architectural interventions (such as pictorial stained glass and sculpture, among others) by Diego Rivera, Jean Charlot, and Fermín Revueltas. The use of public mural painting had its precedent not only in the European religious tradition with which the muralists were familiar as a result of visits to Europe but, more locally, in the painterly decorations of pre-Hispanic architectures. Because of their immense scale and public presence, the possibilities of collective reception for these artistic interventions were significant, in contrast to easel painting which could only be seen by a limited number of people at a time and which was, generally, inaccessible to the public at large. It was clear, therefore, that the majority of Estridentista art intended to reach the masses in a direct and unmediated way. In both cases, their direct and legible iconography was intended to be readily accessible to the majority of the Mexican people through whom social and political change could be effected.[5]

Estridentista art also employed many of the Estridentista literary concepts to deconstruct and denaturalise the image of existing reality. This not only meant that Estridentista artists had artistically to represent and describe a new reality, but also that they needed to find ways to criticise traditional painterly and artistic techniques; a project akin to the one engaged in by the European avant-gardes. In their plastic arts, as in their literature, modified traces of Futurism and Cubism reflected the Estridentista ideals. These influences were clear in their representations of mechanical labour, of geometric formalism, of planimetric decomposition and in the collapse of time and space. Through the use of images, symbols, objects and sensations produced by the modern metropolis, the pictorial and plastic art of the Estridentistas intended to move and awaken its viewers, politically and spiritually, towards the new existential conditions of the present. Art, according to Maples Arce, had the function of enriching the 'vision of a modern life, [contributing] directly to express it and [showing the vision itself] as its result. [...] Generally speaking, all aesthetic manifestations adjust themselves to a new rhythm, a new conception; in the end, to a new sensibility' (Maples Arce 1956: 26-27).

The city and its architecture became the medium that registered the changes that modernity and industrialisation imposed. Because of this, the Estridentista artists focused much of their effort and work on representing

---

[5] An adherence to realist modes of representation, they believed, was essential to the promotion of radical change. In contrast to this, the Russian avant-garde employed an abstract, non-figurative language (seen in the paintings of Malevich and El Lissitzky) that was criticised as elitist and not directed towards the masses.

this new environment and its aesthetic possibilities. As Beatriz Sarlo acutely observes, for the avant-garde 'the new urban landscape, the modernisation of the means of communication, [and] the impact of these processes on traditions [were] the frame and the point of resistance through which the intellectuals articulated their responses' (Sarlo 1988: 26). These tensions were expressed throughout Estridentista work in the opposition between modern sensibilities or concerns and the typical or vernacular techniques that they employed, or the traditional images that they (sometimes) produced. However, the predominant themes of their work were those which defined this new modernity and its effects on the metropolis: modern industry and its factories, the new human or proletariat, the modern city and its buildings and the new sensations produced by these new environments. A description of the art that was exhibited at the *Café de Nadie* clearly describes these themes and concerns:

> The paintings were an incredible show of our pace. Factories raising the flaming arm of their chimneys, assertive and robust in their walls of sweat and work, presented by Fermín Revueltas. Colors looking out the window in an intentional form, medullary balanced, that Ramón Alva de la Canal exhibited. Disaggregated serenity of line which was then the formal investigation of Jean Charlot. Musculatures of working verticals, anxiety of making into drawing the graphic of the moment, which has been the centre of restlessness of Leopoldo Méndez. (Schneider 1970: 86)[6]

Stylistically, many of the Estridentista vignettes which represented these themes also showed an accumulation and agglomeration of flat surfaces interrupted by the rhythmic seriality of windows and openings, a rejection of Cartesian space through the invention and manipulation of perspective laws, a rejection of curvilinear forms, a constant use of severe volumes that appeared to be industrially produced and a use of visual forms that created the effect of interstitial labyrinths. These visual techniques could be compared to the literary techniques that the writers used: accumulation and simultaneity, self-referentiality, irreducible imagery and fragmentation.

The themes of industry and the factory throughout Estridentista work were also used as mediums through which cultural differences could be unravelled. Sarlo described how the avant-garde transformed the meaning of these themes and their cultural use: '[technology and industry] enjoy an intermediary statute: they are there because of what is missing. Because of their presence, one can see, on the one hand, the repercussion of their possible absence and, on the other, the legitimacy of a non-traditional

---

[6] This citation, according to Schneider, is from List Arzubide's book *El Movimiento Estridentista*. During the course of my research, however, I was unable to locate its exact source.

reorganisation of culture' (Sarlo 1992: 13). Germán List Arzubide's *El Viajero en el Vértice* included illustrations by Ramón Alva de la Canal that represented that new industrial world and its effect on traditional modes of artistic production. The woodcut *Postes* (1926) appeared as a formal, abstract investigation until placed within the context of the poem. Because the graphic image operated as a one-point perspective, the image appeared to be infinite as it approached the line of the horizon. The telegraphic medium, which might transmit large amounts of information, appeared always silent since neither the cables nor the posts expressed their communicative function. The abstraction of the image, through the simple elements of the posts, the allusion to the sky and the street, expressed this sense of silence and serenity that simultaneously created a tension through the angled, perspective lines of vision which seemed to propose an invisible force. Similarly, the woodcut *Chimeneas* (1926), also by Alva de la Canal, represented the rationalised and geometricised industry to which these poems alluded. These representations, as mentioned earlier, were not direct reflections of reality, but rather reflections mediated and reorganised by Estridentista concepts and their descriptions of the modern metropolis.

Estridentista images, similar to the literary texts, also defined a new individual or proletariat. This subject was understood as fragmented, mechanised or constructed by the avant-garde and by industry. The painting *El Café de Nadie* (1924), by Alva de la Canal, represented the psychic fragmentation of the modern subject described by Arqueles Vela's novel but also showed the café to be a place that, like the Comala of Juan Rulfo's *Pedro Páramo*, appeared to be inhabited by non-existent and fleeting figures. Through the use of cubist techniques, the space around the central figure of the painting, in this case Maples Arce, was fragmented in such a way that the space of time appeared to change: creating the illusion that the figures that accompanied him were disappearing. Another example of the new representations of the subject was a portrait entitled *Armando Zegri* (ca. 1925) by César Moro, where the figure of a man was constructed from industrial fragments. Similar to El Lissitzky's portraits (such as *The Constructor* [1924] or *Tatlin Working on the Monument* [1921/22]), the portrait of Armando Zegri appeared manufactured by rational and technical processes: the eyes are, for example, carefully laid by a compass and straight-edge. The subject became, in other words, an effect of the forces and means of production.

Architecture was also represented in different ways. We see, for example, in the *Viñeta Estridentista* (ca. 1925) of Alva de la Canal, the use of techniques already mentioned but employed in an exceptional manner. The image completely subverted perspective and manufactured a visual labyrinth through the rhythmic and, seemingly, mass-reproduced windows on the volumes of its modern skyscrapers. Similar techniques were employed in the

July 1926 cover of *Horizonte* by Leopoldo Méndez, though here the buildings represented were vernacular courtyard buildings with tile roofs. Méndez's image demonstrated the Estridentista interest in reconceptualising visuality by altering the perception of the vernacular as something potentially revolutionary (something akin to the photographic project undertaken by Aleksander Rodchenko). It was, however, in the illustration of *Radiopolis* (ca. 1925) by Alva de la Canal that the project of transculturation could be seen most poignantly. In it, we see a synthesis of two interests expressed in Méndez's print: the modern with the autochthonous or vernacular. This image juxtaposed the new technology —physically manifested by radio towers— with a building that combined various pre-Hispanic forms such as the pyramid, massive staircases, and references to the Mayan corbel vault.

It was by attempting to reconceptualise visuality through a foray into the metropolis that Estidentista cultural production was able to position itself within international avant-gardist circles and concerns. Yet, by incorporating referents from their cultural and political milieu, these artists were able to transform seemingly formal and effete investigations into political tools for class consciousness-raising and revolutionary identity formation. As the first internationally oriented movement in Mexico, the Estridentistas played an important part in the formation of later cultural and architectural developments. Its members, central to important artistic circles, continued their investigations and interventions while adapting them to newer and more complex cultural conditions and polemics. These subsequent investigations —by members and non-members alike— yielded forms and imagery based on metropolitan˙ experiences and identities and on increasingly complex notions of subjectivity and communicability. In some cases, the new forms were used to represent the revolutionary character of the Mexican people and its traditions. In others, they were used to show the complex dialectical exchanges that these new forms accomplished with Mexico's venerable traditions. Ultimately, by yielding to the international and the local, the Estridentistas constructed a new avant-gardist system to transform the function of art and revolutionise the city.

Works Cited:

Barthes, Roland (1986) 'The Reality Effect', in *The Rustle of Language* (New York: Hill and Wang), 141-48.

Benjamin, Walter (1970) 'On Some Motifs in Baudelaire', in *Charles Baudelaire: A Lyric Poet in the Era of High Capitalism* (New York: Verso).

Borges, Jorge Luis (1990) 'Ultraísmo', reprinted in Gloria Videla de Rivero, *Direcciones del Vanguardismo Hispanoamericano: Estudios Sobre Poesía de Vanguardia en la Década del Veinte* Vol II (Mendoza: Universidad Nacional de Cuyo).

Hays, K. Michael (1992) *Modernism and the Posthumanist Subject: The Architecture of Hannes Meyer and Ludwig Hilberseimer* (Cambridge MA: MIT Press).

List Arzubide, Germán (1927) *El Movimiento Estridentista* (Jalapa, Veracruz: Ediciones de Horizonte).

'Manifiesto Estridentista Número 2', reprinted in Luís Mario Schneider (1985) *El Estridentismo en México 1921-1927* (Mexico: UNAM).

Maples Arce, Manuel (1956) *Incitaciones y Valoraciones* (México: Ediciones Cuadernos Americanos).

——— (1985 [1924]) 'Urbe: Super-Poema Bolchevique en 5 Cantos de Manuel Maples Arce', reprinted in Luís Mario Schneider, *El Estridentismo en México 1921-1927* (Mexico: UNAM) 189-198.

Rama, Angel (1982) *Trasculturación Narrativa en América Latina* (México: Siglo Veintiuno Editores).

Sarlo, Beatriz (1988) *Una Modernidad Periférica: Buenos Aires 1920 y 1930* (Buenos Aires: Ediciones Nueva Visión).

——— (1992) *La Imaginación Técnica: Sueños Modernos de la Cultura Argentina* (Buenos Aires: Ediciones Nueva Visión).

Schneider, Luís Mario (1970) *El Estridentismo o Una Literatura de la Estrategia* (México: INBA).

——— (1985) *El Estridentismo en México 1921-1927* (México: UNAM).

Simmel, Georg (1971 [1903]) 'The Metropolis and Mental Life', in Georg Simmel et al, *On Individuality and Social Forms: Selected Writings* (Chicago: University of Chicago Press), 324-39.

Tafuri, Manfredo and Francesco Dal Co (1976) *Modern Architecture* vol. 1 (New York: Electa/Rizzoli).

——— (1987) *The Sphere and the Labyrinth: Avant-Gardes and Architecture from Piranesi to the 1970s* (Cambridge MA: MIT Press).

Verani, Hugo J. (1986) *Las Vanguardias Literarias en Hispanoamérica: Manifiestos, Proclamas, y Otros Escritos* (Rome: Bulzoni Editore).

Landscapes of Confusion: The Urban Imaginaries of Néstor García Canclini and Kevin Lynch

Anny Brooksbank-Jones

Abstract

The essay contrasts two examples of the use of photographs to chart residents' imaginary relations with the urban environment. The first is Kevin Lynch's *The Image of the City* (1960), which explores the place of visuality in the construction of cities, contrasting residents' distorted image of the metropolis with the more precise and homogeneous representations of planners. In *La ciudad de los viajeros: Travesías e imaginarios urbanos* (1996), Néstor García Canclini and his collaborators use photographs to chart how residents configure Mexico City in their imagination as they travel across it. Unlike Lynch, however, the authors are concerned less with accuracy or orderliness than with the broader political implications of the individual and collective fictions they encounter. Without new models of citizenship, they argue, urban planners and politicians alike will remain unable to promote new urban imaginaries based on a less alienated, more solidary, vision of the capital.

* * *

> What kinds of travel and travel photography are possible when the travel photographer's old certainties [...] are lost? (Osborne 2000: 184)

> We have a collective perception of the Latin American context through a succession of dispersed and distributed photographs. (Kay 1987: 20)

This essay considers the use of photographs to explore or supplement recurring gaps in the cognitive mapping of the urban environment. In particular, it probes conceptual and other gaps in two accounts of that mapping. The first of these is detailed in *La ciudad de los viajeros: Travesías e imaginarios urbanos: México, 1940-2000*, edited by Néstor García Canclini, Alejandro Castellanos and Ana Rosas Mantecón (1996) and summarised by García Canclini in 'Viajes e imaginarios urbanos'(1997). The second was documented almost four decades earlier by Kevin Lynch in *The Image of the City* (1960).

García Canclini and his collaborators describe a project that uses photographs of Mexico City to chart the ways in which residents shape the capital's identity as they attempt to make sense of its vast, disorderly spaces. They are less interested than is, for example, Carlos Monsiváis in the contradictory and heterogeneous experience of contemporary urban alienation (Monsiváis 1997); what concerns them is how residents work to ward off, contain or reconvert such alienation. Central to these processes, they contend, is the work of images and imagination:

> [D]ebemos pensar en la ciudad a la vez como un lugar para habitar y para ser imaginado. Las ciudades se construyen con casas y parques, calles, autopistas y señales de tránsito. Pero las ciudades se configuran también con imágenes. Pueden ser las de los planos que las inventan y las ordenan. Pero también imaginan el sentido de la vida urbana las novelas, canciones y películas, los relatos de prensa, la radio y televisión. La ciudad se vuelve densa al cargarse con fantasías heterogéneas. La urbe programada para funcionar, diseñada en cuadrícula se desborda y se multiplica en ficciones individuales y colectivas. (García Canclini 1997: 109)

> [We need to think of the city both as a space to live in and as a place to create in our imaginations. Cities are constructed with houses and parks, motorways and road signs; but they are also configured in images. These images may derive from the plans that invent cities and impose an order on them. But the meaning of urban life is also constructed imaginatively, in novels, in songs and films, in press reports, radio and television. The city becomes dense with this accumulation of heterogeneous fantasies; individual and collective fictions multiply and overflow the grid patterns of an urban space designed and programmed for maximum functionality (author's translation).]

They chart these fictions by using visual representations to trace how residents work on their material surroundings, constructing and re-constructing 'las múltiples ciudades de los viajeros' (García Canclini, Rosas Mantecón, Castellanos 1996: 61). In order to maximise opportunities for comparisons and contrasts, the visual representations juxtaposed the Mexico City of the 1990s with the industrial expansion, urban migration and the modernisation of daily life associated with the 1940s and 50s. There were two stages in the preparation of the project.

> En la primera realizamos una selección de fotografías y escenas de películas referidas a los viajes metropolitanos en los años 40-50 y en la última década. Luego seleccionamos 52 fotos, y en un video de 20 minutos editamos escenas de varias películas, que posteriormente exhibimos a diez grupos, cada uno de seis a ocho personas, y les pedimos que las comentaran (García Canclini and Rosas Mantecón 1996: 61).[1]

---

[1] Respondents were invited to undertake three tasks: first, they were asked individually to describe (in no more than three minutes) a typical day; they were then asked to select, as a group, the ten photographs most representative of how they travelled and what travel meant for them, focusing particularly on changes and continuities across the periods and noting any

[In the first stage we assembled a selection of photographs and film clips relating to urban travel in the 1940s, 1950s and the 1980s. We then selected 52 of the photos, and edited together a 20 minute compilation of scenes from various films. These were later shown to ten groups of six or eight people, who were asked to discuss them (author's translation).]

Respondents —made up of delivery people, vendors, traffic police, taxi drivers, students living away from their place of study, and other intensive travellers— were asked which coincided most closely with their personal image or vision of the city, where they noted continuity or change, and of what these changes and continuities consisted.

Accounts of the project have almost nothing to say about responses to the video material. This reflects the practical difficulties of reviewing the material and 'la explícita teatralidad de las películas' which (the authors suggest) inhibited viewer identification' (García Canclini and Rosas Mantecón 1996: 66-67).[2] The focus falls squarely on the selected photographs, which ranged across such routine urban phenomena as traffic jams and pollution clouds, street demonstrations, letterboxes, satellite dishes and advertising hoardings.

The decision to include a group made up of photographers is a rare acknowledgement by the project team of the formal dimension of the visual prompts used.[3] Another such emerges in the decision to focus on the images of only two photographers: Nacho López, the renowned photojournalist who had studied in the mid-1940s with Manuel Alvarez Bravo at the Instituto de Artes y Ciencias Cinematográficas, and Paolo Gasparini, who was working at the time of the project on the Urban Culture Programme at the Universidad Autónoma Metropolitana. The recourse to López is unsurprising: while Cartier-Bresson was haunting Mexico City's shanty-towns in his surreally essentialising quest for the 'decisive moment', López produced a uniquely

---

experiences which were not represented in the photographs; this process was then repeated with the 20 minute video-clip. All 55 films considered for the project were based in Mexico City. Of the 30 films from the earlier period six were excerpted for the video: among them Galindo's *Campeón sin corona* (1945) and *Esquina bajan* (1948), and Buñuel's *La ilusión viaja en tranvía* (1953). Of the later films considered the eight excerpted included Olhovich's *Muñeca reina* (1971), Novaro's *Lola* (1989), Systach's *Anoche soñé contigo* (1991), and *Modelo antiguo* (1993) by Araiza. On the photographs selected, see below.

[2] The two photographers who participated in the group sessions appeared more open to 'el sentido teatral de la vida' [the theatrical sense of life] observing, for example, that 'cada semáforo es un teatro' [each traffic signal is a theatre] (García Canclini and Rosas Mantecón 1996: 82). It is interesting to speculate how different responses to the film clips might have been if (as with the photographs) more contemporary examples had been commissioned.

[3] In the event, professional commitments prevented all but two members from attending, making their contribution of limited value.

powerful constructionist interpretation of his times.[4] Alongside the nationalist symbology of images that testify to his critical engagement with 'la ideología cardenista [...] y la escisión definitiva entre el imaginario urbano y rural' [the Cardenist ideology and the definitive split between urban and rural ideologies] there exists a compelling narrative dimension to López's work.

> Juega con la ambigüedad del registro realista de la fotografía. La naturalidad que surge de dicho sistema se contrapone a las reglas del reportaje convencional que exige la toma neutral, es decir, aquella que no altera o 'construye' los elementos de la imagen. (Castellanos 1996: 50)

> [He plays with the ambiguity of realist photography. The naturalness that results from this approach challenges the rules of conventional reporting, which demands a more neutral shot of its subject; that is, one that doesn't alter or 'construct' the elements of the image (author's translation).]

To the extent that this critique of photographic realism was a powerful influence on the city's photojournalists in the decades that followed —and remains influential today— López's images may be attributed with more than passing significance for the formation of the imaginary cities of the project's respondents. The fact that most of those used in the project were loaned by the Fototeca del Instituto Nacional de Antropología e Historia testifies to their status as part of Mexico's 'patrimonio cultural [...] inmaterial', a patrimony of lived experience enshrined not in Pierre Nora's physical, monumental 'lieux de mémoires' but in 'lenguajes, conocimientos, tradiciones inmateriales, modos de usar los bienes y los espacios' [languages, understandings, non-material traditions, ways of using property and spaces] (García Canclini and Rosas Mantecón 1996: 65). This significance resonates in the images of Gasparini, whose awareness of more fractured photographic responses in recent decades to new cultural and spatio-temporal uncertainties, to unfamiliar modalities of social and political crisis, and to a prevailing loss of faith in 'el "realismo fotográfico" [como] modo de aprehensión y de re-elaboración de ideas comunes, de mitologías cotidianas' ['photographic realism' as a way of apprehending and re-elaborating shared ideas, daily mythologies] is expressed exclusively at the level of subject (Debroise 1987: 49): the young men on buses absorbed in their mobile phones or Walkmans, boys crowding around video-game consoles. It is as if, by treating López's perspective as a photographic 'degree zero', the project could place the question of visual strategy and style in check. By this means García Canclini and his collaborators hoped to confer

---

[4] Despite his constructionist practice, there is no doubt that López's theoretical statements —especially in relation to the indigenous subject— were at times frankly essentializing, as noted by Erica Segre (2001).

cierta coherencia estilística al conjunto de las imágenes y no
complicar excesivamente la de por sí compleja riqueza temática y
escénica del problema. Esta es una de las razones por las que se
usaron fotografías en blanco y negro. (García Canclini and Rosas
Mantecón 1997: 63)

[a measure of stylistic coherence on the collection of images, in
order to avoid complicating further the already complex thematic
and scenic richness of the problem. This is one of the reasons why
black and white photographs were used (author's translation).]

Gasparini's monochrome homage to López stops short of his
model's humanistic complicity, however. It responds rather to the project's
need for 'un material relativamente neutro, que dier[a] una visión "objetiva"
sobre los viajes en la ciudad' [relatively neutral material giving an 'objective'
view of journeys in the city] (García Canclini and Rosas Mantecón 1997: 64).
At issue here is the association of black and white with documentary
neutrality, itself grounded in the convention that black and white is more
discreet, 'more tactful, more decorous than color —or less voyeuristic and
less sentimental or crudely lifelike' (Sontag 1978: 128).[5] The qualifying
'relativamente' and the inverted commas that surround the reference to
objectivity register a contemporary loss of faith in this association. In this
sense it might be argued that Gasparini's respectful pastiche catches the spirit
of its time as faithfully as did López. But this ambivalence is clearer in their
framing than in the photographs themselves; the inverted commas evoke a
literal-graphic 'supplement' or prosthetic that seems designed to invest
Gasparini's derivatively-constructionist images with something of the power
of López's own immanent critique of photographic realism, his 're-
negotiation of the criteria of visibility as well as the modalities of
visualisation' (Segre 2001: 58). From this perspective, the later
acknowledgement that 'el corpus elegido estaba sesgado por el imaginario de
los fotógrafos, de los cineastas y de los investigadores' [the chosen corpus
was inflected by the imaginaries of the photographers, film-makers and
researchers] seems unduly even-handed (García Canclini and Rosas
Mantecón 1996: 64).[6] Given that the project rests on the assumption that

---

[5] On photography's status as *analogon,* a 'message without a code', see Barthes (1981). By
restricting his comments to monochrome press photographs Barthes felt able to bracket the
rhetoric of the photographic image. John Tagg (Tagg 1999) famously takes issue with him,
noting that even the press photograph is not an objective, material emanation of its object but the
material product of a maker and her/his apparatus set to work in specific contexts, by specific
forces, for more or less defined purposes. For a critique of his useful, albeit determinist, analysis
see Price (1994: 9).

[6] The role of the researchers in this process only comes centre stage when García Canclini is
pressed on the subject in the question and answer session that followed the oral presentation of
an abbreviated account of the study later published as 'Viajes e imaginarios urbanos'(1997).

visual images are crucial elements in the construction of the 'discursos imaginarios [que] contribuyen a confirmar el sentido urbano al seleccionar y combinar sus referencias emblemáticas, al darle hasta hoy una unidad y una coherencia imaginarias' [imaginary discourses which help to confirm urban meaning by the selection and combination of their emblematic references, by giving it imaginary unity and coherence up to the present], more sustained and reflexive attention is needed here to researchers' role in the imposition of coherence against the grain (García Canclini and Rosas Mantecón 1996: 64).

This concern for coherence is incongruously prefigured in Lynch's *Image of the City*. Almost 40 years earlier, as García Canclini himself recalls, Lynch had used photographs to explore the significance of visual images in the imaginary construction of cities. His methodology was fundamentally that of an (albeit wayward) urban geographer, and the recourse to photographs is one carefully-circumscribed stage in a highly-structured process. In each of the three cities studied —Boston, Jersey City and Los Angeles— his collaborators began by reconnoitering the designated area on foot before preparing a map —'an abstraction [, ...] the generalised impression that real forms makes on an observer indoctrinated in a certain way' (Lynch 1960: 143)— of what were experienced as the area's key visual elements and their interrelations with other features. This construct was juxtaposed with those of local residents and employees, as they emerged in structured interviews. In the case that concerns us —that of Boston— these analyses were supplemented with 'photographic recognition tests', in which respondents were asked to identify photographs of buildings, streets or interconnections encountered earlier in the project (Lynch 1960: 15). Interviewees

> were confronted with a stack of photographs of the Boston area, taken to cover the entire district in a systematic way, but given to the subject in random order. Several photographs of other cities were inserted in the collection. First the subjects were asked to classify the photographs in whatever groups seemed natural to them, and then they were requested to identify as many of the pictures as they could. [...] The photographs recognised were then reassembled, and the subject was asked to lay them out on a large table as if he [sic] were placing them in their proper position in a large map of the city. (Lynch 1960: 142)

The unselfconscious references to 'real form', to 'recognition' and 'systematic' representations, the assumption that the true image of the city is available to correctly educated eyes, all highlight the chasm that separates Lynch from García Canclini and his collaborators. Both are preoccupied with

---

This apart, references are confined to the passages cited above and a passing allusion to a group of respondents made up of 'investigadores mexicanos' (García Canclini and Rosas Mantecón 1996: 83).

the gap between 'imágenes [urbanas] subjetivas y fragmentarias [y] los diagnósticos globales' [subjective and fragmentary urban images and global diagnoses] (García Canclini 1997: 113). But while García Canclini and his collaborators use photographs to chart the fragmented experience of the city, Lynch and his team use them to test the extent of that fragmentation from the perspective of one who can see the whole. He consequently gives considerably more weight than does the later project to the significance for cities of 'los planos que las inventan y las ordenan' [the plans which invent and order them] (García Canclini 1997).

But Lynch's study is powerfully transitional. On the one hand, his constructionist understanding of signification and the imaginary (uneven though it is) prefigures later developments in cultural geography: on the other, key aspects of the study remain firmly embedded in their time. He is concerned with the impact of uncoordinated urban growth and complexity on residents' sense of emotional and physical security, for example, and with the perceived need for fresh sources of 'identity and structure in our perceptual world' (Lynch 1960: 10). The chilly international climate of the time resonates in references to residents' security, anxieties and fear. It obliquely tensions his belief that the fragmented city could, and should, be remade or reassembled; that the 'landscape of our confusions' could be rendered beautiful, humane and legible if its heterogeneous parts were reconfigured under the tutelage of correctly indoctrinated observers; that the city as a whole could be made visible, recognisable by the application of a single and authoritative visual pattern or image (Lynch 1960: 119, citing Thomas Flanagan). Supported by this image, he insists, citizens would be able to orient themselves accurately and without fear. This, in turn, would issue in a more creative use of space: one designed not 'simply to facilitate routine trips, nor to support meanings and feelings already possessed [but to act] as a guide and a stimulus for new exploration' (Lynch 1960: 109-10). Such an image, he contends

> can furnish the raw material for the symbols and collective memories of group communication. [...] A good environmental image gives its possessor an important sense of emotional security. He [sic] can establish an harmonious relationship between himself and the outside world. [...] Indeed, a distinctive and legible environment not only offers security but also heightens the potential depth and intensity of human experience. (Lynch 1960: 4-5)

Lynch presents residents' fragmented images of their cities as 'soaked in memories and meaning' (Lynch 1960: 1). Whereas nineteenth-century pioneers sought to use photography to create a visual thesaurus of landscapes, sensations and memories, Lynch sees landscape itself as a vast mnemonic system able actively to facilitate romance and the excitement of the new. But this power is bound up with coherence: a coherence constructed by urban planners and realised and internalised by residents 'educat[ed] in seeing' (Lynch 1960: 120). García Canclini and his collaborators explore tactics by which residents work to contain alienation by imposing an imagined coherence on their city's heterogeneity: Lynch seeks an orderly environment that would inhibit alienation by encouraging residents to perceive their surroundings more accurately, acutely and actively.

This equation of seeing and insight, vision and truth, and his faith in the education of the many by the enlightened few, all underline the modern bases of Lynch's world view. The Mexico City project is more heterogeneous: the question of order arises there only as a principled negativity: disorder, insecurity and uncertainty are represented as intractable facts, as the ineluctable consequences of the mega-city's rapid, anarchic growth. The Mexico City project's anthropological perspective approaches individual and collective fictions as an imaginative response to the need to contain disorder; Lynch's urban-geographical perspective views the achievement of an orderly and coherent environment as a precondition for the work of imagination. He makes 'clarity of structure and vividness of identity' the starting point for a poetic and symbolic environment able to serve as a 'continuous anchor' that speaks of 'individuals and their complex society, of their aspirations and their historical tradition, of the natural setting, and of the complicated functions and movements of the city world' (Lynch 1960: 119). Creativity in Mexico City, by contrast, is exercised not in potentially soluble visual puzzles, or in the confident exploration of orderly metropolitan landscapes: individuals' relation to their environment, their aspirations and traditions are produced in the negotiation of routine problems, blockages and hazards. At the same time, García Canclini's focus on the intractable quality of familiar environmental factors —the traffic queues, the impossibly-full bus— underlines the extent to which urban environments, orderly or otherwise, are part of a larger dynamic binding cities and residents in an irregular, continuous and mutual conformation.

Despite their quite different perspectives Lynch and García Canclini both equate photographs with the experience of the city as heterogeneous, 'partial, fragmentary', 'desarticulad[a]' [disarticulated] (Lynch 1960: 2, García Canclini 1996: 112). Those deployed by Lynch's collaborators are designed to conjure particular views of or perspectives on sections of the target cities. In his account of the project, Lynch tends to signal these perspectives in captions: 'Looking up Chestnut Street from Charles Street', from example, 'The thematic unit of Beacon Hill', or 'Scollay Square looking north'. These images purport to be omnitemporal rather than evocations of a decisive moment. City buildings appear in sharp detail, while glimpses of citizens going about their business are rare. Where they do figure it is incidentally and at a distance, caught in unfamiliar and oddly-dislocated poses, as when a particular combination of mirrors reflects back at us an alien profile. Residents appear frozen mid-stride in anonymous rear views in Jersey City's Civic Centre, for example, or glimpsed obliquely at traffic lights in Journal Square. The camera seems to slice through its subjects, abstracting them from continuity and contexts, detaching them from complex meanings, the better to resuture them in an exclusively topographic frame. Combined with the conventionally evidential monochrome, the mundane activities captured here seem strangely out of place, perhaps because the camera assumes the non-reciprocal perspective of the private detective or spy. More synonymous or indexical than metaphorical, these photographs suggest traces or clues (Michaud 1998: 736, Krauss 1985: 211): like Atget's images of Paris, their lack of dynamism and sinister partiality recall the scene of a crime. Where vehicles appear they are invariably parked; it is as if Lynch's photographers, compounding their medium's tendency to freeze its object, had sought to neutralise any movement that might distract attention from the topography. In the process, they create a view of the city as still a-bed, unimagined and unimaginable by its citizens. At stake here is the gap between Lynch's insistence on the role of citizens in the imaginative construction of their city and his geographer-photographers own pre-construction of the city as an assemblage of unanthropologised streets, buildings, bridges.

The images of Mexico City are, by contrast, resolutely heterogeneous and anthropologised. Like David Hockney's 'Pear Blossom Highway', the city appears to be constructed 'from many visual instances of time and space which relate to each other but, like buckled plates, refuse to fit' (Osborne 2000: 164). For, unlike Lynch, García Canclini and his collaborators do not seek 'a consistent image [...] to describe or recollect the city in the absence of the real thing'; they seek something approaching 'the image [or images] used when actually operating in the environment' (Lynch 1960: 154). The role of memory in this process is reflected in the juxtaposition of images by López, reproduced from photographic collections and national archives, with more contemporary —and especially communications— phenomena.[7] To the extent that López's art photographs figure here as documentary while Gasparini's documentary images mimic his model's art, the effect is more ambivalent and less uniform than in Lynch's project. It is also more dynamic, since the interaction of image and frame supports the project's attempt to 'acceder a las formas en que diferentes sujetos —y grupos de sujetos— viven esas condiciones 'objetivas', construyen sus mundos privados en relación con las estructuras públicas' [gain access to the ways in which different subjects —and groups of subjects— live those 'objective' conditions, construct their private worlds in relation to public structures] (García Canclini 1997: 131). Whether delivering beer, queuing for buses, or vending in the heart of a traffic-jam the residents with whom participants are asked to identify are seen negotiating city spaces. By a process that Sontag equates with photographic theft or mugging, the

---

[7] Significantly, the implications of juxtaposing images from the same or different times and spaces are barely considered by García Canclini and his collaborators.

camera confronts us with the unposed (expressive or inscrutable) features of private individuals active —however self-absorbed they seem— in the public sphere (Sontag 1978).

Stripped of human activity, Lynch's images of streets and buildings suggest the unencumbered transparency associated with an idealizing disciplinary perspective. This was in striking contrast with the imaginary maps of the project's respondents:

> The image [produced in individual sketch maps] was not a precise, miniaturised model of reality, reduced in scale and consistently abstracted. [It] was made by reducing, eliminating, or even adding, elements to reality, by fusion and distortion, by relating and structuring the parts. [...] It was as if the map were drawn on an infinitely flexible rubber sheet; directions were twisted, distances stretched or compressed, large forms so changed from their accurate scale projection as to be at first unrecognizable. (Lynch 1960: 87)

Lynch notes, with relief, that 'the sequence was usually correct, the map was rarely torn and sewn back together in another order' (Lynch 1960: 87). But the Mexico City project starts from the assumption that the 'correct' order is unavailable to the residents who travel their mega-city each day. They effectively move from scene to scene, García Canclini contends, from micropolis to micropolis, through urban space that is 'enigmático' [enigmatic], even 'incognoscible' [unknowable], as a whole (García Canclini 1997: 131). Hence the tendency to generate and integrate interpretations from a range of sources —sources that (as Lynch, too, discovered) may be more or less inconsistent, imaginary, and radically opposed to official accounts.

The relevance for both projects of Fredric Jameson's notion of 'cognitive mapping' hardly needs underlining. The 1984 essay ('Postmodernism, or the Cultural Logic of Late Capitalism') in which the term was coined makes Jameson's debt to Lynch explicit.

> In a classic work, *The Image of the City*, Kevin Lynch taught us that the alienated city is above all a space in which people are unable to map (in their minds) either their own positions or the urban totality in which they find themselves. [...] Disalienation in the traditional city, then, involves the practical reconquest of a sense of place, and the construction or reconstruction of an articulated ensemble which can be retained in memory and which the individual subject can map and remap along the moments of mobile, alternative trajectories. (Jameson 1984: 89)

García Canclini alludes to Jameson's account of the project in order to develop his notion of 'pre-cartographic operations' (Jameson 1984: 90).[8] For Jameson, the activities of Lynch's respondents are pre-cartographic to the extent that their 'results traditionally are described as itineraries rather than maps; diagrams organised around the still subject-centred or existential journey of the traveller' (Jameson 1984: 90). For Jameson, Lynch charts imaginary relationships with real conditions. García Canclini has less faith in citizens' ability to fix real conditions, however, and rejects out of hand Jameson's half-hearted defence of Lynch's

> concepción mimética de la correspondencia entre representación y realidad, entre mapas y ciudades, que [...] se vuelve particularmente insostenible si lo que estamos tratando son las relaciones imaginarias que todos tenemos con las estructuras urbanas. (García Canclini 1997: 134)

> [a mimetic conception of the correspondence between representation and reality, between maps and cities, which becomes particularly difficult to sustain when dealing with the imaginary relations we each have with urban structures (author's translation).]

Despite placing terms like 'reales' or 'objetivos', once again, in inverted commas, García Canclini himself cannot wholly avoid this charge; conversely, nor does he always avoid overplaying residents' imaginary at the expense of their material engagement with their city. More central to my argument, however, is his extension of the term 'pre-cartographic' in the analysis of focus-group responses to the body of photographs.[9]

---

[8] There is, of course, an important precedent for this in work on the Latin American megacity. In his *Imaginarios urbanos. Bogotá y São Paulo: Cultura y comunicación urbana en América Latina* (1992) Armando Silva opposes '*el mapa al croquis* [énfasis original]. Gráficamente un mapa puede dibujarse por una línea continua que señala el simulacro visual del objeto que se pretende representar. [...] El croquis, al contrario, lo concibo 'punteado', ya que su destino es representar tan sólo límites evocativos o metafóricos, aquellos de un territorio que no admite puntos precisos de corte por su expresión de sentimientos colectivos o de profunda subjetividad social' [*the map to the sketch*. Graphically a map can be drawn with a continuous line which signlas the visual simulacrum of the object which one aims to represent... By contrast, I conceive of the sketch as 'dotted', since its aim is only to represent evocative or metaphorical limits, those of a territory which does not allow precise places of cross-section because of its expression of collective feelings or feelings of profound social subjectivity] (Silva, 1992: 59-60). Interestingly, García Canclini refers in passing to Silva, while Silva makes no reference to Jameson either in footnotes or in his extensive bibliography.

[9] The use of focus groups reportedly reflected a belief that 'la dinámica grupal reconstituye formas de interacción y elaboración habituales en la ciudad [...] y reproducen los mecanismos de construcción del sentido común en la vida diaria, que son siempre colectivos, nunca individuales' [group dynamics reconstitute habitual forms of interaction and elaboration of the city... and reproduce the mechanisms for constructing common sense in daily life, which are always collective, never individual] (119). The very different contexts in which respondent and commuter negotiations take place certainly weaken this claim, however. Comparing the project's results with larger-scale studies might have helped to explain why, despite the

Of the 52 images considered, the two seen as representative by the most people were chosen by eight of the ten groups: one of men pushing to get onto a bus; the other of a peripheral road clogged with traffic. In all other cases there was little agreement, though all reported feeling that traffic was increasingly disorderly and travel increasingly unsafe. But respondents imagined this disorder and insecurity in different ways. Traffic police saw the city as a place where order could, in theory, be imposed and were more alert to where this was not happening: they commented on the failure to observe traffic lights, for example, or the absence of images of mothers double or triple parking as they dropped off their children at school. By contrast taxi drivers and delivery people tended to see travel as a succession of more or less random complications and problems to be overcome: they drive through red lights, for example, to compensate for blockages elsewhere and park on pavements when nowhere else is available or convenient. They do not attempt to change or explicitly challenge rules. Rather they invent new, tactical ways of getting by. But while

> [u]na estrategia implicaría situar la propia conducta en la búsqueda de mayor racionalidad en la vida urbana, que hiciera posible una mayor gestión de dificultades [los viajeros optan por las] tácticas [... que] son 'operaciones multiformes y fragmentarias' que no buscan producir cambios estructurales. Por eso [...] la táctica es 'una victoria del lugar sobre el tiempo' y [...] 'lo que ella gana no lo guarda'. (García Canclini 1997: 128, citing Michel de Certeau)

> [a strategy would mean relating one's own behaviour to the search for increased rationality in urban life, which in turn would enable better management of these difficulties, the travellers opt for 'multiform and fragmented' tactics that are not designed to bring about structural change. For this reason tactics represent 'a victory of place over time' and 'what they win they do not retain' (author's translation).]

This absence of any larger frame, map or ideology 'which might endow the individual subject with some new heightened sense of its place in the global system' once again recalls Jameson's pre-cartographic mode (Jameson 1984: 92, 90). Unlike Jameson, however, García Canclini is not responding to a perceived decathection of metanarratives in 'pedagogical political culture' (Jameson 1984: 92). He is closest to Jameson when he suggests that the tactics of his respondents are pre-political to the extent that they do not obey any larger rational imperative or seek to address the causes of inequalities; rather, they contribute to the emergence of a type of citizenship that, unable effectively to address the contradictions of modernity, contributes instead 'a la reproducción de la desigualdad sistemática y a

---

consensus-seeking encouraged by small-group dynamics, responses to the photographs proved to be exceptionally diverse.

legitimar la corrupción' [to the reproduction of systematic inequality and to the legitimation of corruption] (García Canclini 1997: 129). Responsibility for problems is displaced onto isolated culprits: immigrants, politicians, shanty-town residents, planners, the unemployed. Such displacements are a way of addressing seemingly insoluble problems, he argues,

> incita[ndo] a ensayar tácticas del pensamiento, 'resolver' en lo imaginario, hacer 'sentir' habitable un entorno hostil. Importa menos saber cómo funciona efectivamente la sociedad que imaginar algún tipo de coherencia que ayude a vivir con ella. (García Canclini 1997: 129)[10]

> [they incite travellers to try out mental tactics, to 'resolve' a hostile environment through the work of imagination, to make it 'feel' habitable. It is less important to know how society really functions than to endow it with an imagined coherence and learn to live with it (author's translation).]

If the journeys of Lynch's residents are definitively 'pre-cartographic' his assessment of their journeys clearly is not. Whereas García Canclini places before respondents individual photographs taken over 50 years, Lynch (as noted) charts the tactics of his own subjects by fragmenting specially-prepared photographic maps. The images used assume a human scale if not a human perspective: he eschews aerial photographs, for example, on the grounds that they are 'both too superficial and yet not generalised enough' (Lynch 1960: 143).[11] This assessment rests on his assumed ability to bridge detailed and generalised views. Mediating between large and small scale, between the abstractly meticulous cartographic representation and the rudimentary portulans, is an ideology that privileges beauty, wholeness and humanity and makes them accessible to the self-confident and visually-penetrating subject.

García Canclini's cartographic claims are more oblique by comparison, and more heavily qualified. When presenting the project's findings to a Buenos Aires audience, he was asked about the difficulty of theorising the heterogeneous and dislocated experience of the megacity from

---

[10] Canclini cites the example of jogging: 'La amenaza de la contaminación, por la cual se piensa que "es suicidarse si vas a correr", se atenúa si "lo podemos ver de esta forma: la contaminación, los alimentos, todo es una forma de intoxicación, y al sudarlo tantito es una forma de desintoxicarnos.   Sí, recibimos algo de eso, pero lo que estamos sacando afuera es lo que nos hace sentirnos mejor' [The threat of pollution, because of which people think that 'it's suicidal to go running', is attenuated if 'we can see it in this way: pollution, food, everything is a form of poisoning, and in sweating it out a little it's a way of detoxing ourselves. It's true that we taken in something of that, but what we are getting rid of is what makes us feel better] (García Canclini 1997: 129).

[11] Compare Beloff's observation that photographs *in general* are too particular to facilitate scientific generalisation (1985: 232).

within it. He replied to the effect that snapshots were the best theorists could offer, that theorists, too, construct their narratives with recourse to particular fragments, in particular contexts (García Canclini 1997). This tactic is evident throughout the study, oriented as it is with reference to diverse and sometimes incompatible sources: metanarratives appear only in wilfully fragmented form; like tweezers, inverted commas hold references to truth or real conditions at a distance. Rejecting the non-reflexive approach of Lynch, or of classic anthropology, he attempts to assimilate his experience of the city to that of other citizens: 'Los actores nos movemos en la megalópolis con "operaciones precartográficas". [...] Los investigadores sobre la ciudad [no] disponemos del mapa global que a los demás les falta' [We actors move in the megalopolis with 'precartographic operations'... We researchers into the city do not have at our disposal a global map which others lack] (García Canclini 1997: 134). This now familiar over-compensation for past presumption inevitably bears its own risks. García Canclini attempts to ward off these too by acknowledging that

> [q]uizás la diferencia sería que tenemos algo así como una aspiración controlada a los mapas. No a uno que abarcara todo, sino a un conjunto de cartas de navegación. [...] No hay estilos metodológicos únicos, de absoluta confiabilidad, que van a dar resultados seguros. Hay que usar varias aproximaciones y ver qué pasa con los hechos, que nos pasa a nosotros en medio de eso. (García Canclini 1997: 134/145)

> [I suppose the difference is that we have something like a controlled aspiration to maps —not to a single map covering absolutely everything, but to a set of navigational charts. There is no single, infallible methodological approach that will yield reliable results each time. We have to use various approximations and see what happens with the facts, and what happens to those of us caught in the middle (author's translation).]

It is this explicit pluralism that enables García Canclini and his collaborators to combine a focus on individual tactics with a penetrating assessment of their implicit political and cultural risks.

To conclude, this exploration of gaps in the cognitive mapping of the urban environment and gaps in the accounts of this mapping has highlighted two different approaches to the mapping process. Lynch's project is cartographic in the sense that it characterises the individual and collective narratives of city residents as fictions or as pathology and insists on planners' role in promoting more orderly imaginings within a clearly-defined set of visual co-ordinates. While García Canclini and his collaborators are no less uneasy with the pre-cartographic or pre-political tactics of their respondents, they display little faith in the fixed co-ordinates of either Lynch or Jameson. Their response is not to leap from pre-to post-cartographic mode, however, from pre- to post-political. Adapting Jameson's critique to new circumstances, they demonstrate the —albeit attenuated— cartographic mediating power of their amalgam of constructionism and subject-centred micropolitics, multiculturalism, and of a traditionally left-informed, macropolitical concern for the public sphere. Like the residents of Mexico City, that is, they make tactical use of the options available; unlike the members of their focus groups, however, the researchers are only too aware of the strategic and political vulnerability of their position.

Works Cited

Barthes, Roland (1981) *Camera Lucida: Reflections on Photography*, trans. Richard Howard (New York: Hill and Wang).

Castellanos, Alejandro (1996) 'Espacio y espejo', in Néstor García Canclini, Alejandro Castellanos and Ana Rosas Mantecón, *La ciudad de los viajeros: Travesías e imaginarios urbanos: México, 1940-2000* (Mexico DF: Editorial Grijalbo), 43-60.

Debroise, Olivier (1987) 'Mexican Photography in the Eighties/La fotografía mexicana en los años 80', in Charles Merewether, *A Marginal Body: The Photographic Image in Latin America/Un cuerpo marginal: La imagen fotográfica en América Latina* (Sydney: Australian Centre for Photography), 48-63.

García Canclini, Néstor (1997) 'Viajes e imaginarios urbanos', in Néstor García Canclini, *Imaginarios urbanos* (Mexico DF: Grijalbo), 107-49.

García Canclini, Néstor and Ana Rosas Mantecón (1996) 'Las múltiples ciudades de los viajeros', in Néstor García Canclini, Alejandro Castellanos and Ana Rosas Mantecón (eds), *La ciudad de los viajeros: Travesías e imaginarios urbanos: México, 1940-2000* (Mexico DF: Editorial Grijalbo), 61-106.

García Canclini, Néstor, Alejandro Castellanos and Ana Rosas Mantecón (eds) (1996) *La ciudad de los viajeros: Travesías e imaginarios urbanos: México, 1940-2000* (Mexico DF: Grijalbo).

Jameson, Fredric (1984) 'Postmodernism, or The Cultural Logic of Late Capitalism', in *New Left Review* 146, 53-92.

Kay, Ronald (1987) 'The Reproduction of the New World/La reproducción del nuevo mundo', in Charles Merewether, *A Marginal Body: The Photographic Image in Latin America/ Un cuerpo marginal: La imagen fotográfica en América Latina* (Sydney: Australian Centre for Photography), 18-21.

Krauss, Rosalind (1985) *The Originality of the Avant-Garde and Other Modernist Myths* (Cambridge, MA: MIT Press).

Lynch, Kevin (1960) *The Image of the City* (Cambridge: MIT).

Merewether, Charles (1987) *A Marginal Body: The Photographic Image in Latin America/Un cuerpo marginal: La imagen fotográfica en América Latina* (Sydney: Australian Centre for Photography).

Michaud, Yves (1998) 'Forms of Looking: Philosophy and Photography', in Michel Frizot et al. (eds), *A New History of Photography* (Cologne: Köneman), 730-38.

Monsiváis, Carlos (1997) 'Identity Hour or, What Photos Would You Take of the Endless City (From A Guide to Mexico City)', in Carlos Monsiváis, *Mexican Postcards*, translated and edited by John Kraniauskas (London: Verso), 31-35.

Osborne, Peter D. (2000) *Travelling Light: Photography, Travel and Visual Culture* (Manchester: Manchester University Press).

Price, Mary (1994) *The Photograph: A Strange Confined Space* (Stanford: Stanford University Press).

Segre, Erica (2001) 'Towards a Reading of Contemporary Women Photographers in Mexico: Issues of Allegory and Identity', in *Journal of Romance Studies* 1.1, 45-68.

Silva, Armando (1992) *Imaginarios urbanos. Bogotá y São Paulo: Cultura y comunicación urbana en América Latina* (Bogotá: Tercer Mundo).

Sontag, Susan (1978) *On Photography* (London, Allen Lane).

Tagg, John (1999) 'Evidence, Truth and Order: A Means of Surveillance', in Jessica Evans and Stuart Hall (eds), *Visual Culture: The Reader* (Thousand Oaks, CA: Corwin Press), 244-73.

Colonising the Land: *Heimat* and the Constructed Landscapes of Mexico's Ciudad Universitaria (1943–1953)[1]

Helen Thomas

Abstract

This essay examines the changing meanings of the provocative German word *Heimat* over the late-nineteenth and twentieth centuries. It explores how *Heimat's* unifying purpose relies on the mythologising of national landscapes, and considers the relevance of the concept in both post-Revolutionary and post-war Mexico. The construction of the University City of Mexico during the 1940s and 50s is used as a case study. The physical realities of the University's original and constructed landscapes are described and assessed as articulations of different political and social relationships with the land.

* * *

Heimat

> The word is always linked to strong feeling, mostly remembrances and longing [for] something very far away, something which one cannot easily find or find again.[2]

By the start of the Cold War in the mid-1940s this definition of the term *Heimat* as something lost seemed all too apt. In reality, though, the German word embodied everything that was abhorrent to the Allies: it resonated with provincialism at its most intolerant and dangerous extreme. Memories of exile and the annihilation of those who had not 'belonged' in Nazi Germany were still raw. Even Lewis Mumford, despite his regionalist sympathies, shuddered at the word 'Heimatsarchitektur' in his 1946 Introduction to *The South in Architecture* (Mumford 1967: 114).[3]

---

[1] We would like to thank the editors of the *Journal of Romance Studies* for permission to reproduce 'Colonising the Land: *Heimat* and the Constructed Landscapes of Mexico's Ciudad Universitaria' which was originally published in: *Journal of Romance Studies* 2.3, 33-44.

[2] Edgar Reitz, director of the sixteen-hour film called *Heimat*, which was screened in eleven episodes on German television in 1984 (cited in Kaes 1989: 163).

[3] What Mumford meant by 'Heimatsarchitektur' is not clear. The official 'style' of the Third Reich was the monumental neo-classicism of Speer. The work of conservative architects

The English language employs a string of terms to capture the meaning of *Heimat*: homeland, abode, habitat, for example. They are all too compact,[4] however, to define a concept employed in contexts ranging from the geographical and spatial (where it evokes a place of origin or lost beginnings)[5] to the spiritual and existential (where it describes the core of the journeying inner self) (Kiryakakis 1988: 5).[6] In all of these meanings it is perceived of as a centre, but an elusive one; in Edgar Reitz's view, "*Heimat*" is such that if one would go closer and closer to it, one would discover that at the moment of arrival it is gone, it has dissolved into nothingness. It seems to me that one has a more precise idea of "Heimat" the further one is away from it' (Kaes 1989: 163).

During the nineteenth and twentieth centuries, this word *Heimat*, like numerous others invented to serve political ends, was reinterpreted many times over. Its core sense, a feeling of belonging together in a place, of being at home, has varied across the spectrum in its implication of complex community inherent in Mumford's desired coexistence of different peoples, to the exclusive racial purity of the Nazis (Mumford 1967).

Heimat's modern presence arose from the separation of Church from State by the French colonisers of German territories at the end of the eighteenth century. The moral structure of Catholicism disintegrated and Church lands were dispersed amongst a new bourgeoisie. A fracture in the previously coherent and mutually dependent social system ensued. Towards the late nineteenth century, during the post-Napoleonic turmoil in Germany, the idea of *Heimat* as a way of unifying previously autonomous principalities

---

reproducing the rural vernacular with no reflective relationship with the urban modernism of the protagonists of *Neue Sachlichkeit* in Frankfurt, Berlin or Stuttgart most clearly fits his narrative. It is unlikely that he was referring to the work of *Neues Bauen* architects such as Scharoun and Häring. Miller Lane (1991) argues that 'heimatlich' architecture, that with rustic siting and reference to regional traditions, was one of a number of styles —including functional Modernism, native regionalism and monumental classicism— that continued simultaneously, even overlapping, throughout the 1930s and 1940s in Germany.

[4] Wickham (1999: 5 and ch. 1) describes the fourteen different semantic configurations of *Heimat*, beginning with its original meaning of farmstead, or farmhouse, going on to expand its basic anti-urban significance. This is evident in the antonym to *Heimat* —*Fremde*, which encompasses words often associated with the modern urban condition: foreign, different, alien, unknown— the experience of otherness is a prerequisite of modernity.

[5] Wickham (1999: 25) describes an early use of *Heimat* as referring to the territory of a community or an individual. The prewar use of the term usually engages with this territorial aspect, and is concerned with geographical origin, parental location, and the symbolic relationship between a particular place and an individual.

[6] In this discussion the geographical import of *Heimat* is balanced against the spiritual journey toward an ideal state, or perfection, as explored in Herman Hesse's *Steppenwolf* where the context is timeless —beyond space and time, one particularly apt in relation to Cold War Abstract Expressionism. Related to this is the internalised intellectual journey of the individual. Wickham (1999: 46) investigates the relationship of *Geist* or spirit to *Heimat* as an internalised rootedness in a place.

began to take on an important role in local and national politics. From 1871, the founding year of the German Second Empire that united twenty-five German States under Emperor William I, the term *Heimat* described an implicit movement amongst regional institutions and councils to revive interest in local history, customs and dialects. These were drawn together at the level of State control to create a new national integrity through using, rather than denying, the provincial. The promotion of local collective life, communal integrity and public morality articulated through a conscious imaging of home subsequently became fundamental to the later Weimar Republic (1918–1933). Several members of the Bauhaus movement had sympathy with the *Heimat* ethic (Applegate 1990: 149). In 1898 Adolph Loos, on the other hand, voiced an early opposition to its use of folk craft and tradition to define local identities:

> One thing nations divided into castes have in common is [a] rigid retention of folk costume [...] But now a new generation has arrived, a generation that has declared war on folk costume. In their struggle they have a good ally: the threshing machine. Its arrival in any village means goodbye to all those picturesque hand-me-downs. They are sent where they belong, to the fancy dress rental store. (Loos 1989: 113)

Loos was referring to the reorganisation of rural communities into more efficient and mechanised units. *Heimat* is striking in a contemporary context for its anti-urban associations. During its early usage it provided a utopian community-promoting antithesis to the experience of alienation inherent in modern city life (Kaes 1989: 165). This opposition between the rural and the urban was originally used to connect geographically dispersed sympathies; later *Heimat* would work to link the provincial reality of the rural with the national aspirations expressed in the urban. Its association with the rural derives from the sources it drew from to define the German nation — localised collective craft cultures as opposed to the high art of the individualistic urban civilisations that had colonised the world in preceding centuries. The result was the 'cultural nation' of Germany, the sum of its parts, rather than a singular 'liberal state' generated from a metropolitan centre.[7]

One of the reasons for the difficulty in making a precise definition of *Heimat* is the deliberately subtle, ambiguous and imprecise way it was employed during the early twentieth century. In order to align a set of

---

[7] The difference between the cultural nation (Germany) and the liberal state (Britain) has its roots within the different approaches to Romantic thought in Germany and England. While the former draws on the collective to define a national cultural identity, the latter defines itself via the products of an individualistic urban artistic elite. This is discussed in detail in Kaiser (1999) who expands on the differences between culture and civilisation.

differences as a whole while allowing them to retain their separate identities there had to be room for interpretation; there could be no prescription. Only in this way could the particular and the general exist simultaneously within *Heimat*'s experiential and emotional construct, one that connected the personal circumstances and memories of the individual with the abstract collective.[8] Thus the primary function of *Heimat* as a cultural idea was to unify: its task was to create an interdependence between the individual, the local, the State and the nation. Its intent was explicitly transcultural: both temporally through its use of tradition and geographically in its aim to synthesise localised cultural identities.

In its promotion of the rural, the land as a tangible reality and as an abstract or symbolic concept played a central role within the prewar sense of *Heimat*. As one postwar commentator put it: '*Heimat* is landscape. *Heimat* is the landscape we have experienced' (Doob 1952: 196). *Heimat*-promoting institutions and legislation drew on a belief within German cultures that the land and intimate experience of it through physical contact were the basis of all knowledge. This was an empirical approach to the world, where all human experience was returned to the local and the familiar (Applegate 1990: 32). By 1916, when an official *Heimat* movement came into being, the term began to represent an expression of the nature of the land itself, with physical geography creating a sense of a national personality. The land belonged to the community, and the restrictions of private ownership were subsumed to serve the collective. In keeping with its sympathy for organic structure the *Heimat* movement was pro-nature. The outdoors became a very important place in the *Heimat* imagination as a communal and public space for the enactment of civic events. Rambling in the countryside was encouraged, and picnicking and open-air displays became popular. The day-tripper and the hiker saw the utilitarian nature of the farmer in a new way, and the rural became the romanticised province of the tourist (Applegate 1990: 63).

Despite the seemingly inward-looking tendencies of the *Heimat* sympathiser, the intrinsic purpose of the concept was the creation of a whole larger than that experienced by the individual. At the beginning of the century the idea of *Heimat* that filtered through German public life and into the subjective world of the private individual enabled the nation as a whole to embrace its position within the world. It was not until later that the communal and nationalist ambitions towards a spiritually and materially prosperous unity inherent in the idea were manipulated and exaggerated towards quite different ends by the National Socialists. Their 'Blood and Soil' rhetoric manipulated all the means of engaging with the urban, the modern and the

---

[8] Kaes (1989: 168) discusses the complex postwar meanings of *Heimat* as an experience of loss (of home and family) and as a vacuum filled with nostalgic memories.

foreign in early *Heimat* thought, which had provided an alternative to the rational and the universal (Wickham 1999: 7).

Heimat and Mexico

Unlike nineteenth- and early twentieth-century Germany, which was defined by its various collective relationships with the landscape, Mexico at that time was conceived of by a tiny and intensely urban social elite. In essence it aspired to be a 'liberal state', strictly maintained under Porfirio Diaz. From the time of conquest civilisation had emanated from Mexico City, which itself was influenced by the urban centres of Europe. Spatial segregation meant that the land beyond the city limits remained more alien than Paris. Surrounding the colonial centres was a vast, uncivilised wilderness largely inhabited by disenfranchised peasants, usually of Amero-Indian descent. The apparent urban complacency of the ruling classes was already rife, however, with the ambiguities that were to fracture Mexico's fragile post-colonial identity and force the presence of the rural into the very heart of the city.

During the nineteenth century national ownership of the land became a factor of international dissent as foreign companies began to build railroads and run lucrative mines in the deserts of the north. Separation of Church and State began to destabilise the precarious systems controlling a monstrously complex social hierarchy, and in 1910 the violent turmoil of the Mexican Revolution was unleashed. By 1920 the Mexican nation was reforming itself in opposition to the pre-Revolutionary Porfirian state and its rational positivist philosophies of government. Like post-colonial Germany in its search for a common past and cultural unity as a reaction to the universalist, rationalist philosophy of the French Enlightenment, post-Revolutionary Mexico became aware of, if not adherent to, the Romantic perception of rural territories within which *Heimat* flourished (Brading 1985: 1-2).[9]

In Germany the rural had preceded the urban. In post-colonial Mexico, however, the centres of colonial control —the cities— had defined the nation. Mexico's rural landscapes had first to be realised aesthetically, therefore, before they could become a 'homeland' for the modern Mexican. This conceptualisation of the rural, within which Mexico's new historical narrative could unfold, was the task of the Muralists in the 1920s and 1930s.[10] Their vast scenes of war and strife were enacted in the 'unhomely'

---

[9] See Brading (1985: 1-2) for a detailed discussion of the Mexican reaction to Porfirian rationalism.

[10] The most famous were Diego Rivera, David Alfaro Siqueiros and José Clemente Orozco. There were other significant contributors to the Mural programme, including Jean Charlot and the architect Juan O'Gorman.

deserts and mountains of Mexico. Painting on the walls of Mexico City's most powerful buildings, they brought visions of the wilderness into the urban imagination. Other painters and photographers, from Clausell and Dr Atl to Alvarez Bravo and Kahlo, began to make sense of Mexico's terrible nature, so unlike its Arcadian counterpart in the domesticated United States. They drew from the example of the open-air schools of painting set up on the fringes of Mexico City, such as one at Santa Anita, from 1913. The classes at Santa Anita began to substitute direct experience of the natural landscape for the closed classrooms of the Academy, sowing the seeds of a *Heimat* sensibility.

An important part of the new revolutionary constitution ratified in 1917, Clause 27 demanded the redistribution of Church land and privately owned estates into collectives managed by peasant communities and families. This meant that the extra-urban areas, their populace and their traditions could no longer be ignored by the urban elites. The social hierarchy began, symbolically at least, to disassemble itself.

Mexicans in power, notably the Minister for Education, José Vasconcelos, began to use the term 'cosmic race'.[11] This was an inclusive phrase that sought to redefine the modern Mexican as a synthesis of Spanish, mestizo and Amero-Indian cultures, and Mexico as a unified hybrid nation. Amero-Indian culture, perceived as both pre-Columbian and ancient, vernacular and popular, permeated post-Revolutionary artistic programmes as a way of achieving this unity.

Indian and vernacular forms became very fashionable amongst the artistic elites and they began to temper international influences with the autochthonous. The studios and paintings of Rivera and Kahlo were crammed with popular artefacts both ancient and modern, and Kahlo famously decked herself in indigenous costumes. Both were avid socialists, promoting the cause of community and equality. Eisenstein brought the connection between knowledge of the land and Indian culture into the international arena through his film *¡Que Viva Mexico!* In 1931 he visited Mexico to film fragments of rural life around the country. Brought together, these formed a montage of regional and geographical diversity that reinforced the tentative beginnings of Mexico's constructed *Heimat*.

The Ciudad Universitaria

The site for the new University City was chosen in March 1943 and was located beyond the affluent villages of San Ángel and Coyoacán that defined Mexico City's south-western edge. It consisted of four patches of cultivated

---

[11] Vasconcelos, Education Minister from 1920 to 1924, was the principal patron of the Muralists.

ejido land belonging to several small villages[12] and large tracts of impassable volcanic rock. This lava landscape was called El Pedregal, and it supported various local myths and superstitions. Described as a place of desolation, loneliness and silence it was perceived as a dangerous wilderness inhabited only by wild animals and desperate men, and home to all manner of Indian magic.[13]

Since the fifteenth century the rocky cliffs of El Pedregal had provided building material for the city and surrounding villages, and the mines frequently turned up archaeological remains that were among the oldest in America. The mined sites that furnished the richest archaeological evidence were the *canteras* of Copilco at the north-eastern limits of El Pedregal, near the village of Coyoacán and the hill at Cuicuilco, an archaic pyramid constructed as early as 1000 BC. These discoveries added considerably to the importance of El Pedregal in the reinvention of Mexico's history. It became a place that represented the rural wilderness with which urban Mexico hoped to engage, and yet was conveniently close to the city, too. It also embodied the important role that the antiquity of Mexico's culture played in North America's postwar perception of itself as historically and culturally independent from Europe.[14]

The location of the Ciudad Universitaria at El Pedregal held immense symbolic power for its architects and government sponsors, amongst them the charismatic and corrupt President Alemán. Both the original and the constructed site that it was to become were seen to represent a new, modern and democratic Mexico. Carlos Lazo, Director-General of works at the Ciudad Universitaria, was especially enthusiastic about the timely discovery of this place. In a talk given on the progress of construction in August 1950, he stated that 'En la localización de la Ciudad Universitaria parece que ha operado un determinismo histórico' (Lazo 1952: 30) [the location of the University City seems to have come about through an historical determinism (author's translation)]. It had special qualities that made it symbolic of its time:

> Bajo esa lava [...] los restos de la cultura más antigua del Continente americano. Sobre ellos, en el centro de México, que es casi el centro del continente; sobre la Carretera Panamericana, es una frontera como lo es México de dos razas, de dos culturas, de dos religiones, está surgiendo en las mejores ciudades

---

[12] *Ejido* is the term used for a plot of land reclaimed by the State under Clause 27 and cultivated either by a single family or as communal village land. The villages would own the rights to lease the land from the State, but they would not own it outright. Thus strict controls over the use of land were maintained.

[13] For a prewar description of El Pedregal, see Fernández de Castillo (1913).

[14] Evidence of this is the interest paid to the pre-Columbian Mexican artefacts by artists such as Barnett Newman and Willem de Kooning after 1943.

universitarias del mundo, por su espíritu y su ambición. No podía, pues, estar más lleno de sentido, de destino y de simbolismo la futura Ciudad Universitaria de México. (Lazo 1952: 177)

[Below this lava [...] lie the remains of the most ancient culture of the American continent. Over these remains, in the centre of Mexico, which is almost in the centre of the continent; over the Pan-American Highway, which like Mexico is a frontier between two races, two cultures, two religions, is being built one of the best university cities of the world, for its spirit and ambition. The future University City of Mexico could not be [...] more full of meaning, destiny or symbolism (author's translation).]

In this speech Lazo, the great road-builder,[15] articulated a desire for unity that transcended the merely national ambitions of pre-war Mexicans such as Vasconcelos. His aspiration for the Ciudad Universitaria as the embodiment of a North American synthesis echoed an essential quality of *Heimat*. He was spinning 'a myth about the possibility of a community in the face of fragmentation and alienation' (Applegate 1990: 29). The parties he wished the Pan-American highway to reconcile were not simply Mexican. They included all of America and specifically the North. The two races, two cultures and two religions that he referred to were not merely the traditional oppositions internal to Mexico: between pre-Columbian and coloniser, Aztec and Spaniard, cosmology and Catholicism. Equally important to Lazo were the differences existing between the Anglo-Saxon and the Latin that were articulated at the desert border between the US and Mexico. As urban Mexicans began to recognise Mexico's geographical and cultural diversity they began to realise a new position for Mexico globally, too. The Ciudad Universitaria, as a large-scale modern project of almost urban proportions, was to represent a country where the dream of modernity appeared to have become a way of life. It was a nationalist project with internationalist aspirations.

Interest in the dramatic qualities of the lava surface at the Ciudad Universitaria has tended to obscure the fact that a large part of the original site was cultivated *ejidatario* land, and therefore home already to a substantial number of peasant subsistence farmers. Their dwellings were free-standing in the fields: drystone walls roofed with overlapping layers of discarded corrugated iron, or tarpaulin-covered, timber-strutted structures mimicking the pitches of the haystacks among which they were situated. Hugging the ground and using the cliffs and outcrops of rock, some shelters

---

[15] Lazo's life work was the construction of the highways linking Mexico City with developing beauty stops, enabling President Alemán's tourist Mexico to flourish. He was responsible for the thoroughfare from Mexico City to Acapulco and promoter of the 'interoceánica' between Veracruz and Acapulco; his routes were followed by the city's most affluent citizens.

were drawn taut on slender posts, while others were made from stone walls buttressing the slope and entered from above through roofs made from iron and timber boards. They were constructed using materials found on or near their site. Sometimes they used lava rock, but often the materials were far from 'traditional' and consisted of urban debris from many sources.

Figure 1: Lava Landscape at El Pedregal
© Hugo Brehme

To build their new university the Rector and his supporters had to remove these people from the land. The *ejido* rights granted to four villages in the 1920s and 1930s that protected them made acquisition of the site extremely complex.[16] After three years of negotiation a Presidential decree announced the expropriation of the land in favour of the University, and defined the terms of compensation for the dispossessed peasants. Besides a lump sum payment the University was to provide comprehensive education for eighty-three *ejidatario* children, give the forty-five *ejidatarios* of Copilco permanent jobs at the Ciudad Universitaria, construct replacement housing for sixty families and provide a primary school.[17]

The outcome of this was a small settlement built for the *ejidatarios*, which were the first buildings to be constructed on the site. The location of the settlement was beyond the eastern boundary of the Ciudad Universitaria

---

[16] The dates for the original expropriation of the lands are as follows: Tlalpan 1929, some handed to Copilco in 1938, San Jerónimo Aculco 1923, Padierna 1938.

[17] For details of the distribution of land see Pani and del Moral (1989: 133-39), which describes the distribution of all land rights and their value, and lists the names of all residents and *ejidatarios* on the site.

on the lava bed itself. Populating the sinuous street layout were sixty houses[18] and a school designed and built by the architect Antonio Pastrana. The *ejidatarios* living in this town still inhabited the same location as they had previously, but they were removed forever from their original environment. Their ramshackle dwellings were destroyed and replaced by a modern architect's interpretation of Mexican vernacular housing. *Heimat* in a personal, geographical and spatial sense became, for them, very far away.

The new houses were hygienically raised above the uneven ground on rubble platforms that were bound on their upper surface by a smooth concrete cap. Their construction used traditional techniques partly disguised by the white render that coated them. Reminiscent of earlier rural buildings by the Ciudad Universitaria architect Enrique del Moral, such as the school at Cosacuarán (1944-1946),[19] load bearing walls of adobe block supported a timber roof structure, with two unmilled timber posts holding up the porch of an external patio. The generic house on top of an abstract plinth replaced the intimate relationship with the ground surface that the *ejidatarios* had experienced in their dilapidated but constantly evolving huts. Their dwellings and their bodies were separated from the ground both physically and metaphorically as they were set to work building the new University campus.

Between 1947, when Mario Pani and del Moral won the University's competition for a master plan design, and 1952, the year of the Ciudad Universitaria's inauguration, the site's complex ground surface was replaced by an organised system of zones and layers, paths and roads. The presence of the natural in the landscapes of the Ciudad Universitaria was deliberately and deeply compromised, in keeping with the modernising aspirations of its planners to provide for an ideal, man-made future. The suppression of nature was at odds, however, with the desire for this future to arise from the fusion of Mexico's diverse histories. These depended upon El Pedregal's links with a pre-Columbian telluric Indian past. Thus the use and definition of the natural at the Ciudad Universitaria was ambiguous. Whilst the existing conditions of the site were cleverly exploited metaphorically, their physical reality was submerged. Personal knowledge of the natural landscape so important within the German sense of *Heimat* would become merely a memory of the *ejidatarios*.

After the dynamiting for construction material and levelling for buildings, roads and foundations the ground surface was carefully

---

[18] This figure is compounded from contract documents related to the construction of the *Unidad Urbana de Ejidatarios* supervised by Lazo in the *Archivo General de la Nación* (AGN) Carlos Lazo Archive box 79.

[19] This used the timber beam and post motif in conjunction with load-bearing walls constructed from various traditional materials. See Pinoncelly (1983: 33). Soon after the construction of the ex-*ejidatario* settlement at the CU, Pani designed a settlement for rural workers in the Yucatan. The individual house units drew heavily on vernacular construction techniques and materials. See Iannini (1999: 46-51) for detailed drawings, diagrams and photographs of the project.

reconstructed. An uneven rocky ground was not deemed either suitable or beautiful, and within the bounds of the campus its presence was largely erased. Immense swathes of land were smoothed and paved using brick, polished volcanic stone, concrete slabs, neat lawns, cobbles and poured concrete. According to Pani and del Moral, the dominant idea was to harmonise natural materials taken from the site and worked by hand with those manufactured elsewhere and brought in.

Figure 2: Artificial Landscape in the Garden of the School of Engineering
© Architecture d'Aujourd'hui 1955

In various photographs of the Ciudad Universitaria, especially of sporting events, the middle distance is populated by trees acting as a buffer between campus and rocky plain, suggestive of an Arcadian landscape —a privileged view available in contemporary Mexico City only in the golf clubs of the wealthy. Like the rural landscapes of early twentieth-century Germany, the newly picturesque grounds of the Ciudad Universitaria became a popular place for weekend picnickers from the city, as well as tourists seeking respite from the heady disorder of the urban centre. The plans for forestation of the Ciudad Universitaria campus aspired to civilise the original wilderness through the planting of imported flora. Lazo asked for government funds to buy 145,000 trees for the site. Many of them were not indigenous, and some, such as the 20,000 eucalyptus trees planted, served to destroy the fragile and complex bioclimate of the volcanic region.

The buildings of the University were carefully sited within the tightly controlled master plan and zoned according to their function: administrative, academic, recreational or residential. Each was named according to its function: School of Engineering, Central Library or Faculty of Philosophy, for example. The vast external spaces of the campus that surrounded the various towers and slab blocks had no names, however, by which to designate them. The largest were conceived of as ceremonial and not 'functional', so within the Functionalist framework they were speechless. The exceptions at the Ciudad Universitaria were the generic names given to the sports fields: football pitch, tennis court, baseball field or *frontón* (a court for a form of pre-Columbian hand-ball still played in Mexico).

Despite this denial of the important and deliberately constructed external spaces of the campus, it was the great variety of axially located squares, courts, gardens, lawns, loggias, underpasses and forecourts that gave the campus its extraordinary character. Their size, their emptiness and relentlessness, their spatial relationships with each other and their separateness from the unusual landscape that they replaced was unprecedented; they were real echoes of the urban dreams of Hilberseimer and Le Corbusier. Three spatial fields at the Ciudad Universitaria are particularly noteworthy. All of them are plinth structures that separate the environment of the campus from the surrounding Pedregal landscape. These artificial ground planes isolate the buildings upon them from the original site and transform them into modernist (sculptural) objects, or monuments. The buildings consequently suffer a deliberate 'sitelessness [...], an absolute loss of place' (Krauss 1994: 280).

The first man-made field to be constructed was the subtly layered sports ground that corralled any irregularity in the surface into a neatly contained compound. Early photographs show it bare from end to end, in stark contrast to the lava beds stretching from its edges, which were visually chaotic in comparison to the abstract composition of the sports field plan. Carefully arranged over this new flat ground made of large precast concrete slabs or in situ concrete articulated by low walls of lava rock that occasionally framed smooth lawns were the structures defining the *frontones,* the football fields and the baseball court. These were constructed before the plinth, early in 1951, and the 'pyramid-like' *frontones* emerged first as ruins from the trampled ground before achieving their pristine edges.

These self-consciously regionalist structures, plus the volcano-like Olympic stadium, were the only architectural elements that made a formal concession to the pre-Columbian legacy of the Ciudad Universitaria site, thus forging a symbolic connection with the ground. The *frontones* and stadium were immensely popular with foreign tourists who visited the Ciudad Universitaria drawn by the formal references to Mexico's, and by association America's, pre-colonial past.

The second important space at the Ciudad Universitaria was the plinth for the Rectory Tower. Located at the edge of a plaza intermittently populated by trees, it overlooked a huge lawn to the East: 'As befits its importance, the building is located at the highest point of the campus in immediate proximity to the main road leading to the city' (Cetto 1961: 68). This and the other huge open spaces of the Ciudad Universitaria had a grand scale that characterised many already existing Mexican urban spaces. This space, defined by the Rectory building and the central Library on its northern edge, and the Museum and Faculty of Architecture to the south, was comparable to the vast central square at the centre of Mexico City. Called the Zócalo, a Spanish word whose English translation is plinth, this is bounded by two of the city's most important buildings: the Cathedral and the National Palace. The Zócalo covered the main temple complex of the Aztec lake city of Tenochtitlán. The destruction of the temple signified the conquering of the Aztecs by rendering their gods homeless; the making of the Ciudad Universitaria plinth symbolised the subordination of Mexico's difficult physical environment and the banishment of natural disaster. The plinth covered the lava bed that, as the product of a massive volcanic explosion, was a reminder of the destructive potential of Mexico City's site: a drained lake surrounded by live and extinct volcanoes in an earthquake zone.

The grand Rectory square at the Ciudad Universitaria was second in size only to the third major space within the campus: the Great Lawn beyond. This was a huge void at the centre of the campus, inhabited only by picturesque clumps of trees. It was compelling evidence of the level of transformation that the original site had undergone; a subtle sign of affluence and domination of the natural world —a lush green lawn— created on a ridiculous scale, beyond functionality. Various murals on the walls of prominent buildings used the external spaces as if they were domestic rooms. The murals narrated the official mythologies, interpreted to highlight their relevance to the new University.

Projecting from the sixth and seventh floors of the Rectory tower, and effectively hung in an outdoor room 500 metres long, a mural by Siqueiros depicting the symbolic shield of the University imposed itself visually throughout the 'Zona Escolar' to the West.[20] Siqueiros made a didactic high-relief panel for the spectator in motion that faced south and on to Avenida Insurgentes. This represents scientists and technicians in the making, a message for the traveller about the University's role in creating the future of Mexico through its democratic education. Other murals told stories

---

[20] Ramírez Montagut (1995: 68) details the subjects of the shield, which was given to the University by Vasconcelos in 1921, as a Mexican eagle and an Andean condor. Siqueiros shows them facing each other and holding on to a ring —unified for all eternity, perhaps, while the original has them twisted away from each other and divided by an image of Latin America above the silhouette of the volcanoes overshadowing the valley and with cacti twisting round them.

of discoveries that made connections between different places and times.[21] These located the Ciudad Universitaria within Mexican history at a moment between the subservient colonial or imperialist past and the free modern future. Juan O'Gorman, for example, tattooed the body of the central library with a complex, erudite iconography that promoted the idea of a national community united by a common hybrid mythology.

Conclusion

The Mexican sense of *Heimat*, sometimes referred to as *Mexicanidad* in postwar texts, was a deeply compromised version of the German meaning. As the Ciudad Universitaria illustrates, ambitions fundamental to *Heimat* — the construction of an imagined community linking the individual to the whole, the importance of local and craft cultures, and the embodying of the national psyche in the land, for example— were symbolic State gestures rather than quotidian structures. Although on the surface the Mexican establishment had sought ethnic, social and cultural unity as a way to define modern Mexico, its means of engagement served to maintain the divisions created during colonisation. The idea of community that had been inherent in the post-Revolutionary constitution found itself dissolving even further into individualism under President Alemán. One time Minister for Tourism, astute land speculator and visitor to Hollywood, he articulated his idea of equality as an ambition for each Mexican to 'have a Cadillac, a cigar and a ticket to the bullfights' (Krauze 1997: 543).[22] He had little concern for Mexicans such as the dispossessed peasant living in the new *ejidatario* town. Even rehoused in his new, hygienic white box the ex-*ejidatario*'s relationship with a unified whole was defined not by a shared sense of 'homeland', but by his position within a hierarchical social and economic system.

Folk cultures were not celebrated as the continuing traditions that formed the basis of a national identity, as they had been in early twentieth-century Germany. Aestheticised and sanitised by an urban elite, they did not actively contribute to the present. They were symbolic representations of either Mexico's dead and ancient past or its exotic otherness. At the Ciudad Universitaria connections with the land were made by way of pre-Columbian references to indigenous, regional cultures in the stylised *frontones*, the Olympic stadium and the murals, and in the abstract interpretations of the vernacular in the *ejidatario* dwellings. These architectural forms and their visual and spatial narratives did not articulate a private local language, or

---

[21] For example Eppens's *The Conquest of Energy* and *The Return of Quetzalcoatl* on the School of Science.

[22] This statement appears to presume the Mexican to have one gender, for one can hardly imagine even the most glamorous Mexican woman with a cigar at the bullfights.

even a national tongue. They sent out universal messages to an international audience proclaiming Mexico's global relevance and equivalence.

Making Mexican nature safe and homely was an impossible feat. The eradication and reconstruction of the useful aspects of the Pedregal site enacted at the Ciudad Universitaria represented, perhaps, one of the few ways of sublimating the terrible aspects of Mexico City's unpredictable natural environment that El Pedregal embodied. In organising and controlling its inhabitants, smoothing the ground, planting vast lawns and thousands of trees, the Ciudad Universitaria was an attempt to make a new, man-made, archetypal home for the citizens of modern Mexico. Many years later Carlos Fuentes would describe this new 'homeland' as an upper-middle-class prison, a place where one of his characters was brought 'by Mercedes to a new house surrounded by walls in the Pedregal district, a house for forgetting, she told herself, because she recognised nothing there, wanted nothing there, and everything she touched she forgot' (Fuentes 1990: 30).

124

Works Cited

Applegate, Celia (1990) *A Nation of Provincials: The German Idea of Heimat* (Oxford: University of California Press).

Brading, David (1985) *The Origins of Mexican Nationalism* (Cambridge: Centre for Latin American Studies, University of Cambridge).

Cetto, Max (1961) *Modern Architecture in Mexico* (London: Alec Tiranti).

Doob, Leonard (1952) *Patriotism and Nationalism: Their Psychological Foundations* (New Haven CT: Yale University Press).

Fernández de Castillo, Francisco (1913) 'El Pedregal', in *Apuntes para la historia de San Angel y sus alrededores* (Mexico City: Impresa del Museo de Arqueología, Historia y Etnología), 144-52.

Fuentes, Carlos (1990) *Christopher Unborn* (London: Picador).

Iannini, Humberto (ed) (1999) *Mario Pani Arquitecto* (Mexico City: UAM).

Kaes, Anton (1989) *From Hitler to Heimat* (Cambridge MA and London: Harvard University Press).

Kaiser, David (1999) *Romanticism, Aesthetics and Nationalism* (Cambridge: Cambridge University Press).

Kiryakakis, Andreas (1988) *The Idea of Heimat in the Works of Herman Hesse* (New York: Peter Lang).

Krauss, Rosalind (1994) *The Originality of the Avant-Garde and Other Modernist Myths* (Cambridge MA and London: MIT Press).

Krauze, Enrique (1997) *Mexico: Biography of Power* (New York: Harper Collins).

Lazo, Carlos (1952) *Pensamiento y destino de la Ciudad Universitaria* (Mexico City: Miguel Angel Porrúa).

Loos, Adolph (1989) [1898] 'Underwear', in *Ornament and Crime, Selected Essays* (Riverside: Ariadne Press), 112-18.

Miller Lane, Barbara (1991) 'The Architecture of Nazi Germany', in *Journal of the Society of Architectural Historians* 50.3, 325-28.

Mumford, Lewis (1967) *The South in Architecture* (New York: DaCapo Press).

Pani, Mario and Enrique del Moral (1989) *La construcción de la Ciudad Universitaria del Pedregal: Concepto, programa y planeación arquitectónica* (Mexico City: UNAM).

Pinoncelly, Salvador (1983) *La obra de Enrique del Moral* (Mexico City: UNAM).

Ramírez Montagut, María (1995) *Interpretación de la teoría de Villagrán García en la Ciudad Universitaria de 1954* (Mexico City: Master's dissertation, Universidad Iberoamericana).

Wickham, Christopher (1999) *Constructing Heimat in Postwar Germany: Longing and Belonging* (New York: Edwin Mellen Press).

Section Three:

Theorising Architectures

Translation Theory and Translational Architectures: Reading between History, Architecture and Cultural Theory

Felipe Hernández

Abstract

This paper creates a link between various disciplinary areas – history, cultural theory and architecture – using the concept of translation as a vehicle. The first sections consist of a detailed analysis of the concept of translation within various discourses. Here, I engage with the work of Walter Benjamin, who elaborates extensively on literary translation, and Jacques Derrida who takes on the Benjaminian notion of translation but moves on to unveil further possibilities. The work of the postcolonial theorists Homi Bhabha and Tejaswini Niranjana is also discussed. Bhabha and Niranjana disclose the political content of translation and approach it as a highly subversive term. Finally, I elaborate on the way Latin American literary and cultural theorists have interpreted the notion of translation in their attempts to study the development of the continent's cultures. In the final section of this essay, the notion of translation is employed in order to examine the contradictions that exist behind the *Museo Cultural Quimbaya* designed by the Colombian architect Rogelio Salmona. It is argued that the lack of a critical process of architectural translation resulted in the building's not responding to the conflictive historical experiences of the people it was designed for. This paper reveals various issues that escape the limitations of traditional self-centred architectural theory which have never been sufficiently theorised in the past or which may have not been theorised at all.

* * *

Introduction

The task of the architect in postcolonial contexts can often be compared with the task of the translator. Such a claim is supported by the fact that the architect needs to carry out a critical mediation between a vast diversity of cultural elements, which are often antagonistic, in an attempt to produce adequate spaces to satisfy the needs of specific societies and cultural groups. However, in architecture, unlike in other areas of cultural theory, translation seems to refer only to the transfer and adaptation of forms, materials and technologies in order to respond to local conditions. The work of Latin American architects such as Luís Barragán, Oscar Niemeyer, Carlos Raúl Villanueva, and Rogelio Salmona, for example, has been praised because it *translates* features from modern Euro-American architectures, and from the architects' own national architectural traditions, in order to produce unique and fascinating buildings that respond to the environmental and physical particularities of the contexts where they are located. Yet, it is possible to argue that despite the formal and spatial qualities of their buildings, they often occlude the convoluted histories and fragmented realities of the peoples for whom those buildings were designed. In turn, Latin American architectural theorists have refused to engage with questions outside the boundaries of architectural materiality in order to study the complex relation that exists between buildings and the variety of users who constantly interact with them. Only rarely has the concept of translation, for example —or, as I indicated in the introduction, other concepts like transculturation and hybridisation—, been used within architectural circles in order to engage with the wider spectrum of social, cultural and political practices to which architecture is intrinsically related. This situation is, admittedly, beginning to change and this volume gives evidence of such a change. For this reason, in the first sections of this paper, I examine the concept of translation within a broader theoretical context. The term translation is used to explain the process of transfer, displacement and transformation of culture across different and contesting cultural sites. Thus, cultural and postcolonial theorists maintain that it disturbs the recognition of cultural authority, and unsettles structures of cultural domination. I argue in this paper that processes of translation open up liminal spaces between and within cultures that bring to light the fissured nature of languages and cultures. In the case of Latin American architectures, the concept of translation reveals areas that have so far remained invisible while, at the same time, prompting a radical re-writing of Latin American architectural histories. In addition, as well as in consequence, the notion of architectural translation could also be used to encourage the production of new architectures and spatialities that would respond more accurately to the complex realities of our cultures and peoples.

In the final section of this paper, the concept of translation provides the basis for an analysis of the *Museo Cultural Quimbaya* designed by Colombian architect Rogelio Salmona. This building has been chosen not only because it was distinguished with the highest architectural prize given in Colombia but also for its cultural specificity. In this section, I challenge the claim made by various architectural theorists according to which Salmona successfully translated features from numerous architectures in order to design the Museum. On the contrary, I argue that there was never a proper process of architectural translation to respond to the conflictive historical experiences of the people for whom the building was designed. In spite of its cultural specificity, it appears that neither Salmona nor Colombian architectural theorists ever engaged with the political dimension of the Museum. At the end of this paper, various issues that escape the limitations of traditional architectural theory will be considered. Some of these issues have not been sufficiently theorised in the past, and others may have not been theorised at all.

Rethinking Translation: Unsettling the Primacy of the Original

It is inevitable to discuss the relation between the original and the translation every time translation, as a practice, becomes the central issue. Within traditional literary translation theory, the original has always been given priority over the translation. However, recent work challenges the latter assumption and tends to unsettle the primacy of the original. In his essay 'The Task of the Translator,' for example, Walter Benjamin maintains that translation is not a passive one-way process that tends to reproduce inoffensively an original in another language. On the contrary, he maintains that it is rather an active and aggressive process that challenges the purity and unity of the original. In so doing, the translator takes advantage of the internal conflict of languages, and their state of flux in order to re-create them.

Since it is assumed that the original is always internally broken — Benjamin suggests that no text has ever been written in one single language, and also that both, languages and texts, are always fractured and impure—, the translator's task is to attempt to reveal the incompleteness and fragmented nature of all languages and cultures through translation. Thus, Benjamin establishes that neither the original nor the translation is a monolithic and static entity. On the contrary, they are independent —yet interdependent— entities by nature, and both follow their own paths of historical becoming.

It could therefore be affirmed that the original becomes simply a point of departure for the translation after which the translation gains its own life. As Benjamin suggests:

> Just as a tangent touches a circle lightly and at but one point, with this touch rather than with the point setting the law according to which it is to continue on its straight path to infinity, a translation touches the original lightly and only at the infinitely small point of the sense, thereupon pursuing its own course according to the laws of fidelity in the freedom of linguistic flux. (Benjamin 1968: 80-81)

If both, original and translation, follow their own independent paths of historical becoming and complement each other, then we can assume that both are equivalent, and that the relation between the original and the translation becomes symmetrical, thus modifying radically the structures that give priority to the original alone. Therefore, the primacy of the original is disrupted.

If in traditional translation theory the original is given a certain priority and always remains at a higher level, theoretical postures such as that of Benjamin tend to eliminate these hierarchical structures and to place both in a similar position. This does not deny the fact that both are related to each other: it has been said that they are interdependent. What this theoretical posture suggests is that, due to the differences and fractures that exist between and within languages, the transfer of content can never be complete, and the process itself will always remain unfinished. Translation stops being only the transfer or transmission of form and content, but could also be understood as *transformation*. For this reason, translation theory becomes fundamental for exploring the dynamics of contemporary cultural communication, especially in situations of cultural inequality. The notion of translation, as reversal and transformation, obtains a certain political value that becomes not only a vehicle, but also a fundamental tool for the continued exploration of culture in postcolonial contexts.

Translation as Transformation: Or Difference in Translation

It became clear in the previous section that translation can also be understood as transformation. Consequently, the concept of difference in translation appears to be transcendental. In other words, the concept of difference is inherently related to the practice of translation for it emerges not only between languages, but also within languages, and, therefore, as something that already exists in the original: an intrinsic fact of every language. As Derrida affirms, 'in a language, in the system of language, there are only differences' (Derrida 1991: 64). That is why Derrida maintains that translation is an impossible yet necessary task.

In his essay 'Des Tours de Babel', Derrida addresses the question of translation as a 'system in deconstruction'. The story of Babel stands for the:

> Irreducible multiplicity of tongues; it exhibits an incompletion, the impossibility of finishing, of totalizing, of saturating, of completing something on the order of edification, architectural construction, system and architectonics. What the multiplicity of idioms actually limits is not only a 'true' translation, a transparent and adequate interexpression, it is also a structural order, a coherence of construct. (Derrida 1985: 165-66)

Derrida's essay can be understood as an intertextual *translation* of Benjamin's essay 'The Task of the Translator' through the narrative of Babel; an addition to and a critique of Benjamin's work —a constructive abuse. Intertextual in the sense that he does not only focus on one text but connects the entirety of Benjamin's work in an attempt to interpret a particular essay. Complementary in the sense that Derrida's re-interpretation of Benjamin's text is then connected to a series of other texts outside the literary field in order to expand its theoretical repercussion. In connecting Benjamin with psychoanalysis, for example, Derrida takes the original text into a much broader theoretical and critical realm. Thus, Derrida translates Benjamin following Benjamin's own posture and proves that translation goes far beyond the transmission of subject matter. One could read Benjamin through Derrida although the texts are different in form, content and significance. As to the practice of translation itself, the deconstructivist approach is seen in the fact that the transcendent value of the original work is refuted so that translation, as self-translation, is the nature of languages. This explains Derrida's earlier affirmation that translation between languages is an impossible but necessary practice. Its necessity relies on the fact that it has to be permanent.

Another interesting aspect of Derrida's discourse is his use of the words: architecture, edification, structure and construction. He obviously identifies himself with an architectural lexicon, but it seems that, here, architecture serves as a negative analogy. That is, architecture and all the architectural words he uses, stands for the opposite of what he is trying to demonstrate, namely the impossibility of finishing, of totalizing, and of completing something. Architecture, on Derrida's usage, would therefore imply a system of totalisation, and the very possibility of achieving completion —the way architects have traditionally understood architecture. However, working within an enhanced architectural field —architecture as a cultural practice and not merely as the *art* of building— Derrida's ideas open up doors for the study of architecture and its intertextual ways of interexpression.

Translation as the Performative Nature of Cultural Communication.

As has been argued, translation is an essential practice within transcultural negotiations. It is important to note that cultural translation does not equal transculturation nor does it replace the complexity of conditions of transculturation.[1] Cultural translation is only one of the processes that takes place within transculturation. It is an intangible but constant process between conflicting historical experiences that enables the transformation of cultures.

Any discussion of issues concerned with cultural translation within postcolonial contexts would be incomplete without a reading of Bhabha's work on the term itself. Bhabha introduces the notion of cultural translation in the light of Benjamin's previous exploration of the task of translation. His

---

[1] See Hernández (2002).

reading of Benjamin is intertextual, following the same route as Derrida. Bhabha also uses psychoanalysis in order to enhance Benjamin's literary work and connects it with a larger sociological context, also inserting some political ingredients. Bhabha maintains that:

> Benjamin's argument can be elaborated for a theory of cultural difference. It is only by engaging with what he calls the 'purer linguistic air' —the sign as anterior to any *site* of meaning— that the reality-effect of content can be overpowered which then makes all cultural languages 'foreign' to themselves. And it is from this foreign perspective that it becomes possible to inscribe the specific locality of cultural systems —their incommensurable differences— and through that apprehension of difference, to perform the act of cultural translation. (Bhabha 1994: 164)

It becomes clear from the above that Bhabha assumes a position similar to Derrida's in the sense that translation is impossible but necessary. What Bhabha suggests, seeing Benjamin through a Derridean lens, is that one way to understand the specific locality of cultural systems is by being aware of the broken and performative nature of cultural languages within themselves. He affirms that 'in the act of translation the "given" content becomes alien and estranged; and that, in its turn, leaves the languages of translation *Aufgabe*, always confronted by their double, the untranslatable —alien and foreign' (Bhabha 1994: 164).

It is in the realm of the untranslatable that Bhabha finds the political content of translation. The elements of resistance that render cultural translation irresolvable and liminal —what Benjamin calls 'the element in translation that does not lend itself to translation' (Benjamin 1968: 75)— become the basis for Bhabha's notions of cultural difference and hybridity. Bhabha looks at the situation of minority diasporic groups living in the centres as well as at the postcolonial relation between the centres and the peripheries at large. He proposes that, since cultural translation can never be total, the elements that do not lend themselves to translation remain in a state of in-betweeness, as stubborn, hybrid chunks that never blend with others and that can never be reconstituted as they previously were. These elements do not seem to belong to any particular cultural formation but exist in all of them as new cultural elements that are both different and differential. They highlight the foreignness of cultural languages, and, at the same time, demonstrate the performativity of translation as the staging of cultural difference.

The notion of cultural difference implies that translation is necessary, while the ambivalence of every cultural language within itself suggests that translation is impossible. That is why Bhabha concludes that 'translation is the performative nature of cultural communication' (Bhabha 1994: 228).

Bhabha's intention is to use the notion of translation in order to unsettle the hierarchical structures that determine transcultural relations in postcolonial contexts. Cultural translation, he maintains, 'desacralises the transparent assumptions of cultural supremacy' (Bhabha 1994: 228). Cultural superiority is here relocated within a more democratic structure of cultural communication in which no culture overcomes another. On the contrary, cultures are seen to complement one another in an agonistic relation. Within this theoretical non-hierarchical structure, inevitable transcultural relations do not result in the elimination of incommensurable cultural differences, but in the negotiation amongst them so that they survive homogenisation. For the aim of cultural translation is precisely to produce cultural differentiation in the midst of our current state of global cultural merging.

The Disruptive Capacity of the Notion of Translation in Postcolonial Theory

From the work analysed thus far, it becomes clear that translation is not only an interlingual process, but a larger cultural matter. In previous sections the notion of translation was taken into the realm of culture in general, and then introduced within postcolonial discourse. In this context, the notion of translation raised important political questions regarding the unequal distribution of power characteristic of the colonial situation in which (traditional) translation was largely used to reinforce the hegemonic position of the coloniser. Since the non-European Other did not historically exist before it was discovered and colonised, its coming into being as historical subject within universal history occurred only through the language and culture of the European. In other words, it appears that for the coloniser, the non-European Other only attained historical subject-hood and voice after a period of apprenticeship in which the people of the colonies learnt the European language(s) and culture(s). Here, translation —mainly literary, but always between differing and contesting cultural sites— serves to affirm the culture of the coloniser as the original. It is thus clear that the practice of translation was an intrinsic part of the strategies employed both to construct and dominate colonial subjects. As Niranjana says: 'translation as a practice shapes, and takes shape within, the asymmetrical relations of power that operate under colonialism' (Niranjana 1992: 2).

For this reason, the total rethinking of translation within postcolonial contexts becomes an important and urgent task. The aim of rethinking translation is precisely to interrupt the effects of colonial translation through strategies of reversal that eliminate the coloniser's cultural authority. In other words, the objective of translation within a postcolonial theoretical agenda is to substitute its subjectification effect for a strategy of resistance.

> The rethinking of translation becomes an important task in a context where it has been used since the European Enlightenment to underwrite practices of subjetification, especially for colonised peoples. Such a rethinking —a task of great urgency for a postcolonial theory attempting to make sense of 'subjects' already living in 'translation', imaged and re-imaged by colonial ways of seeing— seeks to reclaim the notion of translation by deconstructing it and reinscribing its potential as a strategy of resistance. (Niranjana 1992: 6)

If colonial translation is understood as a strategy of domination that serves to erase the violence of colonialism, then postcolonial translation can be seen as the possibility of unveiling the violent and convoluted experiences of previously colonised people that have been occluded by Western historicity.

This reversal should not be confused with essentialist calls for a return to a culturally uncontaminated moment prior to colonisation that are so common in nationalist discourses. The emotional rather than critical position of many nationalist discourses that propound a return to the lost past —the origin— also occludes the violence of the colonial encounter and, therefore, ignores the contesting historical voices attempting to be heard within Western dominated colonial and postcolonial history. The suppression of cultural heterogeneity as intended by nationalist essentialist discourses is comparable with universalising discourses of the centres in the sense that both tend to the homogenisation of the cultural field. Consequently, as Niranjana maintains, nationalist discourses, instead of establishing differences between the coloniser and the colonised, may be complicit with imperialist narratives of universalisation. The process of colonisation, and more contemporary modes of cultural interaction that result from advanced communication technologies, the globalisation of markets, tourism, and diaspora, among others, produced and continue to produce cultural differences that are unavoidable and undeniable. Therefore, instead of propounding a return to lost origins, the postcolonial theorist must engage in a re-writing/translation of history that challenges hegemonic interpretations of Western historicity. This is a deliberate and interventionist —deconstructive— act of translation of history that is no longer concerned with the universalising and homogenising agenda of Western cultural-politics, but with the acknowledgement of differences within a more democratic cultural field. As Niranjana says: 'perhaps postcolonial theory can show that we need to translate (that is, disturb or displace) history rather than interpret it (hermeneutically) or "read" in a textualising move' (Niranjana 1992: 38).

As I have argued throughout this paper, the notion of translation serves to construct a critique to the notion of origin, and, from it, to carry out an anti-essentialist and anti-hegemonic re-writing/translation of history. This is the point of confluence of the various theoretical positions explored so far: the Benjaminian way of reading and translating history presented in the first section, the post-structuralist critique (mainly introduced through Derrida's work on translation), and finally postcolonial discourse. Benjamin offered us a view of translation that challenges the unity and purity of the original. Derrida offers a much more complex theoretical insight that allows for the dismantling of Western cultural hegemony. Postcolonial discourse combines these different but correlated theories in a twofold attempt: a) to make legible areas of difference, contradiction and resistance, and b) to create a space for negotiation amongst those areas of difference and contradiction without striving to eliminate them. Within this frame of ideas, translation becomes a complex culturally disruptive *practice* consisting of a radical re-writing of history from the perspective of the previously colonised peoples.

Appropriating, Translating, and Transgressing in Latin America

It has become clear that literary translation theory serves as a basis for the development of a much larger and more complex inquiry within contemporary cultural theory. The theoretical work of Bhabha and Niranjana highlights the relevance of translation theory in the study of colonial/postcolonial relations because it serves to challenge the superiority of European culture that has always been regarded as the original. It is therefore possible to affirm that colonisation always happens within the realm of translation, and that colonies are always considered copies of the European original —or the effort is to make them into copies. The colonies, as copies, would hence be diminished. That is why Niranjana affirms that the colonial practice of translation shapes and takes shape within asymmetrical relations of power.

For this reason, and despite the fact that postcolonial discourse has not been very popular in the Latin American scholarly context, translation theory has been used as a theoretical tool to examine the relation between Latin American cultures, as part of the so-called periphery, and the cultures of the centres. In the light of the ideas elaborated by the theorists and philosophers mentioned above, translation is seen as a multilateral operation crucial to processes of identity formation. Translation has also become a critical discourse of enormous help for the theorisation of those processes. That is why it has acquired political connotations, or has been the result of sociopolitical circumstances particular to Latin America.

Writers and theorists in Latin America have strong views about translation. Octavio Paz, who in 1992 stood in the forefront of the celebrations of the 500 years of the discovery of America in Mexico, wrote extensively on issues of postmodernism, hybridity, and translation. Although his work on hybridity, which was heavily influenced by the recently published book of Néstor García Canclini (1989), did not have any major political repercussion within the academic arena, his work on translation did. Particularly because it was in keeping with the agenda of most Latin American scholars who were seeking alternative theoretical positions to examine the relation between Latin America and the European coloniser. In 1992 Octavio Paz said that the world appears to us as an accumulation of texts:

> Each slightly different from the one that came before it: translations of translations of translations. Each text is unique, yet at the same time it is the translation of another text. No text can be completely original because language itself, in its very essence, is already a translation —first from the non-verbal world, and then, because each sign and each phrase is a translation of another sign, another phrase. (Paz 1992: 152-63)

Paz's position seems to share with Derrida the idea that languages and texts have been constituted historically as weaves of differences, but written history has been the vehicle for the repression of such differences. However, his explanation resembles more the Deleuzian model of the rhizome in its interminable interconnectability within an undifferentiated and nonhierarchical field (Hernández 2002). Thus, by highlighting the rhizomatic relation between texts, Paz also challenges the notion of the original, and thereby the superiority of the European text in relation to the (Latin) American.

One of the most appropriate ways to explain how translational practice has operated within the Latin American context is through the cannibalistic metaphor used by the Antropofagia movement in Brazil during the early 1920s. Although the case is well known in literary circles, a brief introduction here may be helpful. Some time in the sixteenth century, in the current territory of Brazil, members of an indigenous tribe called Tupinamba devoured a Catholic priest. The event horrified European society, however, for the Tupinambas, it was an act of homage: 'after all, one does not eat people one does not respect, and in some societies the devouring of the strongest enemies or most worthy elders has been seen as a means of acquiring the powers they had wielded in life' (Bassnett and Trivedi 1999: 1). It was also a logical interpretation of the Christian rituals in which the symbolic devouring of the body and blood of Christ is an important part of regular practice.

This event was used three centuries later by Oswaldo de Andrade as a basis for his Manifesto Antropofago. The devouring of the catholic priest served as a cultural metaphor to represent the construction of an identity via the appropriation of cultural elements from other contexts. Devouring implies the selection of what one eats and the subsequent process of digestion. In other words, the actual devouring becomes a violation of the European code, while, at the same time, being an act of homage. The digestive process implied by this cannibal metaphor suggests that, despite the fact that elements have been appropriated, they undergo transformation. Thus, the elements that have been appropriated unsettle the implicit superiority of the European original. As Else Vieira maintains, 'translation entails a double dialectical dimension with political ingredients; it unsettles the primacy of origin, recast both as donor and receiver of forms, and advances the role of the receiver as a giver in its own right, further pluralizing (in)fidelity' (Vieira 1999: 95). It is clear that the metaphor of devouring of the other in order to construct an identity of the self —Brazilian identity in this case— is not a call to return to a lost and unrecoverable past. On the contrary, identity here is dynamic: it is seen to be in a constant process of becoming rather than as a fixed state of being. This dynamic identity results from the interaction between Brazil and the cultures of the centres in an era in which transcultural relations are unavoidable. As Stuart Hall puts it:

> Cultural identity is a matter of 'becoming' as well as of 'being'. It belongs to the future as much as to the past. It is not something that already exists, transcending place, time, history and culture. Cultural identities come from somewhere, have a history. But, like everything that is historical, they undergo constant transformation. Far from being externally fixed in some essentialised past, they are subject to the continuous 'play' of history, culture and power. Far from being grounded in mere 'recovery' of the past, which is waiting to be found, and which when found, will secure our sense of ourselves into eternity, identities are the names we give to the different ways we are positioned by, and position ourselves within, the narratives of the past. (Hall 1994: 394)

As Hall affirms, cultural identities rather than essential are unstable points of identification and imply 'a politics of identity, a politics of position, which has no absolute guarantee in an unproblematic transcendental law of origin' (Hall 1994: 395).

Hall's view is important to this analysis of the notion of translation in Latin America because he sees our identities as *becoming through translation*. Translation has both literal and metaphorical significance within his discourse. Hall recognises the importance of translation in the process of colonisation and maintains that nations in Latin America and the Caribbean share a common history of displacement, transportation, colonisation, and even slavery. This common history not only unifies us across our differences but also indicates the translational character of our cultures. However, despite the fact that most Latin American and Caribbean nations share a similar history, 'we do not stand in the same relation of otherness to the metropolitan centres. Each has negotiated its economical, political and cultural dependency differently' (Hall 1994: 396). Therefore, special attention has to be paid to each particular cultural context. This is an alert to theorists who generalise the Latin American cultural territory —a common trend in the work of Latin American architectural theorists whose work is, consequently, placed under scrutiny. Architectural theorists have demonstrated that they are still committed to the search for a classificatory definition of our architectural identity. They seem to be oblivious to the manifold incommensurable differences that coexist within each one of our cultures and across the continent. That is why it is urgent that architects and architectural theorists engage with a broader range of cultural theory in order to escape from the severely enclosed and self-isolating realm of architecture. This would allow architects to respond more precisely to the reality of Latin American cultures not only theoretically but also in practice.

In sum, I want to suggest that translation, in the Latin American context, does not only imply transformation but also, and more importantly, *transgression*. It stresses the need for the creation of a cultural politics of difference in order to undertake, and make visible, the complex negotiation among the different sociocultural and political positions that coexist within our own cultural spaces, and, also, between Latin America and the metropolitan centres. Translation here is therefore associated with a re-reading and re-writing of history so as to bring to light the non-linear course of our own history, the fragmented nature of our cultures and the antagonism that characterised —currently and historically— the interaction between cultural fragments.

[Mis]Translating Architecture: The Unseen Side of the Museum

The theories examined thus far reveal numerous issues that have not been carefully addressed by architects and architectural theorists in Latin America. However, these issues have an enormous potential to return political agency to both the practice and the theorisation of architecture because they escape the rigid materiality of the building and connect architecture with a broader range of social and cultural circumstances.

In this section, I will put to work the various theories on translation studied above. I will take advantage of the subversive capacity inherent in the notion of translation in order to undertake a specific case study: the *Museo Cultural Quimbaya* which is located in Armenia, capital of the department of Quindio, Colombia. Translation theory will thus provide the tools to unveil aspects of this particular building that have never been examined before. Its very name, *Museo Cultural Quimbaya*, implies various translational processes. It creates a link with a specific indigenous group, the Quimbaya, and, by extension, with the convoluted history of indigenous people in Colombia at large. It also implies physical processes of translation, in the sense of the displacement and transportation of objects that are considered to be representative of the Quimbaya culture. These objects were transported from various museums in Bogotá to the new building designed for their display. Above all, the notion of translation allows us to see the *Museo Cultural Quimbaya* as the possibility to make visible and audible the voices of contemporary indigenous groups that have been discriminated against as a minority throughout the history of Colombia and which are, today, exceptionally underrepresented. The arguments that will be discussed in this section put under scrutiny architects and architectural theorists' commitment to, and understanding of, the realities of Colombian cultures and societies.

Given the fact that the Quimbaya culture is not well known internationally, I will take a brief historical detour in order to introduce it before discussing other issues in greater detail. The Quimbaya was a small indigenous group that inhabited the central Andean region of the current territory of Colombia along the shores of the river Cauca. Precisely because of being situated along the river on fertile soil, and given the favourable conditions of the local climate, the early Quimbayas developed advanced agricultural as well as mining techniques in an area that was rich in gold deposits. That is why the members of the late Quimbayas became excellent goldsmiths and craftsmen producing refined objects in clay, textiles and, more importantly gold. Some of these objects were kept for many years in the *Museo del Oro* [Gold Museum], in Bogotá, although the vast majority is held in private collections or has been traded on the international market.

Like other indigenous groups in Colombia, and across Latin America, the Quimbayas had to endure the Spanish conquest and colonisation. As mentioned above, Spanish colonisation consisted mainly of the forceful conversion of indigenes to Christianity, for which it was necessary that they learn the Spanish language —that is why Niranjana and Hall affirm that these were subjects living *in* translation. This was the means to impose new socio-political and urban structures with which to dominate and, ultimately, eradicate completely indigenous cultures. The violence of colonisation, as well as the consequent fragmentation of indigenous histories, is thus resolutely engraved as an inherent part of the Quimbaya culture. These are, nonetheless, issues that have not been properly dealt with in Colombia either theoretically, socially, politically or architecturally. The Quimbaya Cultural Museum was an opportunity to deal with this part of Colombian history. Yet, by focusing on an unproblematic display of assorted pre-Columbian objects, the Museum contributes to occlude the true history not only of the Quimbayas but also of other indigenous groups in Colombia and Latin America.

The history of the *Museo Cultural Quimbaya* begins, in the early 1980s when the central government of Colombia commissioned the building with a view to commemorate the 500 years of the discovery of America. This was a time when numerous indigenous groups across Latin America were campaigning ferociously for the recuperation of what was allegedly theirs, in particular, the land. Indigenous people were also demanding participation and inclusion within the hegemonic institutions of the nation for they had been, and continue to be, largely discriminated against. In fact, indigenous groups did not have representation in the Colombian Congress until 1991, one year before the celebration of the discovery.

Therefore, it is not coincidental that the government proposed to build a museum in Armenia, the geo-political centre of the Quimbaya group prior to the arrival of the coloniser, in order to symbolise the return of their cultural heritage —represented in an impoverished collection of pre-Columbian objects—, to the place where it belongs. Thus, the *Museo Cultural Quimbaya* can be considered as a token to appease the protests of indigenous groups in a moment of political tension. However, contemporary indigenous people, including those of Quimbaya descent, did not participate in the design of the Museum, nor were they given spaces to perform their cultural practices or to exhibit their current art work.

The building for the Museum was designed by Rogelio Salmona between 1983 and 1984. In 1988, the Museum was awarded the Colombian National Prize for Architecture in the 'best building' category. According to Colombian architectural theorists such as Germán Téllez and Ricardo Castro, the Museum is exceptional for it successfully combines elements from different architectures. There is, for example, a succession of courtyards which appear to be inspired by Spanish and North African architectures but which also remind us of early colonial architecture in Latin America. There are also streams of water, or 'atarjeas' —mentioned by Ricardo Castro in his essay in this volume—, that run throughout the whole complex which, along with the use of brick as the main cladding material, are associated with Moorish architecture as in the case of La Alhambra.[2] Téllez goes further so as to link the triangular skylights of the Museum with various 'postmodernist' Euro-American architectures fashionable at the time. In addition to this feature, commentators admire the fact that the geometry of the building, in plan and elevation, is clearly dictated by the principles of modern architecture. However, and interestingly, never has a commentator mentioned

---

[2] For a more detailed description of the museum, see Téllez (1991). See also Ricardo Castro's book on Salmona (1998) and his essay included in this volume in which he elaborates on the similarities between the 'atarjeas' used by Salmona in the *Museo Cultural Quimbaya* and those in the Alhambra.

any relationship between the Museum and the Quimbaya culture —neither literally, nor metaphorically nor politically. I am by no means suggesting that the building should have included pre-Columbian architectural features or that wood and straw should have been used as the main construction materials in order to recuperate a long lost past. I have maintained that such a task is not only unachievable but also an equally inappropriate critical posture. I am highlighting the fact that there has never been the intention to link the Museum with the culture it attempts to represent —at least not beyond its mere name.

Salmona opted to design a traditional museum. Following functionalist principles, the building consists of a sequence of galleries rationally arranged around a succession of central courtyards where objects can be displayed and contemplated passively, as if they were art objects. The location of the building in a shallow depression and the constant whisper of the water are aimed at conveying a sense of peace and tranquillity; a sense of admiration for the site and the building as an object of art in its own right. The problem lies on the fact that Salmona's unproblematic selection of a rational and serene architectural language occludes the violence of colonisation and the history of destruction and subjugation suffered by the Quimbaya culture and other indigenous groups in Colombia, as well as in the rest of the continent. The Museum does not commemorate, nor does it bring to light, the genocide of thousands of indigenous people and almost the totality of a culture. Furthermore, the *Museo Cultural Quimbaya* does not help to reveal the current situation of minority indigenous groups which, as I have insisted throughout this section, are severely discriminated against and under-represented. More alarmingly, it does not offer an opportunity for contemporary indigenous people to make visible and audible their claims, which could have been achieved simply by providing spaces for indigenous people to congregate, or for contemporary artists to work and to display their work.

Another aspect of the Museum that clearly did not receive the necessary attention was the way in which indigenous objects are displayed. In keeping with the functionalist and modernist arrangement of circulations and galleries, the exhibits are placed within glazed cases embedded in the walls or on plinths lit indirectly from the ceilings as if they were art objects exhibited in a museum of modern art. The lighting of the galleries does not add any dramatic effect nor does it highlight the religious and domestic character of most of the objects displayed. In fact, the lighting arrangement is almost identical to the one used in the *Museo de Arte Moderno de Bogotá* also designed by Salmona. The fact that objects are displayed as if they were art objects to be contemplated for their beauty estranges the perception of the pieces, which are pre-Columbian objects symbolically returned to the place where they belong. The result is a contradiction between the exhibited objects and its immediate surroundings. Therefore, the Museum banalises and exoticises *Quimbaya* craftsmanship. It is banalised because its real significance is taken away from it, and exoticised because it is presented as what it is not: art work. This tension is even more acute given the fact that such objects appear to be out of context although they are exactly in the place where they were created more than a thousand years ago. It is also the place where their creators were massacred, abused, and acculturated. The conflict between the exhibits and architecture is therefore not only a curatorial inconsistency, but also an architectural problem that arises from the inadequacy of the spaces provided for their display. In this case, there seems to have been a lack of interest —or, perhaps, a lack of knowledge— in searching for alternative ways to display indigenous craftsmanship while, at the same time, responding to the historical realities of the *Quimbaya* and other indigenous cultures.

Thus the *Museo Cultural Quimbaya* can be seen as a conciliatory initiative offered by the government of Colombia in order to moderate the animosity of indigenous groups at the time. Architecturally it is a simple and unproblematic solution whose programme is only concerned with functionalist and aesthetic issues yet not with the realities of the sociocultural group to which it was addressed. For this reason the Museum could also be understood as a patronizing response to indigenous claims. The government decided to move the collection of *Quimbaya* craftsmanship from one official institution to another, which, albeit in the place where the *Quimbayas* lived, does not provide spaces for the re-articulation of differences, nor create possibilities to call contemporary discrimination to a halt. The *Quimbaya* culture is 'exhibited' in the Museum, but this will happen according to vertically imposed structures created by the elites. As a result, the *Museo Cultural Quimbaya*, reinforces social and political hierarchies, obstructs socio-cultural integration and continues to conceal the tortuous history of transcultural relations in the country. In a project like this, with an enormous degree of political specificity, it is necessary that architects transgress the limits of architecture as building in order to engage with much broader issues. Sociopolitical specificity implies that architects (that is practitioners, theorists and also students of architecture) need to respond to the particularities of specific cultural contexts and groups within the space of specific Latin American nations. It is also necessary to rethink —in the sense of translate, transform and re-codify— the architectural programmes they address, in this case, the museum, which can no longer be taken unproblematically as a global institution. In fact, this is the most remarkable failure in the case of the Quimbaya Museum: the straightforward appropriation of the Museum as an architectural programme that is globally applicable. It is true that various features were successfully appropriated from different architectures so as to create a new building that undoubtedly achieves a high degree of formal sophistication and architectural elegance. However, the very notion of the *Museum* was never properly translated. If, as stated at the beginning of this paper, the task of the architect is comparable with the task of the translator, then, architects ought to reveal through their buildings the fragmented nature of Latin American cultures as well as the convoluted histories of its peoples. For this reason, I maintain that the *Museo Cultural Quimbaya* was a missed opportunity to engage with the past and the present realities of the *Quimbaya* and other indigenous people, and to reveal and problematise their history. A task that Salmona clearly did not undertake and, which, architectural theorists have not been able to discuss.

This case study shows how theories of translation —and other notions such as hybridity and transculturation— open new areas of inquiry for architecture and offers the tools to reinforce previous theoretical models that were incapable of tackling them. This is nonetheless not an arid and fruitless theoretical effort disconnected from the design and construction of buildings. On the contrary, since it makes visible the inability of traditional architectures to respond to the specificities of particular Latin American sociocultural environments, Colombian, in this case, it leads to the reassessment of the way buildings are designed. In other words, the notion of translation not only reveals aspects that escape the limits of architectural materiality but also provides the tools to undertake a continued and more radical exploration, theoretically, formally and technologically so as to provide architectural solutions that respond more accurately to the convoluted histories and fragmented realities of Latin American people.

Works Cited

Bassnett, Susan, and Harish Trivedi (eds) (1999) *Post-Colonial Translation: Theory and Practice* (London: Routledge).

Benjamin, Walter (1968) *The Task of the Translator*, in Hanna Arendt (ed), *Illuminations*, trans. Harry Zohn (New York: Schocken Books), 71-82.

Bhabha, Homi (1994) *The Location of Culture* (London: Routledge).

Castro, Ricardo (1998) *Salmona* (Bogotá: Villegas Editores).

Derrida, Jacques (1985) 'Des Tours de Babel', in Joseph F. Graham (ed), *Difference in Translation* (Ithaca: Cornell University Press), 165-207.

———— (1991) 'Différance', in Peggy Kamuf (ed), *Derrida: A Derrida Reader* (New York: Columbia University Press), 59-79.

García Canclini, Néstor (1995 [1989]) *Hybrid Cultures: Strategies for Entering and Leaving Modernity*, trans. Christopher L. Chiappari and Silvia L. López (Minneapolis: University of Minnesota Press).

Hall, Stuart (1994) 'Cultural Identity and Diaspora', in Patrick Williams and Laura Chrisman (eds), *Colonial Discourse and Postcolonial Theory: A Reader* (New York: Harvester Wheatsheaf), 392-403.

Hernández, Felipe (2002) 'The Transcultural Phenomenon, and the Transculturation of Architecture', in *Journal of Romance Studies* 2.3, 1-15.

Niranjana, Tejaswini (1992) *Siting Translation: History, Post-Structuralism, and the Colonial Context* (Berkeley/Los Angeles/Oxford: University of California Press).

Paz, Octavio (1992) 'Translation of Literature and Letters', trans. Irene del Corral, in R. Schulte and J. Biguenet (eds), *Theories of Translation from Dryden to Derrida* (Chicago: University of Chicago Press).

Téllez, Germán (1991) *Rogelio Salmona: Arquitectura y poética del lugar* (Bogotá : Escala Ltda.).

Vieira, Else (1999) 'Liberating Calibans: Readings of Antropofagia and Haroldo de Campos' Poetics of Transcreation', in Susan Bassnett and Harish Trivedi (eds), *Post-Colonial Translation: Theory and Practice* (London: Routledge), 95-113.

Cement and Multiculturalism

Adrian Forty

Abstract

Concrete is generally seen as a material that has obliterated local differences, and made everywhere seem the same. In Latin America, and particularly Brazil, though, a regionally distinctive architecture was developed using the medium of concrete. This essay explores how, in the Brazilian context, concrete was used to signify modernity, and yet in such a way as to resist the processes of globalisation through which modernity was known and manifested. The essay contains a detailed discussion of the cultural implications of concrete in one building in particular, the Faculty of Architecture and Urbanism at the University of São Paulo, designed by Vilanova Artigas.

* * *

Cement, a fine grey powder found throughout the world. When combined with, sand and aggregate, steel, water and labour, it is used to make concrete, a universal construction material often held responsible for obliterating nature, and for making everywhere seem the same. Concrete can be described as 'a monocultural medium,' whose effect is to homogenise all cultures. The question is, can a material which is everywhere the same, and which makes everywhere seem the same, also be effective in allowing the articulation of local or regional differences? Under what conditions might this happen?

Cement is a particularly complex case for considering this, because it is not any old medium, but _the_ medium of modernisation. For every country starting out on the journey from backwardness, the opening of the first cement plant was always a historic moment, marking one of the first steps on the ladder of modernisation. The arrival of the capacity to produce cement at once delivered up to that country a constructive capacity that gave it parity with the most developed economies. Though a country may not be able to afford anti-AIDS drugs, or the latest in missile technology, the means to produce cement gives it the means to make infrastructure, roads and buildings that are more or less as good as those in the most advanced economies. Even in countries almost entirely lacking skilled labour, the versatility of cement makes it possible to produce plausibly 'modern' constructions.

The acquisition of cement technology allows access to a global discourse of construction, in which the most backward country is just as well able to speak as the most advanced. However, if we are to pursue this linguistic analogy a little further, we find that this global discourse of cement presents certain peculiarities. But first we need to distinguish between cement and concrete, which up to now I have confused: whereas cement is a product, a commodity, which can be made, bought and sold, concrete is a process —it is a compound made from sand, cement, steel and human labour, in which the finished result owes everything to the manner of combining these various ingredients. The early pioneers of concrete realised that, while the way to profit from cement lay in controlling its supply, the way to profit from concrete lay in establishing a monopoly over the techniques for using it. The early history of concrete is all about patents, for one or another system of using it; it was the ambition of every engineer to patent a technique of concrete construction, and the most successful in this strategy was the French firm of Hennebique. When a country acquired a cement production plant and the means to build in concrete, it was immediately confronted with an existing international network of patent methods of concrete construction; while a country newly endowed with cement had in theory the means to produce the most advanced work, in practice it was constrained by the systems available to it. It is in this sense that, when we talk about the 'global discourse of concrete' in the first half of the twentieth century, it applies quite specifically to the currency of available techniques for building in concrete; and, of course, in a developing country it was not always possible to buy the best or the latest patents, so while it was theoretically possible for that country to speak in the global language offered by concrete, in practice its limited access to the range of systems available world wide caused it to speak in an impoverished vocabulary. In short, the features of the global discourse of cement are that while concrete offered access to modernity, it also limited the range of expression available to countries newly empowered with the means of speech in this medium because of the monopoly established by first-world countries over techniques of using it. In these circumstances, there was undoubtedly an incentive in such countries to invent new systems and techniques, outside those already current in the global market of concrete technology.

In thinking about this contradictory feature of concrete —that it at once allows, but at the same time denies access to modernity— Brazil offers us a particularly rewarding opportunity for investigation. There are two things that everyone knows about Brazilian architecture in the twentieth century: the first is that it is famous for its concrete, and the second is that Brazil was the first country where a *national* version of international modern architecture was developed (Banham 1962: 36). Let us look at the basis for these two pieces of received knowledge. First of all the claim that Brazilian architecture is defined by concrete. Of course this is not a uniquely Brazilian feature —it is true of other Latin American countries— but let us look at it in relation to Brazil. It is indeed the case that one of the most startling aspects of the extraordinary period of economic growth that Brazil experienced in the 1950s through to the early 1970s was a remarkable expansion in the production of cement. We can outline the history of cement in twentieth-century Brazil as follows. A significant number of concrete structures appeared in Brazil from early in the twentieth century, mostly through the supervision of European-born and trained engineers. Brazilian expertise in building in concrete developed rapidly, and certainly by 1940 was acknowledged in both Europe and the United States. The cement for these buildings was imported, and although the first cement plant was set up in Brazil in 1926, the majority of the cement consumed in the country continued to be imported until after the Second World War. The preference for concrete over steel construction can be explained by the fact that Brazil had no steel mills capable of producing rolled steel until after the Second World War; all constructional steel had to be imported, and cost more to import than did cement. In the 1950s, import substitution policies encouraged overseas suppliers of the cement consumed in Brazil to set up plants in the country, and within a relatively short time, almost all the cement used in Brazil was produced domestically. 'It should be noted', wrote the 1965 Survey of the Brazilian economy, 'that Brazil is exceptionally well equipped to produce cement on a large scale' (Brazilian Embassy 1965: 110). By 1959, Brazil was producing 3.7 million tons of cement, and importing a mere 29,000 tons, or less than 1% of domestic production. By 1966, production had increased to 6 million tons, and then, in the next ten years, the Brazilian economy's great boom, more than trebled to 19.1 million tons in 1976 (Brazilian Embassy 1966: 140; Baer 1995: 77). It is perhaps not surprising that this extraordinary increase in cement production should not have had some effect upon architecture. Nonetheless, we might ask why it was that Brazil, and Latin America in general, more than anywhere else in the world —say the Soviet Union, or Japan— became known for concrete.

   If we turn to the second received truth about Brazilian architecture —that Brazil created the first national version of international modernism— the historical moment when this was noticed for the first time was the 1939 New York Worlds Fair, where the Brazilian pavilion designed by Costa and Niemeyer was specifically intended to represent the 'Brazilian spirit'. But the full recognition of the Brazilian identity of the new architecture of the country came four years later with the Museum of Modern Art's exhibition and accompanying book, *Brazil Builds*. Now the peculiar feature of the whole Brazilian effort to create a national version of modernism is that it relied for its recognition upon critics in other countries, and of these, by far the most important was the United States. The story of how *Brazil Builds* made Brazilian architecture known to the rest of the world —and to Brazilians themselves— has been told before, most recently and comprehensively by Zilah Deckker. But there is a particular point to this episode, which is that to a large extent the 'Brazilianness' of Brazilian architecture was discovered by the Americans, and certainly relied upon American command over the diffusion of news and information to make this known throughout the rest of the world. One might say that the 'Brazilianness' of Brazilian architecture was in effect an American creation, a creation that served American political purposes at that particular moment in the Second World War. To some extent also Brazilian architecture's reputation for concrete was also set in train by *Brazil Builds,* which stated: 'Modern Architecture in Brazil has always relied on reinforced concrete' (Goodwin 1943: 104). I want to suggest here that whatever objective basis for the truth of Brazilian architecture being both concrete and national, the fact that we know it in these terms is an effect of the American mediation and diffusion of these particular features. And the significance of this, as far as Brazil is concerned, is considerable, for it establishes American authority over the global discourse of concrete. However original the Brazilian architects might have been, however effective they may have been in inflecting the global language of concrete architecture with a Brazilian accent, ultimately the success of this project relied upon how it was represented to the rest of the world. The extraordinarily widespread influence of *Brazil Builds* ensured that the Brazilians invariably found the terms in which they used concrete controlled by rules set elsewhere. Brazilian concrete could never be more than a dialect, shall we say, of a language regulated by authorities located in the First World. From a Brazilian point of view, the identification of 'Brazil' through the medium of concrete was not necessarily a benefit, for it immediately drew Brazil into a global discourse in which it was, unavoidably, the weaker party, the object rather than the subject.

I want now to look at the various strategies developed by Brazilian architects and designers in the use of concrete to represent their national identity, bearing in mind their dependent status within the global discourse of concrete. There are, I think, three distinct strategies that we can identify.

1. The first was to build in concrete what in other countries would have been built in another material. This was the strategy for which Brazil was best known in the late 1920s and early 1930s. A good example is the Martinelli building in São Paulo of 1929, which looks like a North American skyscraper, but rather than being built of steel, as any American skyscraper would have been, it was built of concrete. Its 'Brazilianness' relies upon the substitution of concrete for steel. Whatever technical ingenuity was required to achieve this result, in cultural terms it is a piece of mimicry, a case of 'almost the same but not quite', in Homi Bhabha's phrase. As a means of representing

Brazilianness through the medium of concrete, it can be regarded as not particularly successful.

2. The second strategy was the one developed by the architects from Rio de Janeiro, the so-called Carioca school, of whom Niemeyer, whose reputation eclipses that of all other Brazilian architects in the twentieth century, is the best known. The prime feature of this strategy was the use of thin, curvy sheets of concrete, and an avoidance of orthogonal shapes. Apart from Niemeyer, the best known exponents of it were Jorge Machado Moreira and Affonso Reidy. In 1955 Joaquim Cardozo, Niemeyer's engineer, summed up what he saw as the main features of this Carioca style: 'It is clearly a tendency towards wide surfaces made into true concrete *sheets*. I say *sheets* because they form thin layers that suggest an intimate lightness that greatly resemble envelopes of hot-air balloons and dirigibles' (Segawa 1997: 299-300). When one sees works like Niemeyer's Pampulha church, or the pedestrian bridge over the road to Reidy's Museum of Contemporary Art, or the school at Pedregulio, one can see what Cardozo meant.

As a strategy for defining 'Brazilianness' the Carioca school's use of thin sheets and curved shapes was in a sense highly successful —this is certainly what most people outside Brazil have come to think of as Brazilian modernism. However, it also carried with it certain drawbacks, the principal one of which was that it owed its definition as the 'Brazilian style' to an external agency, the Museum of Modern Art in New York. Whatever it meant to be 'Brazilian' was being determined by someone outside Brazil, in New York, with control over worldwide information systems. Furthermore, the Carioca school's success at indicating 'Brazilianness' relied upon doing something different with concrete from what was being done by architects and engineers in other countries. The strategy relied upon the fact that their work was unlike the accepted norms of concrete construction produced elsewhere. In other words, the success of this strategy relied upon the presence of a pre-existing cultural 'other', from which the Brazilians could assert their difference, but upon which they were inescapably dependent. To have made a distinctive way of using concrete the defining feature of 'Brazilianness' drew Brazilian architecture into a situation where, given the global nature of concrete architecture, it was bound to find itself in a position of dependency.

3. The third strategy for the development of a Brazilian architecture out of the monocultural medium of concrete sought explicitly to avoid this position of dependency. It is best exemplified by the work of the São

Paolo's 'Paulista' school of architects, and in particular that of Vilanova Artigas. I want to look at one building that allows us to talk about this strategy, and this is the Faculty of Architecture and Urbanism FAU at the University of São Paulo.

The FAU, designed by Vilanova Artigas, was started in 1962 and finished in 1969. It is a work whose significance extends far beyond its immediate purpose as a school of architecture. A massive block of concrete sits upon twelve spindly legs. There are enormous cantilevers at the corners, the cantilevers exaggerating the weight of the mass above, relative to the delicacy of the legs supporting it. I know of no better demonstration of Ruskin's principle of 'superimposition', of 'heavy on light', than this, where we see a dead weight carried upon visibly active supports. If we look at the piers, seen face on to the facade, they are a continuation of the surface of the block above, formed into inverted triangles, whose apex would just touch the ground were they not truncated by having merged into a slender pyramid, whose tip just reaches to the bottom edge of the concrete box above. Seen from face on, the piers look reasonably substantial, though their attenuation in the middle —the very opposite of the entasis of the classical column— diminishes their bulk. But when the piers are seen not face on, but from the side, their shape changes into elongated pyramids rising from the ground, diminishing to a needle point where they touch the mass of the concrete box above. These piers, which are wholly 'active' in the Ruskinian sense of the word, are the result of some fairly ingenious engineering: Artigas and his engineer went to a great deal of trouble to create the effect of so much being carried on so little.

Now let me say at once that what I find remarkable about this building is the contrast between on the one hand the extreme elegance and sophistication of the engineering of the structure, and on the other hand the crudeness of the execution, for the concrete work itself appears rough, and impoverished, the product of backwardness. This is a rare conjunction, for generally speaking architects and engineers have tended to take the view that technically advanced works should be executed skilfully —it is as if the technical excellence of a work runs the risk of being compromised if there is a visible lack of skill in the execution. While there are plenty of works where the roughness of the execution is visibly apparent —one may think of Le Corbusier's *béton brut* works of the 1950s, the first Unité d'Habitation at Marseilles, or the monastery of La Tourette— these works were not distinguished by *technical* virtuosity. It is relatively unusual to find a work that like the FAU is simultaneously primitive and at the same time technologically sophisticated. It is the implications of this, in the Latin American context, that interest me, for it provides a very distinct and unusual

Adrian Forty

commentary on the three connected themes of Latin America, concrete and modernity.

Figure 1: Faculty of Architecture and Urbanism, FAU
University of São Paulo, Brazil
©Adrian Forty

The building is certainly knowing about the global discourse of concrete —for example the device of twisting the axis of a pier through 90 degrees had already been done by Nervi— but at the same time it responds to the specific condition of Latin American economies. Equally, the building shows a familiarity with the already established 'Carioca' style: what appears at first sight to be a large concrete block sitting on legs, turns out, when one examines it from the corner to be a wafer thin sheet of concrete enclosing something (an open volume) within, so it does, in a sense, conform to what Cardozo had defined as the 'Brazilian style' by working in thin sheets of concrete. Where it differs however, from the Carioca-style concrete sheets is in being, firstly, demonstratively flat and, secondly, exceedingly raw. As we have already said, what we see in this building is an odd combination of sophisticated technical expertise and, on the other hand, crudeness of execution. While we might see this combination as being for purely aesthetic effect, it has been suggested that we can also see it as an attempt to absorb the backwardness of Brazilian labour and lack of industrial productive capacity (Recaman 2000: 12-13). The combination of the primitive and the sophisticated that one sees here can be differentiated from the European 'Brutalism' with which it has sometimes been compared; Le Corbusier's

Unité at Marseilles (though not that at Firminy) was crude because of the low level of skill of the largely Algerian labour force, but there was no compensatory refinement of the engineering. Rather what we see here is a building which makes use of the one material that Latin America has in abundance, unskilled labour, but which, by combining it with Latin America's other resource, human inventiveness, suggests a strategy for the endemic Latin American economic crisis. If the synthesis is awkward, it must be in some sense an expression of the futility of *any* solution to the problems of Latin America, to the *impasse* of development. Instead of achieving development by importing capital, processes and techniques from first-world countries, the strategy that is represented here acknowledges the backwardness of the Brazilian economy and proposes to work within the recognition of that backwardness. While the result might be more gradual, and in the short run less productive, the results of this approach were thought by some economists at the time more likely to lead to social integration than the other approach to development that used foreign investment to set up advanced manufacturing industries.

The interpretation of the FAU as 'an attempt to absorb the technological deficiencies of Brazilian building techniques' (Recaman 2000: 13) is corroborated by the known intentions of Artigas. Artigas had been trained as an engineer, and took pleasure in technological innovation: his Londrina bus station was the first concrete shell construction to be built in the whole of the Americas, North or South. At the same time Artigas was a communist and hostile to United States involvements in Latin America. He was also a strong critic of the Carioca style promoted by *Brazil Builds* precisely because this version of Brazilian architecture had been 'made' by the Americans; likewise he was critical of the influence exercised by Le Corbusier upon the Carioca school, because of the dependent status in which it cast Brazilian architecture (Deckker 2001: 200-01). Artigas's alternative works with the acknowledged 'facts' of Brazilian building —concrete, abundant unskilled labour, lack of productive capital— and used these to develop a version of 'Brazilianness' that was not dependent upon a first-world model, but at the same time seems redolent of the heroic futility of all attempts to modernise the Brazilian economy.

The question of the 'Brazilianness' of Artigas's concrete is amplified by the dispute over whether his and the other São Paulo architects' work could be described as 'Brutalist'. The apparent similarity of some of the São Paulo buildings to European 'Brutalist' works encouraged some critics to refer to the Paulista school as 'Brutalist'. Interestingly, Artigas himself rejected this, possibly a little too emphatically. As he put it 'The ideological content of European brutalism is something other. It brings with it a cargo of irrationalism...' (Artigas 1988, quoted in Segawa 1999: 150), where architectonic form, despite its appearance of technical determinism, was in fact arrived at through arbitrary or accidental aesthetic choices. The gist of the objection seems to have been that from the standpoint of Brazil, European Brutalism was an expression of melancholy, the work of a civilisation that had all but destroyed itself in World War II, and whose use of technology was always now tainted by knowledge of its own capacity for self-destructiveness. In this respect, European Brutalism was artificial: although European countries in the immediate post-war period had had to deal with material shortages, this was never more than a short term problem that did not justify the prolonged aesthetic 'austerity' of Brutalism into the late 1950s and 1960s. But for Brazil, these conditions did not apply —not only had Brazil not been destroyed by the War, but neither had it ever enjoyed a process of advanced development before. Far from having to deal with the ruination of an advanced economy, the problem for Brazil was to achieve an even half-advanced level of economic development to start with; seen in this context, the use of raw concrete finishes was not, as Segawa puts it, 'a technological "front", but the most advanced technology that Brazilian architects had' (Segawa 1999: 150).

Seen in this light, Artigas's FAU not only makes a statement about the social relations of production in Brazil, but also implies some resistance to the global discourse of concrete. Building in concrete, as Brazilians had to do, encouraged critics inside and outside Brazil to compare their work to concrete architecture in other parts of the world —the 'natural' effect of concrete is that it unites all nations, puts each in relation to the other. Any attempt by an individual country to develop a separate identity always predicates an 'other' on which this difference is based— and, in the politics of development, this 'other' will be the developed world. Brazilian architecture, working in concrete, was drawn into a global discourse, in which, given the transcultural medium of concrete, there was always a tendency for it to be cast as dependent in relation to the more developed world. In all three of the strategies described we see the peculiar difficulties faced by architects in a country on the periphery where they aspire to represent aspects of that country's identity through the medium of concrete; although their chances of success were limited, the results could nonetheless reveal a certain originality.

Figure 2: Faculty of Architecture and Urbanism, FAU
University of São Paulo, Brazil
©Adrian Forty

Adrian Forty

Works Cited

Baer, W. (1995) *The Brazilian Economy, Growth and Development*, 4th edn. (Westport Conn. & London: Praeger).

Banham, R. (1962) *Guide to Modern Architecture* (London: Architectural Press Press).

Bhabha, H.K. (1994) *The Location of Culture* (London and New York: Routledge).

Brazilian Embassy (1965) *Survey of the Brazilian Economy* (Washington DC).

———— (1966) *Survey of the Brazilian Economy* (Washington DC).

Deckker, Z.Q. (2001) *Brazil Built, The Architecture of the Modern Movement in Brazil* (London and New York: Spon Press).

Goodwin, P.L. (1943) *Brazil Builds, Architecture Old and New 1652-1942* (New York: Museum of Modern Art).

Prebisch, R. (1971) *Change and Development – Latin America's Great Task* (New York, Washington & London: Praeger).

Recaman, L. (2000) 'The Stalemate of Recent Paulista Architecture', in *AA Files* 41, 9-17.

Segawa, H. (1994) 'The Essentials of Brazilian Modern', in *Design Book Review* 32/33, 64-68.

———— (1997) 'Oscar Niemeyer: A Misbehaved Pupil of Rationalism', in *Journal of Architecture* 2.4, 291-312.

———— (1999) *Arquiteturas no Brasil 1900-1990* (São Paulo: Edusp).

Syncretism, Wonder and Memory
in the Work of Rogelio Salmona[1]

Ricardo L. Castro

Abstract

This essay explores the significance of the work of Colombian architect Rogelio Salmona using as interpretative strategies the concept of syndesis —from the Greek, meaning a process dictated by the urge to bind together— and syncretism —also from the Greek, meaning combination of various beliefs or practices. Additional connections —such as the idea of 'wonder' emerging from literature and particularly the work of Cuban writer Alejo Carpentier, 're-creation' considered by Salmona himself as the basis for making architecture, the incorporation of landscape in the architectural work as expressed in both the Western and Japanese (Shakkei) traditions of place-making, and finally a deep passion for the practice of architecture— help the critical weaving of this essay, in itself representative of the concept of syndesis.

* * *

Commenting on the work of Gilles Deleuze and Félix Guattari, philosopher John Rajchman, states: 'We must always make connections, since they are not already given'. He adds: 'In other words, to make connections one needs not knowledge, certainty, or even ontology, but rather a trust that something may come out, though one is not yet completely sure what' (Rajchman 2000: 6). I believe that Rogelio Salmona's architecture is ultimately about connections —a concept wonderfully summarised by the ancient Greek word *syndesis*— which traverse physical and temporal borders. Herein lies part of its syncretic (*Webster's* 1974: 1182) character.

The following thoughts attempt to describe aspects of the work of Salmona that encapsulate what I will call a syncretic practice. Rather than being founded on precepts and norms, this practice seeks to establish an appropriate context, idoneous,[2] as it were, to a serendipitous[3] search and discovery through making. As such, this practice promotes connections, and there are many in this short essay. These connections come from various

---

[1] I would like to acknowledge here my colleagues and friends Rhona Kenneally for her criticism and editorial assistance and Robert Mellin for bringing to my attention the concept of syndesis and for his editorial suggestions.

[2] *The Compact Oxford English Dictionary* (1971: 1370) defines the concept as follows:
Ideonity [ad. late L. idoneitas, tatem, f. idoneus...] Fitness, suitableness or aptitude.
Idoneous a. Now rare [f. L. idone-us fit, suitable+-ous.] Apt, fit, or suitable.

[3] Umberto Eco in one of his recent works (1998) offers an alluring and insightful exploration of the concept.

Ricardo L. Castro

fields reflecting a line of thought that I have favoured as an architect and educator. For many years now, the work of artists and writers has been a source of inspiration and action in my teaching, learning, and research.[4] Moreover, I have sometimes been fortunate to work closely with some of them (Castro, 1997).

Despite his long and prolific architectural career, Salmona (Castro 1998) remains at the interstice of contemporary architectural history (Frampton 1982: 82). He is, unmistakably, one of the silent architects (Smithson and Smithson 1989: 5), whose work may well be described as belonging to what post-colonial critics call 'the periphery'.[5] Salmona's œuvre is one of the most significant of those produced on the American continent during the second half of the twentieth century.[6] His buildings[7] and architectural complexes display great presence and robustness and speak of a particular reality always related to a sense of place.[8]

---

[4] This is not, by any means, a new practice. Vitruvius (1960) is the first theoretician who introduces the idea of the architect exploring other fields. Peter Collins (1965) discusses extensively, in Chapters 21 and 22, the influence of Literature, Criticism, Painting, and Sculpture on Architecture. Finnish Architect Juhani Pallasmaa's recent article 'Six Themes for the Next Millennium' (1998: 74-79) was inspired directly by Italo Calvino's *Six Memos for the Next Millennium* (1993).

[5] As pointed by Ashcroft, et al. (1998): 'This has been one of the most contentious ideas in post-colonial discourse, and yet is at the heart of any attempt at defining what occurred in the representation and relationship of peoples as a result of the colonial period' (36). Another critic, Hans Ibelins (1998) points out: 'It is precisely because so many phenomena are associated with globalisation that its capacity to explain specific conditions is so limited [...]. Nonetheless, the multiplicity of aspects that can be linked to it, only serve to highlight the fact that there are good reasons for regarding globalisation as the dominant theme of the 1990s, exerting all kinds of direct and indirect influences on contemporary mentality. The consequences of this are no less noticeable in architecture'(9).

[6] Salmona, like Sigurd Lewerentz in Sweden, Dimitris Pikionis in Greece, José Antonio Cordech in Spain, just to mention a few of the silent architects, has translated pragmatic and poetic concepts and intentions into physical form. These result from the architect's deep communion with, and understanding of the materials and processes, the landscape, as well as of the historic-cultural context in which his architectural intervention takes place.

[7] Salmona's œuvre, includes such notable examples as the Torres del Parque (1967) in Bogotá, the Presidential House for Illustrious Guests (1981) in Cartagena, the Quimbaya Cultural Museum (1983) in Armenia and the National Archive of the Nation (1992) in Bogotá.

[8] The concept of place has been recently explored in depth from a philosophical and historical perspective by Edward S. Case (1997). John Urry (1995) has explored the theme from a sociological vantage point. From a literary perspective, place has been particularly analysed by Paul Carter (1988) and J. Hillis Miller (1995). David Harvey (1990) provides an enlightening analysis of the contemporary condition of place throughout his book. Particularly fascinating is his reading of the movies Blade Runner and Wings of Desire as representatives of the way we currently experience space and time.

Concurrently with the last phase of the Latin American literary boom,[9] a new expressive architectural wave manifested itself in many of the regions south of the Rio Grande. These regions are peripheral to the architectural practices supported by an intelligentsia positioned within an imaginary strip stretching along the Eastern seaboard of the United States, particularly New York and Boston, towards Europe in the East and to Japan and Hong-Kong in the West. One of the significant practices to emerge from the boom of Latin American architecture is that of Rogelio Salmona.[10] Like the work of Eladio Dieste in Uruguay, Juvenal Baracco in Peru, and Luís Barragán in Mexico, Salmona's architecture is marked by a distinct individualism. Salmona's prolific œuvre has been produced within the confines of his own country but his fame resonates throughout the Ibero-American world. Moreover, the significance of Salmona's architecture is, I believe, the result of two important aspects: its *syncretism* and its power to provoke *wonder*.

One definition of syncretism is 'the combination of different forms of belief or practice' (*Webster's* 1974: 1182). Syncretism is a powerful idea, particularly well suited to the characterisation of an architectural pursuit. Such pursuit, informed by various sources is able to extract ideas and inspiration from them, to be used critically in the form-making process and its ultimate product, architecture. This is a far cry from a mere copying or mimicking. Used frequently in such fields as religion and philosophy, syncretism may also serve to describe practices in other realms.

The idea of *wonder* can be best expressed by a concept emerging from literature. In several of his essays and novels the Cuban writer Alejo Carpentier addresses, describes and analyses architecture in a highly suggestive and imaginative prose aided by a conceptual strategy which he names as 'lo real-maravilloso' [the marvellous-real] (Carpentier 1967: 58-70).[11] This notion serves as a tool with which to approach and understand that syncretic reality that seems to exist throughout Latin America. The marvellous-real is essentially a strategy, a technique which 'is [...] designed to sharpen our awareness of the astonishing richness of observable reality' (Shaw 1985: Preface). It follows that the concept of the marvellous-real, first conceived of as a strategy to describe existing reality, is also appropriate to

---

[9] It is through the expressive realm that societies assert their identities. An obvious example is the recent boom in Latin American literature through which many facets of the Ibero-American nations in our continent —virtually unknown to those in the North until recently— have been unveiled to the world. The work of Alejo Carpentier, Gabriel García Márquez, Octavio Paz, Carlos Fuentes, and Jorge Luis Borges, to name a few, are eloquent examples.

[10] For full details about the biography of the architect see Germán Téllez (1991: 48-59).

[11] There are numerous publications on the subject. A comprehensive analysis is provided by Alexis Márquez Rodríguez (1982: 29-178).

describe its making.[12] Salmona, unknowingly, mines the same vein as Carpentier, constructing a reality as vivid and engaging as that of the writer but this time made of tangible elements and materials. Salmona's architecture is also an ideal dwelling for *Mnemosyne,* the Greek Classical Goddess of memory and the mother of all muses. It is *Mnemosyne* that permeates Salmona's highly evocative architecture, triggering recollections of distant locales and buildings in those who experience it. The architect has incorporated in his buildings the spirit of other architectural practices, those that have astonished him through a lifetime of understanding and making form and places.

For Salmona, the process of design is based on experiences, the impact of forms, landscapes and the manner in which they are inhabited. He considers architecture to be based on a continuous process of *re-creation* of those aspects and things that, at a particular time and in a particular place, produced an impact on us. As he points out:

> To make architecture is to remember to re-create. It is to continue in time what others have in turn re-created. It is a revival of elements that already exist. The courtyards, courtyards, 'atarjeas' or troughs, the thresholds, and the transparencies cannot be reinvented. Architecture is in tacit agreement with history, since every work informs the next one; it is the result of a continuous practice in search for the essence. (Salmona 2000: see Appendix)

Salmona is in the forefront of those who, rigorously and critically, refer to the past without trying to imitate it. In this manner he is unwittingly following the steps of Carpentier, who had celebrated the existence of readily available material for the artist who could, just by being alert, seize the marvellous reality that surrounds us.

Salmona's architecture engages with all levels of landscape and doing so it creates a true sense of place. Place is, as Ignasí de Solà-Morales (1997) tells us, '[...] recognition, delimitation, the establishment of confines' (Solà-Morales 1997: 97). Moreover, Salmona's architecture is designed to respond to those elements that are bounded by telluric limits —the horizon, the sky, the mountains in the background— in an attempt to expand the liminal condition of the place. It is an effort directed to recuperate the classic notion of the limit, which according to the Greeks was where things began to

---

[12] Having acknowledged this, care must be taken, however, to distinguish between this concept and both 'surrealism' and 'magic realism', two similar generative paradigms. Magic realism, so much in vogue today, is used to describe the work of several significant Latin American writers. Suffice it to mention Gabriel García Márquez (Nobel Prize 1982), Isabel Allende, Julio Cortázar, Carlos Fuentes and Mario Vargas Llosa. Although distinct, the three concepts do share a common denominator: the aspect of the marvellous. Their difference is in the origins of the marvellous. Carpentier himself elucidated this issue eloquently in his lecture, 'Lo barroco y lo real maravilloso'. See Márquez Rodríguez (1982: 185-93).

manifest themselves, to appear once more.[13] It is at the Sanctuaries of Delphi and Dodona where this concept acquires its full expression. This symbiosis of landscape and architecture has been a constant characteristic of Salmona's works. It can ultimately be understood as an impulse to encompass wherever possible the three natures,[14] which English theoretician, John Dixon Hunt has identified as components of a landscape.[15] If the Classical Greek ideals of architectural composition resonate in Salmona's architecture, the same can be said of the Japanese tradition of enclosure and *Shakkei,* or borrowed scenery.

This understanding of the landscape resonates also at the intimate scale. Thus, for instance, the appearance of moss in the joints of a brick wall, the action of water over a surface, the demise of a landscape by wind forces and other similar occurrences that leave a trace of nature on the architecture, eventually reducing it to a ruined state are phenomena that Salmona understands well. He is able to control the weathering process through the choice of materials and construction processes that work in unison with the elements. Salmona is aware of the ephemeral quality of architecture when measured in telluric terms, hence his constant impulse to work with, not against, these telluric forces (Holl et al. 1994). At another level, perhaps remote, this fascination with the history and forces of nature speaks of entropy, a concept which was dear to land-art artists such as Robert Smithson and Michael Heizer.

The ultimate task of design is the production of form, claims Christopher Alexander (Alexander 1964: 15). This form is the result of a process of differentiation that takes place at various levels ranging from those dealing with ecological concerns to those of a symbolic nature. Between these extremes we find functional and social, as well as experiential

---

[13] Martin Heidegger points out: 'a space is something that has been made room for, something that is cleared and free, namely within a boundary, Greek *peras*. A boundary is not that at which something stops but, as the Greeks recognised, the boundary is that from which something begins its presencing. That is why the concept is that of *horismos*, that is, the horizon, the boundary' (Heidegger 1971: 154).

[14] John Dixon Hunt discussed the issues extensively in a series of lectures organised at the Université de Montréal in the fall of 1993. On this occasion he presented the concept of the three natures for the first time. Dixon Hunt departs from the concept of alterum natura, originally coined by the Roman philosopher and orator Cicero to describe nature. Besides Cicero's *alterum natura* —the first nature— constituted by the untamed parts of our world, Dixon Hunt conceives a second and a third nature. While the second nature comprises that part of the landscape that is used for cultivation of agricultural produce and cattle-raising, the third comprises the garden. The latter is the nature that approaches architecture most immediately. Only on special occasions does architecture seem to engage in a dialogue with all three natures. Significant examples are the Baroque palaces with their hierarchical differentiation that goes from the building to the parterres, the bosquet, the selvatico and ultimately to infinity. For more on this aspect see Norberg-Schulz (1975: 286-320).

[15] The concepts of landscape, along with those of scene and nature have had a profound evolution throughout history. See Yi-Fu Tuan (1974: 129-49) and James Corner (1999: 22-26).

elements. At the centre of all these processes it is the body, our bodies that become the point of reflection. The fact is not new. As far back as the first century BC, Vitruvius (1960: 72), the Roman architect and writer of the first architectural treatise, imparts a significant piece of advice founded on the relation of the body and architecture.[16]

Figure 1: La Nueva Sata Fe de Bogotá
© Ricardo Castro

Since Vitruvius' time, the body has often been the focus of attention of theoreticians of architecture as well as practitioners.[17] Thus the central position that the body plays in the conception and making of Salmona's architecture should come as no surprise. This concern is reflected in three aspects: the choice of materials, the notion of intimacy, and the kinetic quality of his work.

---

[16] Vitruvius points out: 'The design of a temple depends on symmetry, the principles of which must be most carefully observed by the architect. They are due to proportion, in Greek analogia. Proportion is a correspondence among the measures of the members of an entire work, and of the whole to a certain part selected as standard. From this results the principle of symmetry. Without symmetry and proportion there can be no principles in the design of any temple; that is, if there is no precise relation between its members as in the case of those of a well-shaped man. For the human body is so designed by nature that the face, from the chin to the top of the forehead and the lowest root of the hair, is a tenth part of the whole height; the open hand from the wrist to the tip of the middle finger is just the same [...]' (Vitruvius 1960: 72).

[17] The recent preoccupation with the body constitutes a good example. It appears in many fields from literature to architecture (Cary and Kwinter 1982; Feher et al. 1989; Scarry 1985, 1988; Serres 1985, and Stafford 1994).

In one of his short essays, the Argentine writer Julio Cortázar (1983: 22-24) formulates a new way of climbing stairs: going up backwards. In this manner, he claims, the world encompassed by our vision becomes clearer and larger with every step until, at the top, we can view the true horizon. This marvellous architectural allegory can be interpreted as a strategy to discover new facets of the world, provided we are ready to follow an unorthodox plan of action, and remain always open to serendipity. Salmona's buildings also embody hidden paths that permit serendipitous encounters and discoveries. The displacement along each one of their directions constitutes a totally different experience: the return complements the reaching of the objective for it is then that the path, with its inherent characteristics, acquires a new dimension. Returning along the tacit paths in Salmona's buildings is like climbing stairs 'à la Julio Cortázar'. His architecture is a vehicle that enhances our bodies' kinetic and experiential possibilities.

In *Six Memos for the Next Millennium*, Calvino (1993: 9) cites a marvellous aphorism by Ovid (1958): 'Knowledge of the world means dissolving the solidity of the world'. The process of liquefying this solidity may well lie in the act of dwelling, of experiencing. Salmona points out:

> Given its complexity, architecture is not only an aesthetic fact. Architecture has to be lived in; it has to be dwelt in. As we move through built spaces, through architectural spaces, we receive visual, olfactory, auditive, and haptic (tactile) stimuli. They are corners that preserve the emotions and memories of the world. We live in these souvenirs as the stars do in the firmament, always attracted among them.
>
> Gabriel García Márquez said in one of his interviews that to make literature one has to look back, look at one's own literature. One must study it and know it to be able to track at what historical moment we are at the moment of writing.
>
> I agree. The same applies to architecture. It is convenient to look back before stepping forward. Would it not be a waste to disregard the great works of universal architecture? And being American architects, to disregard the great open pre-Hispanic complexes, the subtlety of colonial architecture, the richness of the crossbreeding or *metizaje*, the simplicity of popular architecture, and the innovations and social content of Modern Architecture?
>
> Yes, indeed. It is convenient to look back, but one must know that at the right moment the gaze has to be withdrawn. It is a matter of recreation and transformation. Not of copying. (Salmona 2000: see Appendix)

Pathos is the Greek word for emotion. It is a word that conveys multiple meanings, some positive others negative. It is a word with a long history. Pathos refers to experience, to event, to accident, to those things and people that seem to mark us as individuals for a lifetime. A poem, any poem, aptly summarises the idea of emotion. It is about an emotion experienced by the poet who, moved by the presence of natural elements and forces, creates literary form. In turn, it creates pathos for us the readers. Consider this extraordinary passage by Gabriel García Márquez in which the writer, referring to Aureliano Segundo, one of the characters in *One Hundred Years of Solitude*, makes us aware of the evocative power of rain:

> He amused himself thinking about the things he could have done in other times with that rain which had already lasted a year. He had been one of the first to bring zinc sheets to Macondo, much earlier than their popularisation by the banana company, simply to roof Petra Cote's bedroom with them and to take pleasure in the feeling of deep intimacy that the sprinkling of the water produced at that time. (García Márquez 1970: 322)

Figure 2: Casa de Huéspedes Ilustres, Cartagena de Indias
© Ricardo Castro

Like poetry, architecture is, above all, about pathos. It is about the impact that natural and human-made dwelling forms have on us. This pathos is the force that nourishes architectural creation. As Vincent Scully has pointed out: 'to make anything in architecture, which has always been a large-hearted art, it is necessary to have loved something first' (Scully 1962: 42). To have loved something implies to have formed an emotional bond with that something, to have had a pathetic relationship with it. Pathos is ultimately about experience. Salmona is captivated by these concepts, whose implications David Abram has clearly articulated: 'Only by affirming the animateness of perceived things do we allow our words to emerge directly from the depths of our ongoing reciprocity with the world' (Abram 1996: 56).

A component of pathos is the idea of passion. It should not come as a surprise that the concept of passion is one of the basic themes of classical mythology and universal literature.[18] The concept is also intrinsically related to a meaningful practice of architecture: first it is a demanding process; second it is an extraordinary force that moves humans to make exceptional things or to do extraordinary feats. It is the passion for the 'quehacer', the everyday making, that nourishes Salmona's practice as well as his success. It is also his willingness to follow the arduous path of a demanding profession in which constraints are increasingly the norm rather than the exception. It is finally his ability to involve his work in a process of *syndesis,* that is, a process dictated by the urge to bind together (*Webster's* 1974: 1182), to make connections, as it were, in the manner suggested by Deleuze and Guattari. And is it not ultimately syncretism —transcultural, to locate this query within the limits of this collection— a typical example of *syndesis*?

---

18 For an enlightening analysis of the passions among Classical deities and mortals see Calasso (1993).

Appendix

An Architectural Experience

Lecture given by Rogelio Salmona *at the School of Architecture*
McGill University
28 March, 2000

I
Introductory Remarks (original version in French)

I would like to thank McGill University's School of Architecture for this generous invitation to present my work. I would also like to thank all of you ladies, gentlemen, and dear friends for your presence in this auditorium this evening.

I must say that it gives me a great satisfaction to have returned to Canada to be amongst you.

I want to communicate to you, with images and words, the emotion that I experienced when, in a given place in Colombia, I had to resolve an architectural composition.

What I am trying to do with architecture, which, as pointed out by Le Corbusier 'is a gesture of the spirit more than a trade', is to offer to the society to which I belong a sensitive and intelligent answer, if possible, to both its material and spiritual needs.

I would like to show you with simplicity the goals and the solutions, the experience that I have accumulated after 1960, when I returned to Colombia after having worked for more than nine years in Le Corbusier's 'atelier' in Paris. It is effectively in his studio that I had all the necessary time to ponder on the architecture I had to make (not the one that I could make) upon my return to [South] America. It is this experience and its itinerary that I will try to communicate to you this evening.

II
An architectural Experience (original version in Spanish)

Architecture is a way of seeing the world and of transforming it. It is a cultural fact that proposes and, in certain instances, provokes civilisation. It is an intelligent synthesis of experiences and spaces, and of a handful of nostalgia.

It is also the gaze that traverses with rigour and enthusiasm the little things of life, that sublimates the everyday, that resolves for example, the function of a window because through it the landscape comes indoors, or the design of a courtyard which allows man to discover the stars and to limit the infinite.

And architecture owes as much to the everyday as to the most spiritual elements in art. It helps resolve man's small problems, but, at the same time, it is in charge of the great themes of civilisation and of the great works of universal culture. It transforms nature and moulds the city. It is the pulse of a place and a meeting-place for reason and poetry, for clarity and magic.

But this wisdom is not only knowledge. It is a spiritual heritage that emerges when a given stimulus excites memory, awakening the souvenir.

Architectural knowledge, therefore, is nothing less than the fruit of a continuous theoretical and project search; a work through which one attempts to capture —although this cannot ever be fully accomplished— man's dream to create his own place or, as Gaston Bachelard would say: his own niche in the world.

To make architecture is to remember to re-create. It is to continue in time what others have in turn re-created. It is a revival of elements that already exist. The courtyards, *atarjeas* or troughs, the thresholds, and the transparencies can not be reinvented. Architecture is in tacit agreement with history, since every work informs the next one; it is the result of a continuous practice in search of the essence.

It constitutes a deep cultural act, since it is not possible to recreate the unknown. On the contrary, it is wisdom that permits choice and selection, and this is the great moment of creation. The moment in which, as happens in music, one begins to compose, to transform what exists, to elaborate the form, to define the particular spatiality of each work. It is the moment that establishes architecture's spirituality.

Given its complexity, architecture is not only an aesthetic fact. Architecture has to be lived in; it has to be dwelt in. As we move through built spaces, through architectural spaces, we receive visual, olfactory, auditive, and haptic (tactile) stimuli. They are corners that preserve the emotions and memories of the world. We live in these souvenirs as the stars do in the firmament, always attracted among them.

Gabriel García Márquez said in one of his interviews that to make literature one has to look back, look at one's own literature. One must study it and know it to be able to track at what historical moment we are at the moment of writing.

I agree. The same applies to architecture. It is convenient to look back before stepping forward. Would it not be a waste to disregard the great works of universal architecture? And being American architects, to disregard the great open pre-Hispanic complexes, the subtlety of colonial architecture, the richness of the crossbreeding or *metizaje*, the simplicity of popular architecture, and the innovations and social content of Modern Architecture?

Yes, indeed. It is convenient to look back, but one must know that at the right moment the gaze has to be withdrawn. It is a matter of recreation and transformation. Not of copying.

To withdraw the gaze, but also to keep it deeply when one traverses the centenary plazas, the forgotten courtyards, the galleries and entrance thresholds that have witnessed history's parade, to find in the silence its own resonance. To keep the gaze in order to measure and draw all those places that move us so we can keep them in the memory so we can one day remember their measures, echoes, resonance to compose, recharging the architectural work with emotion, the surprising spaces, the meeting places.

Memory helps to find the way of poetry. It helps to discover that it is possible and necessary to compose with the material, with light and shadows, with humidity, with transparency and skewed views, to achieve an enriched spatiality for the senses.

Different from the other arts, architecture, substantially abstract although utilitarian in material terms, is conditioned by the events and the context of which it is part. One of its characteristics is that it has to have a clear concept of reality, that is, it must be able to evaluate what is its own; must know how to extract from the bottom of its own geography and culture the solutions that best fit the needs and behaviours. Architecture should never drift away from its time or its people. But it must go beyond.

It must propose spaces that induce emotion, which can be apprehended with sight but also with the senses of smell and touch, with silence and sound, luminosity and penumbra and the transparency that can be traversed allowing the discovery of unexpected spaces.

As for me, I prefer the architecture that allows me to hear the resonance of the emotions, and I am moved by those architectures that allow a glimpse of the trembling hand that builds them and constructs them, with its doubts, its mistakes and attempts like silent notes in the final result.

Above all its doubts. Doubt always generates discovery, it allows distancing from ideological schemes, it forces thought and the seeing of things with the eyes without prejudice.

Doubts but also certainties. One of them is the nearing, ever closer, to the place where architecture is composed and is constructed. To know how to interpret this is a way to enrich it.

Architecture, then as functional problem, efficient, as a cultural act, collective and historical, but also architecture for the landscape, and architecture for the senses.

The best architecture is, I believe, that which transforms without modifying, that unveils slowly with emotion and that is capable of proposing spaces that enchant, make one happy and surprise. That is profound poetics.

Translated by Ricardo L. Castro.

Works Cited

Abram, D. (1996) *The Spell of the Sensuous* (New York: Vintage).

Alexander, C. (1964) *Notes on the Synthesis of Form* (Cambridge: Harvard University Press).

Ashcroft, B., G. Griffiths and H. Tiffin (1998) *Key Concepts in Post-Colonial Studies* (New York: Routledge).

Calasso, R. (1993) *The Marriage of Cadmus and Harmony* (Toronto: Vintage).

Calvino, I. (1993) *Six Memos for the Next Millennium* (New York: Vintage).

Carpentier, A. (1967) *Tientos y Diferencias* (Montevideo: Arca).

Carter, P. (1988) *The Road to Botany Bay: An Exploration of Landscape and History* (New York: Alfred A. Knopf).

Case, E. S. (1997) *The Fate of Place* (Berkeley: University of California Press).

Castro, R. L. (1998) *Rogelio Salmona* (Bogotá: Villegas Editores).

―――― (1997) 'A Draft of Shadows', in *On Experiencing the City* [on line] (Montreal: Galerie Optica). Available from: http://www.wherever.com/sites.htm (accessed 9 February 2003).

Cary, J and S. Kwinter (eds) (1982) *Incorporations* (New York: Zone).

Collins, P. (1965) *Changing Ideals in Architecture* (Montreal: McGill-Queen's University Press).

Corner, James (1998) 'Operational Eidetics: Forging New Landscapes', in *Harvard Design Magazine* 6, 22-26 .

Cortázar, J. (1983) *Ultimo Round* (México DF: Siglo XXI).

de Solà-Morales, Ignasí (1997) *Differences* (Cambridge, Mass: MIT Press).

Eco, U. (1998) *Serendipities: Language and Lunacy* (New York: Columbia University Press).

Feher, M. et al. (eds) (1989) *Fragments for a History of the Human Body* (New York: Zone).

Frampton, K. (1982) *Modern Architecture and the Critical Present* (London: Garden House Press).

García Márquez, G. (1970) *One Hundred Years of Solitude,* trans. Gregory Rabassa (New York: Avon Books).

Heidegger, Martin (1971) *Poetry, Language, Thought* (New York: Torch Books).

Harvey, D. (1990) *The Condition of Postmodernity* (Oxford: Blackwell).

Holl S., J. Pallasmaa and A. Pérez-Gómez (1994) *Questions of Perception: Phenomenology of Architecture* (Tokyo: A+U).

Ibelins, H. (1998) *Supermodernism: Architecture in the Age of Globalization* (Rotterdam: NAi Publishers).

Márquez Rodríguez, A. (1982) *Lo barroco y lo real-maravilloso en la obra de Alejo Carpentier* (Mexico: Siglo XXI).

Miller, J. H. (1995) *Topographies* (Stanford: Stanford University Press).

Norberg-Schulz, C. (1975) *Meaning in Western Architecture* (New York: Praeger).

Ovid (1958) *The Metamorphoses* (New York: Penguin).

Pallasmaa, Juhani (1998) 'Six Themes for the Next Millennium', in *Architectural Review* no. 1169, 74-79.

Rajchman, J. (2000) *The Deleuze Connections* (Cambridge, MA: MIT Press).

Salmona, R (2000) 'An Architectural Experience', unpublished text of a lecture given at the McGill School of Architecture, Montreal on 29 March.

Scarry, E. (1985) *The Body in Pain* (New York: Oxford University Press).

Scarry, E. (ed) (1988) *Literature and the Body* (Baltimore: John Hopkins University Press).

Scully, V. (1962) *Louis I. Kahn* (New York: George Brazillier).

Serres, M. (1985) *Les cinq sens* (Paris: Bernard Grasset).

Shaw, D. (1985) *Alejo Carpentier* (Boston: Twayne Publishers).

Smithson, A. and P. Smithson (1989) 'The Silent Architects', in *Sigurd Lewerentz 1885-1975: The Dilemma of Classicism* (London: Architectural Association).

Stafford, B. M (1994) *Body Criticism* (Cambridge, MA: MIT Press).

Téllez, G. (1991) *Rogelio Salmona: Arquitectura y poética del lugar* (Bogotá: Universidad de Los Andes y Escala).

Tuan, Yi-Fu (1974) *Topophilia* (Englewood Cliffs, NJ: Prentice-Hall).

Urry, J. (1995) *Consuming Places* (New York: Routledge).

Vitruvius Pollio, M (1960) *The Ten Books on Architecture*, trans. Morris Hicky Morgan (New York: Dover).

The Compact Edition of the Oxford English Dictionary (1971) (Oxford: Oxford University Press).

Webster's New Collegiate Dictionary (1974) (Springfield, MA: G & C Merrian Co.).

Niemeyer's Casino and the Misdeeds of Brazilian Architecture[1]

Carlos Eduardo Dias Comas

Abstract

The architecture produced in Brazil between 1936 and 1945 is customarily taken to represent a [Brazilian] National or Regional Modernism, which, in turn, is considered to be a corollary to Le Corbusier's work. That vision is challenged in this paper by an unprejudiced analysis of one of the most representative buildings of this period: the Casino at Lake Pampulha, designed by Oscar Niemeyer in 1942. Along with an analysis of the building itself, the theoretical basis behind it, which appears to have been set by Lúcio Costa in his essays and memoirs of the preceding decade, will also be analysed. The complexity of the interchange between Brazilian and European culture is highlighted, with due emphasis on the relevance of the anthropophagic metaphor put forth by writer Oswald de Andrade in 1928.

* * *

Remembrance of Types Past

Niemeyer's Casino at Lake Pampulha (1940-1942) sits on top of a promontory. Reception and gambling occur within an almost square box, inside a hypostyle hall and a mezzanine. Dancing and entertainment take place in the oval drum on stilts, a restaurant above, a bar below. The T-shaped block to the right of the box shelters the kitchen over a loading dock and two service rooms. Box and block succeed each other facing the avenue and truncating the promontory. Almost centralised, the trapezoid marquee that shelters the incoming car extends an arm to frame the feminine statue, a hand to reflect the block projection. The incoming branch of the internal access road aligns with the loading dock, the exit with the gallery carved in the opposite side of the box. Endowed with a high cornice to hide stage equipment, the drum crowns the promontory and dominates the lake. Box and drum define a square of almost equal arms, an expansion of the box roof slab creating an open porch between them. Almost as high and long as the box, the block stands subordinate a half floor below.

The three volumes are cleverly imbricated. Inside the box, the nave adjoining the block includes a full-height reception area before a three-level

[1] We would like to thank the editors of the *Journal of Romance Studies* for permission to reproduce 'Niemeyer's Casino and the Misdeeds of Brazilian Architecture' which was originally published in *Journal of Romance Studies* 2.3 (2002), 73-87.

circulation and service spine. Two metres above reception level, a gallery runs along a closed strip with toilets, antechambers, access to the kitchen, service stairs and office. Administration stands above the strip. Dressing-rooms are at dock level. A narrow spiral staircase next to the reception provides a quick link between hall and gallery. At midpoint, the gallery becomes a landing for the ramps between hall and mezzanine, running straight and parallel to the entrance facade. Beyond the box, the gallery splits in two curved ramps around the stage, one of them widened to link kitchen to restaurant. The circulation scheme is completed by an internal staircase linking dressing-rooms to upper stage and an external one linking restaurant to porch and adjacent bar.

Figure 1: Casino at Lake Pampulha
© Carlos Eduardo Dias Comas

Otherwise, articulation between box, drum, block and marquee guarantees four tripartite elevations, each with a central projecting element on stilts. Access is frontal, but obliqueness enlivens the overall conception. Elements of composition occupy nested L-squares whose axes are perpendicular to the radius of the curve made by cars before reaching the marquee. The relationship of drum and box resembles the relationship between the homologous figures of block and marquee. Diagonal symmetry is reiterated in the articulation of the L-shaped mezzanine with the almost square hall and reception. The L-shaped residential arrangements of Le Corbusier come to mind but so does the diagonal relationship between the theatre and the gambling room at the Monte Carlo Casino renovation by Charles Garnier. In fact, the relationship between drum, promontory and lake recalls Garnier's towers by the sea, while the prominent role of the ramps inside recalls his Paris Opera staircase. But the approach from the land celebrates the wedding of the car and of the suburb in the manner of Le Corbusier's Villa Garches near Paris and Villa Savoye at Poissy, the marquee recalling both the guardian's lodge at Garches and the ediculae at the hostel Le Corbusier designed for the Salvation Army in Paris.

Debts to Garnier are in the way of an allusion, though. No doubt that this is Modern Architecture. The independent structural frame and brilliant planning combine to afford maximum transparency. Transparency makes evident the reciprocity between inside and outside; at the same time it shapes a display window or a lighthouse, conveniently oriented towards the lake, the neighbouring airport and the access highway from Belo Horizonte. Opacity is reduced to the cornices, to the block, to the wall separating block from box and to the two-bays-wide panel in the box's entrance facade. The panel limits and announces the mezzanine while balancing the mass of the block. The verticality of the free-standing columns is reiterated by the closely spaced iron mullions framing the glazed pane behind. An imposing portico stands next to domestic stratification. The marquee floats over thin steel rods, the glazed pane curves below the mezzanine and both add to the display of compositional freedom between cantilevered flat slabs, supports and walls as a constituent principle of Modern Architecture according to Le Corbusier. The narrow divisions yielding curved glazing at the Villa Savoye extend to straight panes. There, curved glazing was a function of vehicular access. Here, it precedes a lateral veranda for enjoying the lake view, engaging in private conversation or checking losses and gains —while recreating a common feature of late-nineteenth-century town houses in Brazil.

This is Corbusier-related Modern Architecture, but with a twist of its own. The balanced symmetry of the entrance facade rephrases the void between two solids, a scheme so prominent in earlier buildings by Niemeyer and Lúcio Costa: Rio's Ministry of Education (1936-1945), the Brazilian Pavilion at the New York World's Fair (1938-1939) and the Grand Hotel at Ouro Preto in south-eastern Brazil (1940-1944).[2] The theatrical opposition between the horizontality of the Pavilion street facades and its verticality towards the garden is now compressed in a single frontal view. The contrast between horizontal bulge and vertical recess in the Hotel's street elevation is now condensed in a shallow space. The extroversion of the mechanism of the free plan reappears in the porch sustained by one free-standing column: the glazed pane doubles to follow the staircase, boasting a minimum thickness and veiling an interior, already unusual due to a triangular and mixed line

---

[2] Costa's projects and essays can be found in Costa (1966 and 1995). An account of the Brazilian Pavilion at the New York World's Fair can be seen in *Album comemorativo do Pavilhão Brasileiro de Nova York* (Anon 1939).

geometry. The curve is not an episode, as at the Ministry, a leitmotif, as at the Pavilion, or a minor landscape incident, as at the Hotel, but a leading lady subtly subordinated to the boxy hero. As in the Ministry or Pavilion, instances of baroque-like fusion of elements contrast with the classically clear articulation of elements: the curvilinear expansion of the box's flat roof slab disappears in the drum cornice, the drum's floor slab becomes an inclined staircase, the blank panel and the mezzanine floor slab meet as a folded sheet. Contrast is reiterated in materials chosen for both pragmatic and representational reasons: the travertine cladding of columns, borders of slabs, cornices and walls reinforces the aura of stately elegance associated with symmetry and a colossal order, while the industrial tiles with an Empire pattern cover parapets, blending seriality with local domestic overtones.

Exterior sobriety gives way to excitement inside. The subversion of Corbusian themes goes on. At Garches and Savoye, the square double-height space limited by the L-shaped slab is a quiet patio. Niemeyer fashions a rigorously sparkling scenery for the rituals of mundane dissipation. Columns are silvered and shiny. Ramps flaunt marbles or green and yellow onyx. Bronze mirrors clothe the gallery wall, tying together box, block and drum. Unlike the gnostic sect mentioned by Jorge Luis Borges, Niemeyer does not seem to think that coupling and mirrors are abominable because they multiply the numbers of men. Each visitor discovers a twin among a duplicated forest of columns and realises he cannot escape being both spectator and actor in a circuit that maximises the opportunities of seeing and being seen. In the restaurant, plywood panels, carpeting and vertical slats upholstered in tufted pink satin absorb sound; the glass dance floor lit from below waits for Ginger and Fred. Niemeyer shows that Modern Architecture can deal with play as well as work, night as well as day. A former student, like the five-year-older Costa, of Rio's National School of Fine Arts, the Republican successor to the Imperial Academy of Fine Arts, Niemeyer validates Guadet's equation of good architecture with correct composition endowed with a proper programmatic character, aware of the affinities between Garnier, Guadet and Le Corbusier. While composition is based now on the skeletal frame, as Le Corbusier wished, characterisation still complies with strategies codified long ago by Quatremère de Quincy, extolling the crystallisation of a suitable emotional mood to aid performance but prioritising fidelity to type. Thus Niemeyer remembers that a casino was first a recreation cottage and then a suburban villa. Aware of the beauty of the site, he chooses to present the casino as a free-standing building composed by a regular prismatic nucleus and projecting bodies on opposite sides: a villa-belvedere.

Figure 2: Entrance Facade, North-East
© Carlos Eduardo Dias Comas

Prime examples are the Casino in the Vatican Gardens and the Rotonda near Vicenza. Concluded in 1562, the Pirro Ligorio design for Pius IV was based on late Renaissance notions about the old Roman villa; the Palladian masterpiece was designed between 1566 and 1571 for a prelate returned from his Roman office. In papal land, an elliptical patio is surrounded by four orthogonal blocks: two equal and opposite porticoes, a two-storey loggia and a higher and longer block. In Venetian territory, a regular drum inscribed into a square box is surrounded by four identical porticoes. Later on, in 1638, Venice would sponsor the first casino in the modern sense, an establishment dedicated to gambling against a bank operating under government concession. In 1671, a collateral development of the type takes place in Vaux-le-Vicomte, a palatial villa south-east of Paris that fixes its own panorama. The prism is now rectangular between court and garden. Superseded by depressions at the front and sides, the projecting body appears as a half-drum from the garden. The arrangement turns into a neo-classical cliché. In Rio, the half-drum is circular in the house of Grandjean de Montigny and elliptical in the house of the Marchioness of Santos, the former built for himself by the first director of the Brazilian Imperial Academy of Fine Arts' course of architecture, the latter owned by a mistress of Pedro I, who founded it. A century later, within the rectangular box of the Villa at

Garches, the drum becomes a small roof incident, the projecting body a lateral orthogonal porch. The rather more relaxed Villa Savoye adopts a square plan: the drum persists as an echo, fragmented and central on the ground floor, shaped as an off-centre screen in the solarium, but the projecting bodies are replaced by four horizontal windows. Among the Four Compositions, Garches is the pure prism that satisfies the spirit, opposed to the easy, picturesque and lively play of volumes of the Villa La Roche in Paris; Savoye is the prism carved to subsume La Roche within Garches.

Le Corbusier said of La Roche that it could always be disciplined by classification and hierarchy. Endowing the peripheral projecting body with traditionally nuclear features and thus eliciting ambivalent readings, Niemeyer intensifies both exuberance and discipline, informality and ceremony. Updating of the villa type accompanies the review of its origins and history. The box might be read as rectangular and neo-classical (drum and marquee corresponding to the dining room and porch of Grandjean) or square and Renaissance (drum, marquee, block and veranda corresponding to the four blocks of Pirro or the four porticoes of Palladio). Or rectangular as in Palladio's Malcontenta in Venice, and Garches or square as at Rotonda and Savoye, but always enhancing the role of the car as an indispensable Modern device. Otherwise, displacement of the drum from the box hints at the end of an evolutionary process. And if the square between drum and box recalls the renovation by Garnier, the square between mezzanine and drum evokes the additive play of La Roche, imbricated with a carved box *à la* Savoye. Crossing La Roche and Savoye, Niemeyer proposes a fifth, hybrid composition. In a second turn of the screw, he adds appendices, reinforces symmetry and generates another instance of spiritual satisfaction to show that adhesion to the villa-belvedere is not restricted to the exterior.

Circulation in the box is effectively cruciform, but the corridor leading to the block is kept closed for security reasons. The mirror wall redresses the situation, because the duplicated ramp restates the cruciform nature of circulation and thus reinforces the typological assertion. The cross is a secondary but vital feature of the Vatican Casino and the Rotonda. Migration of activities to the borders of quadrants and the normative horizontality of Modern Architecture inhibit the emphatic celebration of the centre via a drum or dome, but do not disallow that centre's transformation into a crossroads, the landing from which vision can dominate the two halves of the gallery, the ramps, their specular image and, by extension, the design structure. Thanks to the mirror, the landing is the memory of the absent dome, the inversion that signals a different time, the revelation of a transitory centre. Simultaneously, mirror and flat ceiling join to stress that production of symmetry is a duplication operation, not a centralising activity. Equality only becomes hierarchy with the addition of a third term. Without a pediment, the colonnade denotes equivalence rather than privilege, seriality rather than centrality. Without a dome, the crossroad looks forward to departure rather than arrival.

Niemeyer does not miss the opportunity of summarising in a simple wall the sensational scenography and the intellectual appeal. After all, reflection is also 'the turn of consciousness upon itself to examine its own content through the agency of reason', 'meditation and reconsideration'.

French Cuisine and Other Pleasures of the Flesh

As Borges points out in 'Pierre Ménard, autor del Quijote', meaning depends on context (Borges 1996b). Brazil's cultural marginality and Niemeyer's links with Costa impinge upon the reading of the Casino. At first an exponent of the neo-colonial manner, Costa turned to Modern Architecture in his rejected design for the Fontes mansion (1930), in which long stretches of glazed panes protected by climatically responsive wood blinds assimilated the Corbusian horizontal window to a characteristic element of internal or rear galleries in colonial and imperial Brazilian houses. He then built some International Style houses (1931-1933) with Gregori Warchavchik, a former assistant to Piacentini. Nevertheless, in parallel, individual projects for townhouses, the Monlevade Company Town and the Coelho Duarte Estate (1931-1934), Costa tried to blend a cosmopolitan, abstract, Corbusian-based Machine aesthetic and a Perret-inspired classicist rational structuralism by references to a vernacular architecture with a kindred authenticity and formal simplicity. Shuttered horizontal windows, reinforced mud or trailing rubble walls, monopitch tiled roofs and trelliswork panels renewed a rational and national building tradition while adding to a Modern set of elements of architecture. Fragments of pilotis turned into verandas, balconies, pergolas, expanded and/or porous ground floors renewed a Brazilian typological tradition while adding to a Modern set of elements of composition. Balanced symmetry relative to a diagonal axis enlivened orthogonality and landscape architecture elements guaranteed compositional definition.

The Revolutionary Government of Getúlio Vargas seized and started centralising power to accelerate the modernisation of Brazil (1930). Costa began promoting Modern Architecture during a brief stint as director of the School of Fine Arts (1931). 'Reasons for the New Architecture' (1934, in Costa 1966: 17-41) was written after the Vargas regime became consolidated and the modernist intellectual Gustavo Capanema was appointed Minister of Education. In it Costa hailed Le Corbusier as the twentieth-century Brunelleschi. Endorsing Guadet's idea of originality as doing better what others have done well, Costa remarked that personality in architecture, if not a crime, was not a recommendation. Corbusian work was the paradigm to follow, a compositional renewal validated by socio-cultural and technological change. The New Architecture which it posited was the legitimate heir to the academic tradition. It restored the clarity and the objectivity of composition of a Greco-Roman world encompassing Portugal, Spain and their American colonies, in which baroque preserved its composure even at its most delirious. In the memoir explaining his project for Rio's University City (1936, in Costa 1966: 67-85), Costa enlarged the argument by proposing that two opposing concepts meet and complement each other in Modern Architecture: the rationalism of the Greco-Roman strand beside the 'expressive' Gothic-oriental exemplified by Le Corbusier's Palace of the Soviets. Costa's design for the university, in which Niemeyer collaborated, proposes the Aula Magna as a smaller version of the Palace, to be developed by Le Corbusier himself, framed by a colonnaded portico whose stark monumentality points to de Chirico and Piacentini (Costa 1966 and 1995).

Figure 3: Lake Facade, South-East
© Carlos Eduardo Dias Comas

Costa was keen on rebutting attacks on Modern Architecture as International, or Jewish, German or Slavic and therefore un-Brazilian. His feelings about Brazilian architecture seem akin to those of Borges on Argentine literature. Borges believed the Argentine tradition was 'all of Western culture' and then suggested that Argentines are or might be like Jews who 'are outstanding in Western culture because they act within that culture and, at the same time, do not feel tied to it by any special devotion'. He extended the reasoning to all South Americans, who were capable of handling all European themes 'without superstition' (Borges 1996a: 272).

In that light, the Casino's erudite allusions, sundry paraphrases and premeditated quotations vindicate a classical inheritance and a French legacy. Pedro I, who proclaimed Brazil's independence and founded its Academy of Fine Arts, was a Bourbon and Bragança; Le Corbusier replaced Grandjean as a father-figure. But Brazilians knew better than Europeans that family ties are seldom free of tension. Fathers feed their sons and feed on them. Saturn, son of Uranus, devoured his: Saturn castrated and exiled Uranus only to die later at the hands of Zeus. Parricide is a rebellion against the diet established by the father and a prerequisite for individual maturation and the cyclical revitalisation of the world. Since guilt has to be placated, parricide turns into sacrifice, cannibalism into the vehicle for communion. Eat the slaughtered body to get to the soul: knowledge, assimilation and enlightenment ensue. The cultural anthropophagy theories put forward by the Brazilian literary and artistic vanguard impressed Le Corbusier in his first South American trip of 1929 (Le Corbusier 1960: 17).[3] In Oswald de Andrade's *Manifesto antropofágico* of 1928 the devouring of Bishop Sardinha by the Tupinambás in 1554 is hero-killing rather than parricide, the slaughter of an enemy one chooses to eat for his virtues instead of a father one did not select (de Andrade 1995). Nonetheless, as aborigines, Tupinambás stand for forefathers later decimated by the Portuguese without the benefit of ritual. The point is that Brazilians cannot escape being at the very least half-Western, whatever their race or ancestry, through genetics, transculturation and acculturation. Their mixed heritage justifies their claim to draw on the whole of Western culture as well as to contribute to it. Indeed, Gilberto Freyre (1946) credited the Portuguese aptitude for tropical colonisation largely to its mixed cultural heritage, encompassing Romans, Goths, Arabs and Jews.

Costa, Niemeyer and their circle were concerned with the representation of a modernity based on tradition and the affirmation of national identity within Western culture, as posited earlier by de Andrade and other intellectuals. The concern was not particularly novel nor exclusively Brazilian. It could be argued that the ideological construction of a national identity through shared traits such as language was not antagonistic to industrial-based modernisation, but rather its handmaiden. Representation of a national identity through architecture had been one of the key disciplinary issues of the nineteenth century, no matter how inconclusive the answers. For different reasons, the problem resurfaced after World War I in Germany,

---

[3] Le Corbusier (1960: 17) reports his conversations with the young intellectuals of São Paulo (presumably Oswald de Andrade and his wife, the painter Tarsila do Amaral). The Manifesto was republished in de Andrade (1995).

Italy, Russia and Scandinavia. All were latecomers to industrialisation compared to England, France or the USA; none was unaware that cultural integration was needed to develop an internal market. Modern Architecture aligned itself with machine-sponsored cultural integration, but was under siege in Italy, outlawed in Russia (1931) and Germany (1933). If the appointment of Capanema opened the possibility of government patronage, the building of his Ministry and the University City being known to rank high on his agenda, there was no doubt that both projects were likely to involve highly charged problems of symbolism.

Costa was fully aware of the many threads of the European vanguard when he singled out Le Corbusier —as hero and then godfather— to be consultant to the Ministry and the University City. The academic underpinnings of Corbusian work made it possible to present Modern Architecture as a true style, in the sense of a coherent, construction-grounded, limited set of elements of architecture and elements and principles of composition. Costa argued that it did not belie the equation of architecture with qualified construction. The skeletal frame that the Dom-ino scheme and the Five Points made the normative condition of the new architecture was not just any kind of frame, but one employing a cantilevered flat slab to make feasible and visible a free plan and a free facade.[4] Costa saw that the free plan stood for a dual order: a topological reasoning commanding the disposition of walls according to functional convenience and a geometrical, unitary reasoning commanding the repetitive location of supports within the stratified space of flat parallel slabs. Classical stability and picturesque improvisation might co-exist if not accord, without ruling out the use of symmetry in its original meaning of commensurability. Costa understood that the Five Points alluded to the Five Orders and implied a tripartite articulation of the free facade, while the very expression Dom-ino spoke of domesticity, the game-like character of architecture, the authority of self-imposed rules without which no game can begin. This would explain, paraphrasing Quatremère and Guadet, how the style could adapt to display both local and programmatic character, although the absence of ornamentation and a factory-like aspect suited house as well as palace and was international (for technology knew no bounds) (Quatremère 1788, 1832; Guadet 1900).[5]

---

[4] The Dom-ino House, or Maison Dom-ino, was a reinterpretation of the Hennebique structure that Le Corbusier carried out in collaboration with his friend Max du Bois. Simple and inexpensive, it was used by Le Corbusier in most of his mass housing projects in the 1920s and 1930s. The Five Points were the architectural principles that he extrapolated from the development of the Dom-ino House.

[5] A princeps edition of Quatremère de Quincy (1788) can be found at the National Library in Rio, probably brought by Grandjean de Montigny. Both the Encyclopédie and the Dictionnaire Historique d'Architecture (1832) were key texts for the Brazilian Academy of Fine Arts. Costa paraphrases Quatremère's strategies for programmatic characterisation in the entry character

Moreover, Le Corbusier was already qualifying his International Machine aesthetic. Smitten by the voluptuousness of the Rio landscape, he mingled echoes of a meandering river, a serpentine trail and a Georgian crescent in a curvilinear inhabitable viaduct (1929) that added a twist to the Linear City proposal of Soria y Mata. In the Errazuris and de Mandrot houses (1931), scarce resources and remote sites justified the use of local materials and borrowings from a Mediterranean vernacular. In the metropolitan context of Paris, the Surrealist paradoxes in the Beistegui apartment (1930–1931) joined the rubble walls in the Swiss Pavilion (1930-1932) and Porte Molitor buildings (1931-1933) to show Le Corbusier condoning the conjunction of building technologies of distinct evolutionary stages. The thermal failures of the Salvation Army glazing led him to sketch accordion-like, horizontally pivoting panels for Barcelona and mucharabieh-like grilles for Algiers (1933), to be called *brise-soleil*. Meanwhile, the Italian Rationalists stressed the affinities between minor Italian architecture of the past and the modern spirit since 1932 (See Etlin 1991: 300-04).[6] Popular architecture was now a formal source as authoritative as construction, engineering, industry or painting. Costa was not alone: Modern Architecture was no longer a question of new technologies and materials, but a linguistic breakthrough.

Now, academic theory opened two ways of tackling the problem of national identity. One was the revival of a characteristic indigenous style, more often than not Gothic. The comparison made by Guadet between the French Cour du Louvre and the Italian Cancelleria suggested a more sophisticated approach. Almost contemporary, both are Renaissance buildings with similar functions and both have bays of similar width and height, yet they look different because the proportion of windows per bay is greater in the former, as the climate demands. National character was tied to compositional differentiation within a style, more precisely, within an imported style, as Guadet clearly states the French building's debt to Italian art. Thus national characterisation could be conceived in terms of characteristic elements —a highly perforated wall, and characteristic attributes— relative transparency, instead of a characteristic style (Guadet

---

when he says that Brazilian Modern buildings might achieve local character by particularities of plan and elevation (such as patios and galleries), choice of materials and surface treatment (such as rubble or whitewashed walls) and by the use of appropriate vegetation. The treatise by Guadet (1904) was given to Costa, when he was seventeen years old, by his father and became his bedside book (unpublished interview with the author, 1987).

[6] Brazilians were quite knowledgeable about what was going on Italy, given the importance of Italian immigration since the beginning of the nineteenth century and commercial relations with the Mussolini regime, besides the fact that Warchavchik and Rino Levi had been educated in Rome. Piacentini came to Rio in 1935 as a consultant for the University City project and was the architect chosen for the Professors' Building Committee. Costa's insistence on the arrival of Le Corbusier might have been motivated by a desire to oppose the Italian's political clout. See also Santos (1987).

1900: I, 106-09). The neo-colonial movement was justified by the idea of a characteristic national style, while art deco buildings ornamented with Indian motifs explored the idea of the characteristic national element. Neo-colonial could be dismissed as not being modern, while art deco could be dismissed as being both insufficiently modern and superficially national.

Projects such as Monlevade showed that it was easy to assimilate Modern elements of architecture to characteristic elements of vernacular Brazilian architecture. It was harder to prove that Modern Architecture could rival the great historical styles, given so many proclamations of rupture with the past and lack of built evidence other than residential work, the occasional exhibition pavilion, school or sanatorium. It was not enough to say that forms had to change so that the old spirit might live, that fidelity to tradition implied its betrayal. Corbusian proposals for Geneva and Moscow advanced an answer but did not set the question. Neither, in Italy, did Terragni's Casa del Fascio (1933-1936), a glass house recalling both the urban palazzo with its central courtyard and farms whose L-shaped wings open on to a loggia enclosed by a wooden grid. As of 1934, more examples were needed to show that Modern Architecture could deal pragmatically and semantically with any kind of programme, modern or old, monumental or otherwise. Costa's stress on symmetry was symptomatic. If it spoke of his interest in the representative role of government buildings and hence signalled a concern with national characterisation; it also fitted into a wider interest in programmatic and typological characterisation —ultimately a preoccupation with the rhetorical capabilities of Modern Architecture.

National character was in itself a programmatic requirement in the Ministry of Education and Brazilian Pavilion projects. The Ouro Preto Hotel had to face an eighteenth-century setting. But the Casino programme was low on 'national' content, and it shows. *Azulejos* (ceramic wall tiles) do not appear as hand-painted panels updating a characteristic feature of the richest Luso-Brazilian elevations. Sun-breakers are conspicuously absent, and so are the depth and texture they add, whether alveolate, lacy or corrugated. The drum answers both to functional and situational characteristics; Guadet had already noted the influence of site over programme. Otherwise, curves are minor elaborations that could be related to expressionist or Dada precedents. Allusions, paraphrases and quotations delimit a typological lineage whose impact subsists in the exclusion of the neo-classical Brazilian precedent or lack of awareness of the author's prior work. Niemeyer's design might well exemplify a Modern Glass Casino by the water: it hints at a site such as Cap Ferrat or Portofino —not too windy and enjoying less than extreme temperatures during at least one season of the year— to justify the amount of area on pilotis.

Figure 4: Lake Facade, South-West
© Carlos Eduardo Dias Comas

Delimitation of a typological lineage also relates to programme in Ministry, Pavilion and Hotel. Framed by a colossal contemporary order of circular columns, the former's forecourts recall the Campidoglio and Versailles, three-sided squares shaped by civic palaces, which might constitute a type of profane monument. The pilotis is a hypostyle hall and a propylaeum, evoking Egyptian and Greek temples, which might constitute a type of sacred monument. Affinities with the Bauhaus bridge speak of common educational purposes. With Guanabara Bay in the background, the curvilinear volumes of the superstructure materialise almost literally the Modern metaphor of the building as a ship, the ship of State propelling the Nation. The U-shaped 'parti'[7] of the Pavilion recalls nineteenth-century plantation houses near Rio such as Colubandê, a *hôtel particulier* —their common Roman source. From the street, the cantilevered bending gallery is a stratified fragment of Le Corbusier's curvilinear megastructures; Melnikov's Russian Pavilion at the 1925 Paris Exposition, a seventeenth-century ranch in São Paulo and a sixteenth-century fort in Salvador are evoked in the elevated terrace between curved ramp and staircase, forecourt and garden, gallery and

---

[7] 'Parti' is the Beuax-Arts term for the overall conception of a work of art as well as the formal solution chosen to actualize it.

Carlos Eduardo Dias Comas

trapezoidal auditorium. From the garden, the gallery is a sparkling Crystal Palace behind a colossal colonnade of steel supports clad by a bow-shaped metal sheet: gallery tied to auditorium as Colubandê is to its chapel. Domesticity and deflated pomp alternate theatrically, as befits the ephemeral stage of a fair. Like the nearby eighteenth-century Governor's Palace, the Ouro Preto Hotel is an extrusion. A two-to-three-storey-high stockade of square pillars and public rooms supports the cellular seriality of private balconies behind blue trelliswork. Domesticity and rustic monumentality overlap in a fractured block resembling a cut geode, as befits a mining town. In all cases, the Brazilian precedents might be overlooked without major damage to the conveyance of programmatic character, whether specific or generic; the Doric severity of the Ministry, the Ionic elegance of the Pavilion, the Tuscan plainness of the Hotel, the Corinthian luxury of the Casino surely added to the competitiveness of Modern Architecture in relation to the classical tradition, exemplifying diversity of feeling within a similar compositional framework.

These buildings do comprise a corpus, albeit their appearance varies more than that which Le Corbusier gave to his Four Compositions. For instance, the porous base is shown in different guises irrespective of programme, exhaustively demonstrating the plastic potential of balanced symmetry. Reduced to a transparent pane between marquee and double-height hall at the Casino, the central void acts as portico and passage joining two similar courts at the Ministry, forecourt and garden at the Pavilion, front and back porches divided by a pierced concrete block screen at Ouro Preto. It even appears as entry and service porches separated by a frescoed stone wall in a retreat house design that Niemeyer produced for none other than de Andrade (1939). Walls mask peripheral supports to reappear behind them under a cantilevered slab; slabs project and recede, truncating columns or enhancing their full height in a multilevel space. Thus all buildings disclose the free plan mechanism at ground level, in contrast to its concealment behind an external wall, as in Garches, or a colonnade, as at Savoye. They counteract such exhibitionism with the reiterated display of a colossal contemporary order, itself a result of the independent configuration of flat slabs on different levels. A recurring ambivalence is the offspring of an impulse that exacerbates both stasis and dynamism, both immodesty and decorum, compared to other Modern work. Locational clues are stronger when the four buildings are seen together, but compositional interest does not depend upon representation of any kind of genius loci (Comas 1989, 1991, 1999, 2000, 2002).

Woe to the Vanquished: Winner Takes All

To say that these buildings belong to a regional or national modernism is a half-truth, the by-product of a diffusionist view that misses or dismisses their complexity as much as the challenges of the 1930s (Curtis 1996; Frampton 1980). Economic depression upset machinolatry and cosmopolitanism. Never-suppressed regionalist and nationalist trends grew stronger after the 1929 Crash. And the technical failures of many Modern buildings hit the news, just at the time when aerodynamics was making the Machine aesthetic of the 1920s look worn. Whatever the international congresses on Modern Architecture said, the zeitgeist was no longer an ally. Gaps in the orthodox account of its birth opened wide. There was very little 'Modern' in older industrial nations, apart from villas for the smart Bohemia of Paris and Los Angeles, and Russia was not industrialised at all. International was the act and not the fact. Criticisms that Modern Architecture was German, Slavic or Jewish were not built on fantasy alone. To become truly international, it had to expand its typological and technological range. Reality discredited beliefs in a technological and formal Darwinism. In order to survive, Modern Architecture had to embrace technological eclecticism, even if as a transitional stage. It had not so much to dissociate itself from, as to qualify, its machinist basis. Loss of innocence had to be compensated for by a gain in wisdom: birth and puberty are equally awesome thresholds. Of course, some like their meat raw. But that does not mean one should prefer raw to cooked. Or justify contempt for cooking.

Another version of a fetishist cult of the original uncorrupted by diffusion is the derivative label. Of course, debts to Le Corbusier have been acknowledged by Costa and Niemeyer, even exaggerated as a political strategy. This has been successful to the point that now even Brazilians credit Le Corbusier with the authorship of the Ministry of Education design, although evidence proves that he was no more and no less than a consultant in the process, and that the building is in crucial ways the antithesis of his ideas for another site.[8] Otherwise, attributing to Le Corbusier the invention of the pilotis, the horizontal window, the glazed facade, the roof garden, the butterfly roof and the sun-breaker is either historical myopia or bad faith. It suffices to look at the Ducal Palace in Venice, department stores in Paris, Gaudí in Barcelona and the Muslim and Mozarabic mucharabieh. Equally, Juan O'Gorman's studio for Diego Rivera in Mexico (1932-1933) used constructivist industrial imagery and Ozenfant echoes mixed with a cactus fence, vivid colours and *brise-soleil* before the latter appeared in Algiers or Barcelona. Such examples do not discredit him: who would blame Michelangelo for using the same Orders as Bramante? Admitting that the free

---

[8] Browne (1988) dismisses it as a transplant.

plan, in the sense of the visible independence of walls and columns, is a Corbusian find, why is Mies not scolded for adopting it so late in the Barcelona Pavilion? Le Corbusier was the greater authority, admittedly, but he was less a catalyst than a corroborator of convergent efforts during the first half of the 1930s, in Brazil and Mexico as well as in Italy and Finland, where Alvar Aalto incorporated farm reminiscences into his own wood and masonry house (1934-1936).

Apart from Costa's reservations with regard to originality, there was no Corbusian precedent for the assemblage of horizontally mobile cement louvres framed by concrete fins like giant venetian blinds that shields the glazed north facade of the Ministry. The same applies to the Nursery's vertically mobile curtain of cement slats. At the Pavilion, the mucharabieh changes material (steel instead of wood), scale (huge pores) and manufacturing process (handcraft to serial production). Ouro Preto sports a trelliswork version of the movable vertical slat, and the pierced concrete block that screened its porches had been patented in 1930 as *combogó*. Le Corbusier's first elaborate *brise-soleil* was designed for the Algiers skyscraper (1938), after seeing the final plans of the Ministry. Its figurative and definitely Surrealist superstructure is probably a forerunner of the magnificent roofscape of the Marseilles Unité d'Habitation, as nothing remotely approaching it was present in previous Corbusian buildings, drawings or sketches. One would need blinkers not to perceive the debts of the Harvard Carpenter Center to the porous base of the Ministry and the curvilinear ramp of the Pavilion, or the connection between Lever House in New York and the expanded base of the Ministry. After all, Niemeyer was a member of the design team for the United Nations building (1947).

Costa and Niemeyer and a dozen others were engaged in the definition of a typological identity that, as of 1942, already suggested a Brazilian Modern style. As Costa observed, a style is born and refined out of the repetition of a few forms. In another demonstration of the way context produces meaning, porosity, exuberance and ambivalence were taken by many as 'natural' expressions of a climate, a temperament, a psychological and geographical landscape, instead of one 'conventional' reading among several. Had it really been so idiosyncratic, the style would not have been so influential.[9] Yet the very idea of style was felt to be a betrayal of Modern

---

[9] To recall only architects and Modern works of distinction already built or being completed concurrently with the Casino: Affonso Eduardo Reidy, Jorge Moreira and Carlos Leão, who were members of the Ministry team, the latter having designed on his own Rio's Pedro II College (1937-1938); Marcelo and Milton Roberto, authors of the seminal headquarters for the Brazilian Association of Press (1936-1938) and the Santos Dumont airport (1938-1944) in Rio; Attilio Correa Lima who deesigned the Seaplane and the Coastal Boat Passenger Stations also in Rio (1937-1938); Luis Nunes and Saturnino de Brito who designed respectively the Olinda Water Tower (1936) and the Anatomical Laboratory at Recife (1940); and Vital Brazil, author of

Architecture. Most critics made peace with the International Style (1932) label, but 'formalist' and 'decadent' are labels still applied not so much to the Ministry (since it was attributed to Le Corbusier) or the Hotel (a compromise, when not ignored) as to the Pavilion and Casino, because of their hedonist, 'frivolous' curves, not to mention the immoral purpose of gambling. (Similar curves in Aalto are praised as humane and organic and no one condemns the Colosseum as architecture because Christians were put to death in the arena.) This Tartuffe-esque argument is usually entangled with the idea that backward countries should not be squandering money on Art. It might even reach the point where the functional segregation of artists and public in the Casino is equated to the class divisions of Brazilian society (Frampton: 1980). Oddly enough, Euro-American arrogance at its most impudent and hypocritical finds an echo in all 'nationalist' and 'regionalist' theories that deplore an 'imported modernity', when it is not shocked because Modern Architecture did not eliminate the abyssal distinctions between the country's rich and poor.

A subtler attack is to call the Pavilion and Casino a lyrical but facile prelude to deeper Corbusian work.[10] The less than exhaustive analysis of the Casino here might suggest that what seems facile about it is only a matter of less than satisfactory critical attention. The Pavilion and Casino can be said to be villas like Garches and Savoye. But Le Corbusier is strict about treating Garches as a suburban palace full of Florentine gravitas and giving to rural Savoye the allure of a skinny and small Trianon, both classical in feeling given the formal autonomy of its architectural elements. The Brazilians explore the interstices between pure house and palace, collision and co-presence of the domestic and the monumental; ambivalence in another guise. They juxtapose baroque episodes of fusion with classical bits of individuation and then turn Corbusian containment inside out: urchin-like complication outside, simplicity within. At the same time they indicate how to define a quasi-closed urban block, a latter-day Palais Royal at the Fair, and, as in Monte Carlo and innumerable German spas before that, they use gambling to anchor garden suburb development. House and palace play again in the Hotel; the Ministry rises stately in the quasi-open block. Yes, a degree of cruelty creeps in as Utopia is rejected, and the world is accepted almost as it is. But then, assimilation is never complete either in hero-killing or parricide: the amount of denial necessarily implied by the killing is reiterated in the refuse that accompanies digestion.

---

the Esther apartment building in São Paulo (1936-1938). The Brazilian influence was acknowledged in some of the most interesting Latin American projects completed after the war, such as the University City of Caracas, the University City of Mexico and the Quinta Normal Housing Estate in Santiago de Chile.

[10] This is the case in an otherwise interesting piece on Oscar Niemeyer by Buchanan (1988).

The Casino marquee weighs over thin steel. Its arcuated arm strikes a delicate note against the dominant orthogonality, plundering the guardian's lodge at Garches to frame Zamoisky's statue. At Monte Carlo, gamblers traditionally touched the knee of a bronze horse for luck. At Pampulha, the reclining statue is a female figure, bringing to mind that it was a goddess who ruled over luck, fate and opportunity in Latin mythology. Fortune had the power to raise the unworthy mortal and lower the mighty; she controlled the destiny of every living being by bestowing fertility on men, plants and animals and was shown as a blind woman holding a helm, to steer the course of the world, and a cornucopia, for the riches that she could bring from the horn of Amalthea, the she-goat that suckled the boy Jupiter, the plenty promised by the god to the family who owned the animal. Oddly enough, the arcuated arm might pass as a stylised horn or as the crescent or bow that were nocturnal Diana's attributes. In the directly opposite point of the building, transposing a feature of the entrance at the Salvation Army, the double supports delineate the V of Victory. 'Si non è vero, è ben trovato' [if it is not true, it is a good invention]. Hedonism never meant absence of brains.

Works Cited

Anon. (1939) *Album comemorativo do Pavilhão Brasileiro de Nova York* (New York: H. K. Publishing).

Borges, Jorge Luís (1996a) 'El escritor Argentino y la Tradicion', in *Obra completa* (Buenos Aires: Emecé), 267-74.

——— (1996b) 'Pierre Menard, autor del Quijote', in *Obra completa* (Buenos Aires: Emecé), 444-50.

Browne, Enrique (1988) *Otra arquitectura en América Latina* (Mexico: Gustavo Gili).

Buchanan, Peter (1988) 'Formas flotantes, espacios fluidos', in *AV* 13, 28-35.

Comas, Carlos Eduardo (1989) 'Arquitetura moderna, estilo Corbu, Pavilhão Brasileiro', in *AU* 26, 92-101.

——— (1991) 'Prototipo, monumento, un ministerio, el ministerio', in Fernando Pérez Oyarzun (ed), *Le Corbusier y Suramérica* (Santiago: Ediciones Arq), 114-27.

——— (1999) 'Le Corbusier: os riscos brasileiros de 1936', in Yannis Tsiomis (ed), *Le Corbusier e Rio, 1929-36* (Rio: Centro de Arquitetura e Urbanismo), 26-31.

——— (2000) 'Modern Architecture, Brazilian Corollary', in *AA Files* 36, 3-13.

——— (2002) 'O passado mora ao lado', in *Arqtexto* 3, 31-40.

Costa, Lúcio (1966) *Sobre arquitetura* (Porto Alegre: CEUE).

——— (1995) *Registro de uma vivência* (São Paulo: Empresa das Artes).

Curtis, William (1996) *Modern Architecture since 1900* (New Jersey: Prentice Hall).

de Andrade, Oswald (1995) *A utopia antropofágica* (São Paulo: Editora Globo).

dos Santos, Cecília Rodrigues (1987) *Le Corbusier e o Brasil* (São Paulo: Tessela/Projeto).

Etlin, Richard (1991) *Modernism in Italian Architecture, 1890-1940* (Cambridge MA.: MIT Press).

Frampton, Kenneth (1980) *Modern Architecture: A Critical History* (London: Thames and Hudson).

Freyre, Gilberto (1946) *The Masters and Slaves: A Study in the Development of Brazilian Civilization* (New York: Alfred A. Knopf).

Guadet, Julien (1900) *Élements et théorie de l'architecture* vol I (Paris: Librairie de la Construction Moderne).

Le Corbusier, Charles (1960) [1930] *Précisions sur un état présent de l'architecture et de l'urbanisme* (Paris: Vincent Fréal).

Quatremère de Quincy, A.-C. (1788) *Encyclopédie méthodique d'architecture* (Paris: C.J. Panckoucke).

———— (1832) *Dictionnaire historique* (Paris: Librairie d'Adrien Le Clère).

Trope of the Tropics: The Baroque in Modern Brazilian Architecture, 1940-1950

Sandra Isabella Vivanco

Abstract

In a naturally phenomenological land, filled with contrast and excess, it is no wonder that the first hybrid architectural products were Baroque churches. These were designed to honour and comfort the converts and to instil awe and fear into natives and sceptics. However, the characteristic *mestizo* aesthetic, resulting from the native artisan's traditional craft used to built such baroque churches, would prove hard to classify according to existing European canons. Consequently, it would be recorded in history as provincial and bastardised. Contrary to this generalised association, I am proposing the Baroque as a lens through which we may re-examine Latin American Modernism to understand it as a symptomatic process of transculturation and hybridity now exacerbated by globalisation. Three hundred years before the wave of rationalism swept through Latin America during the first decades of the twentieth century, the first examples of Baroque architecture opened the doors for an architecture deviating from the canon. It is an architecture that can be seen as a native improvisation on ecclesiastical high drama. Yet, this sensibility reappears at the dawn of Brazilian modernism in Cândido Portinari's tiled murals or *azulejos*, Affonso Reidy's undulating housing block of Pedregulho and the seductive yet schematic minimalism revealed at Oscar Niemeyer's Pampulha.

* * *

Allegories are, in the realm of thoughts, what ruins are in the realm of things. (Benjamin 2003: 178)

Introduction

Drama. From the *retablo* to the *telenovela*, a theatrical, sensorial, high-contrast aesthetic permeates the cultural production of Luso-Hispanic America, which finds its origins in the tragic mass genocide of native populations under the guise of the 'discovery' of the New World. Historically characterised by great social disparity and a highly, almost painfully corporeal perception of reality, Latin America's artistic production cannot easily ignore the trauma of slavery, missionary conversions, language erasure, dictatorship and repression.

To attempt entry into this exuberant and ambiguous culture, one needs to internalise its vigorous vegetation, the 4/8 beat of drums that provide the tempo and sounds of life in Latin American cities, the telluric pulse of natural phenomena, and the extreme power imbalance often rooted in illiteracy and poverty. Within a lush landscape, filled with socio-political and economic contrast and excess, it comes as no surprise that the first hybrid architectural products were Baroque[1] churches. Designed to welcome the converts and to instil awe and fear in natives and sceptics, the flourishing architectural production reached its apex in the *plateresco* and *churrigueresco* churches of the eighteenth century. The characteristic *mestizo* aesthetic, combining the native and African artisans' traditional craft and available materials with imported aesthetic principles, would prove hard to classify according to existing European canons and would be recorded as provincial and bastardised.

Contrary to this more generalised association, I am proposing the Baroque as a lens through which we may re-examine Latin American modernism to understand it as a symptomatic process of transculturation and hybridity. The term transculturation, as defined by the Cuban interdisciplinary scholar Fernando Ortiz (1881-1969), describes a category that explores crucial moments —of construction and destruction— throughout the history of colonialism and post-colonialism. By its very definition and processes, transculturation resists essentialism. The *real maravilloso* [marvellous real] —as coined by another Cuban writer Alejo Carpentier (1904-1980)— the Baroque and hybridity are notions dynamically related to projects that sought to define the national cultures of Latin America. The Baroque was profoundly marked by the world that it sought to justify: a fabric of different histories in which different time frames are interwoven with no legible hierarchy.

Baroque as Post-Modern

In its natural interdisciplinary and multi-cultural condition, the Baroque offers a postmodern avenue of inquiry into modern Latin American architectural production. The legacy of Iberian colonialism compelled the nascent Latin American nations —particularly Brazil, Cuba and Mexico— to negotiate conditions of modernity informed by mannerist and baroque culture, which they translated, transformed, and circulated back to the European metropolis. In this sense, the Baroque problematised the negotiation of Modernity in Latin America and provided a conduit from which its contested values and languages spilled into Postmodernity.

---

[1] The Baroque architectural tradition I am referencing is Southern European, specifically Luso-Hispanic.

Postmodern theatricality and artifice are interrelated and have important sources in the Baroque. In contrast to the quest for order, harmony and naturalism in form, so privileged by the Renaissance and its mystification of Classicism, the Baroque in Latin America, from its origins up to its current vital expressions, nurtures pose, adores and repels the simulacrum, and upholds and underlines artifice in social ritual as intrinsically theatrical.

The Latin American Baroque —by its very elasticity and overwhelming capacity to register, accommodate, and contaminate— led to the creation of paradoxical tropes of cultural identity. The Baroque has surfaced in Euro-American architectural criticism as a cliché homogenising cultural differences among regions and nations. In fact, the Baroque is simultaneously multiple, allegorical and in flux and is by definition porous, ductile and highlights numerous specificities.

Baroque in the Brazilian Historical Imaginary

During the 1930s, it was the *Barroco Mineiro* (Baroque architecture from the Brazilian mining region of Minas Gerais) that was chosen as the natural precedent for Modern Architecture in Brazil. In opposition to the neoclassical nineteenth century, the colonial cities of Ouro Preto, Diamantina, Olinda and Recife were first presented as important frames of cultural reference by Lúcio Costa, the architect and critic who provided the theoretical base for Brazilian Modern Architecture.

Costa's theoretical stance was that modern architecture did not need to break completely with the past but on the contrary, it provided the opportunity to abstract the true spirit of traditional architecture. Brazil was positioning itself as a modern nation and, simultaneously, trying to recover its history. In this process, the Baroque was granted privilege. In the translation of the Brazilian modernist project, identity is not found in the past but projected into the future.

The absence of significant pre-Columbian architecture in Brazil made possible the positioning of the Baroque as autochthonous. It also highlighted its condition as the first noteworthy hybrid architecture in the Americas. It is precisely this absence that allowed Brazilians the creative freedom that fuelled their early modern architectural production. In fact, European Baroque was to the Renaissance and Classicism what Brazilian Modernism was to the International Style. In other words, these movements represented a reaction against the homogenising and globalising tenets of Neo-Classicism and International Style Modernism respectively.

Shortly after the arrival of Spaniards and Portuguese on American shores, forts and churches were erected, the first to defend and the second to display, both to embody colonial power. These buildings were literally *translated* from Europe to assist in the process of cultural domination in Latin America.[2] Built with native and slave labour and imported design, the churches were often placed directly on top of pre-Columbian temples, as is the case with the church of *Santo Domingo* built over the Inca temple of *Coricancha* in Cuzco, Perú or with the Cathedral in Mexico City built over the sacred Aztec site of *Tenochtitlán*. About this cultural clash, Marina Waisman writes:

> The symbiosis of such dissimilar elements —Colonial and Native— resulted, during the three centuries under European domination, in an original architecture that, starting from European models, adapted these to local conditions, techniques, material, site, scale, seismic problems and so forth and, in certain periods like the eighteenth century, transformed their primary spatial meaning by way of the fantastic treatment of interior surfaces. (Waisman 2000: 4)

Ouro Preto, formerly known as *Vila Rica* (Rich Town) is arguably the centre of Brazilian Baroque history. As the capital of Minas Gerais, it was the richest area of the country in the eighteenth century, due to the gold, diamonds and other precious stones mined there. Two influential religious buildings built in Ouro Preto —the *Igreja de São Francisco* (1772-1794) and *Nossa Senhora do Carmo* (1766)— achieved seamless continuity between art and architecture. Some of the strategies used were: the obfuscation of traditional boundaries between sculpture and building; the excess of gilded contoured surfaces; and the expressiveness of facial features and garment folds in the representation of saints of mixed ethnicity. The histories of these two churches are laden with race and class overtones too complex to be properly analysed within this essay.

Their author *Aleijadinho* (1738-1814), trained both as an architect and a sculptor, transformed churches into sculptures and sculptures into churches.[3] The palpable pain, the rippling intensity in their clothing as well as the haunting facial expressions of the saints which inhabit these sacred spaces articulate the social struggles inherent in colonisation. His work dealt with racial violence and power struggles in sublimated fashion. This sublimation is evident in the frequent occurrence of images of the flagellation of Christ, a scene from the Passion that can be understood as an allegory for slavery. Aleijadinho, the son of a Portuguese architect and an enslaved African woman, was canonised by Lucio Costa and other intellectuals as the first

---

[2] *Translating* is used here in the Benjaminian sense, both as transferring —temporally and spatially— as well as furthering the life of the original.
[3] I am thankful to my colleague and dear friend Henry Drewal for this reflection.

Brazilian architect because he embodied the Brazilian values of miscegenation and nationalism:

> A contradição fundamental entre o estilo da época —elegante e amaneirado— e o ímpeto poderoso do seu temperamento apaixonado e tantas vezes místico, contradição magistralmente superada, mas latente e que, por isto, de quando em quando extravasa, é a marca indelével da sua obra, o que lhe dá tonus singular e faz deste brasileiro das Minas Gerais a mais alta expressão individualizada da arte portuguesa do seu tempo. (Costa 1995: 529)

> [The fundamental contradiction between the style of that era — elegant and mannerist— and the powerful impetus of his passionate and often mystical temperament, a contradiction masterfully surmounted, but latent and that, because of this, every so often overflows, and is the indelible mark of his oeuvre, which gives it its singularity and makes of this Brazilian from Minas Gerais the highest and most individualised expression of Portuguese art of the times (author's translation).]

Eight years before Costa was named Director of the *Escola Nacional de Belas Artes* (National School of Fine Arts) in 1930, he had visited the city of Diamantina and written about the lessons hidden in the houses and churches lining the cobble-stoned streets. Costa thought:

> Acho indispensável que os nossos arquitectos deixem a escola conhecendo perfeitamente a nossa arquitetura da época colonial — não com o intuito da transposição ridícula dos seus motivos, não de mandar fazer falsos móveis de jacaranda, os verdadeiros são lindos —, mas de aprender as boas lições que ela nos dea de simplicidade, perfeita adaptação ao meio e à função, e consequente beleza. (Costa 1995: 68)

> [I think it indispensable that our architects leave school with a perfect knowledge of our colonial architecture, —not wanting ridiculously to transpose its motifs, not to commission ersatz furniture made of jacaranda, however lovely the originals— but to learn from it sound lessons in simplicity, perfect adaptation to setting and use, and its resulting beauty (author's translation).]

Baroque and Modernism: An Antagonistic Relationship

In opposition to its European counterpart, technology was not the impetus behind Brazilian Modernism, nor was it the primary objective behind

Baroque architectural production. There was no love affair in Brazilian Modernism with mass production, speed and standardisation. On the contrary, the emphasis was on the individual character and philosophy that shaped the architecture. A search for cultural specificity via an established dialogue with local conditions such as landscape and craft was vital to the formulation of an original modernist language.

It is important to note that the intellectual leaders of the architectural avant-garde were the same people in charge of the preservation efforts that set out to construct a national architectural past. Members included Mário de Andrade —a leader in the 1922 *Semana de Arte Moderna* (Modern Art Week), a key event that raised the national artists' consciousness around the crafting of a national identity informed by modernism but based on native values and aesthetic experimentation— as well as Joaquim Cardozo —poet, historian and the structural engineer who gave coherence to Oscar Niemeyer's formal gestures. The *Semana do 22* (Week of 22) condensed many of the influences of the European avant-garde with which Brazilian intellectuals and artists had been directly in contact. One of the event's leaders, the writer Oswald de Andrade, proposed in his *Manifesto da Poesia Pau-Brasil* (Brazilwood Manifesto) (1924) an *export-quality* poetry that would not emulate foreign aesthetic canons but be derived from Brazilian history, popular culture and everyday life.

A manifesto was crafted at the *Semana do 22* where Oswald de Andrade advanced the term *Antropofagia* (Cannibalism) to describe the Brazilian cultural process: a system that ingested, digested and expelled foreign influences, especially European, melding them together with local native traditions to generate what is generally acknowledged as 'Brazilianness'. As has been pointed out by the art critic Paulo Herkenhoff, *Antropofagia* is 'the foundational myth of twentieth-century Brazilian culture. It refers to the historical forging of bodies during the making of the Americas —by violence, by sexual encounters, by gender politics, by the anatomy lessons of science, by religion, and by art' (Herkenhoff 2001:134). The painter Tarsila do Amaral, who did not participate in the *Semana* but was an influential member of many avant-garde artistic projects, played with Europe's ancient fear of cannibalism in her 1928 painting *Abaporu*, where an out of scale native, a cannibal no doubt, foregrounds sun-drenched cacti.

This ambivalent relationship between tradition and modernity, or more precisely between national identity and the International Style, is further highlighted in Brazil by the fact that it was precisely young modernists who were ultimately responsible for the formulation and instrumentation of the SPHAN —*Serviço de Patrimonio Histórico e Artístico Nacional* [National Agency for Historic and Artistic Patrimony]. Founded in 1938, this federal agency ensured the cataloguing and preservation of traditional as well as modern cultural patrimony. Significantly, one of the first buildings to be protected by SPHAN was the 1936 Ministry of Education and Culture (MEC), which is generally acknowledged as the first government sponsored modernist building in the Americas.

The MEC was undoubtedly the star of the 1943 New York Museum of Modern Art exhibit *Brazil Builds* which ignored the concept of *Antropofagia* and instead focused on the 'brilliant tropical adaptation of the International Style' (Goodwin 1943: 81-103). The exhibit and accompanying publication sought to establish the new 'American' modernism while legitimising Brazil through its architectural production, as a valuable North American cultural ally. In a strange turn of events, the accompanying exhibition catalogue was in fact the first international document to infer Brazilian Modernism's connection to its Baroque past. From its pages, one can glean the following common architectural principles, which I will use as a basis for the formal and spatial comparison between Baroque and Modern Brazilian Architecture:

1. Elaborate formalism, including inside and outside inversions, which heighten the mystery of the architectural promenade.

2. Generous discrepancy between interior and exterior boundaries, causing *poché* space to be as figural as the architectural object.

3. Scenographic sense and hyper-awareness of spatial theatricality.

4. Integration of art and architecture, where ornament becomes one with wall and structural elements become one with sculptural *retablos*, rendering the religious narrative almost experiential.

Lúcio Costa's influential writings strongly argued the case for the parallel existence of conservation and modernism as truly Brazilian. I will attempt to show how this sensibility is apparent at two different sites: Affonso Reidy's undulating housing block at Pedregulho and the seductive yet schematic minimalism evident in Niemeyer's Pampulha. Cândido Portinari's tiled murals or *azulejos* will be highlighted in both projects.

Pampulha, Pedregulho and Portinari's Role

The two Brazilian projects, Pampulha and Pedregulho, share the above-mentioned concerns as well as the premise that the work articulates architecture and landscape concurrently.[4] The programmatic concerns are not

---

[4] During the decades around World War II, there were many projects by Latin American

only characteristic of the times but are also representative of modernist ethical values such as the citizenry's right to government-sponsored leisure and affordable housing.

If the aforementioned MEC in 1936 and the creation of the nation's capital Brasilia in the late 1950s define the beginning and end of government-sponsored modernism in Brazil, Pampulha presented to the world in 1942-1943 the promise of a modern *Brazilian* architecture. Dreamt up by the great visionary and multi-faceted character Juscelino Kubitschek, then governor of Minas Gerais and later to become Brazil's president, Pampulha was fashioned as a nearby resort in an effort to modernise the appeal of his native city Belo Horizonte. Eighteen years later, Kubitschek would display the same kind of assertiveness exponentially at Brasilia, where the sky was the limit to the consuming desire not only to construct national identity but to do so by creating a landscape more fantastic than the surrounding one.

Because Kubitschek had been impressed by Oscar Niemeyer's 1938 modernist hotel in Ouro Preto, he decided to invite the young architect to propose four buildings: the dance hall, the casino, the yacht club, and the church. Niemeyer responded by creating a surreal landscape of curvilinear forms and rolling hills to anchor the artificial lake in which reflections of the buildings are overlaid simultaneously with multiple site views creating a strangely serene atmosphere.

The foundation was laid at Pampulha for the formation of a cosmopolitan, yet profoundly local, modern architecture that informed and influenced the rest of the world. Niemeyer's manipulation of reinforced concrete, in tight collaboration with Cardozo, proved that creative freedom and structural rigour did not have to be mutually exclusive. In fact like Reidy, Candela and Borges, it is tectonic knowledge that informed their spatial investigation. The result is a series of sculptural gestures that are laced around the constructed body of water, sometimes framing the landscape and sometimes transforming it by ingestion.

Of the four buildings, the *Igreja de São Francisco* [Church of St. Francis] best illuminates my position. At Niemeyer's St. Francis, the ceremonial space in the church is trapezoidal in plan and covered by a parabolic vault that is in turn capped by a higher vault of slightly bigger radius hovering over the altar. Only glass is allowed to bridge the gap between the smaller and the larger vault that connects to three other vaults

---

architects informed by the principles mentioned above. Max Borges in Cuba and Félix Candela in Mexico are two architects who, although fascinating and under-researched, fall outside the scope of this paper. Candela's oeuvre stands on its own within the history of Mexican modernism due to the intimate relationship between tectonics, function and intention found in his architecture. It is not surprising that Borges collaborated with Candela prior to his 1952 Tropicana Club in Havana which like Candela's Church of La Milagrosa of 1953 delights in the experiential as a by-product of formal virtuosity and in the blurred boundary between inside and outside.

defining the sacristy. This scenographic 'trick' allows light to dematerialise the vaults and make them look as if they were floating. At Pampulha, reinforced concrete was pushed to the limits of its physical properties: it did away with the structural grid, simultaneously explored its own plastic and structural potential, and finally remained exposed.

Looking at Portinari's tiled murals, it is evident that their indiscriminate appearance inside and outside subjugated the readability of the walls as structure and helped to blur the boundary between exterior and interior. The mural at the altar depicting St Francis was the uncontested interior focus and the exterior mural, which referenced Baroque ecclesiastical architecture, brought an otherworldly scale to the back wall of the church. At the time, Portinari was considered the most important painter in Brazil. After his first collaboration with Costa, Niemeyer, Reidy et al. on the MEC, he had a solo show at the New York MOMA in 1938 and shortly after was commissioned to paint a mural at the National Library of Congress in Washington DC.

Niemeyer's overly discussed fascination with the curve was formally established at Pampulha as a reference to tropical landscape and sensuality, and as an affront to the formal rigidity demanded by the prescriptive International Style. Niemeyer has spoken about Le Corbusier's enthusiasm for Pampulha and how he once chose to compliment Niemeyer by telling him 'you do the Baroque very well'.[5] What an irony that years later, Le Corbusier would be utterly offended by critics' assertions that Ronchamp had Baroque inspiration!

Pedregulho, the complex by Affonso Eduardo Reidy of 1947-1952, furthers the exploration initiated by Niemeyer in Pampulha. It consists of three residential blocks, health centre, school, market and laundry room, gymnasium and swimming pool. The project was designed to house almost five hundred families in one and two bedroom apartments connected by a single loaded corridor. Characteristic of many successful partnerships in Brazil, Pedregulho was conceived collaboratively with the structural engineer Carmen Portinho.

The origin of this complex, within the modernist utopia of centralised subsidised housing and support facilities, was a paternalistic initiative aimed at revolutionising domestic life as well as facilitating the re-education of lower-echelon city employees. Its formal departure point can be traced back to Le Corbusier's Marseille block of 1946 as well as his studies for the urbanisation of Rio de Janeiro of 1929. However, Pedregulho exceeds all expectations. By mediating classic rationalist principles with Baroque playfulness vis-à-vis local conditions of site and building programme,

---

[5] Interview with Oscar Niemeyer. The interview was conducted by the author in the architect's studio in Rio de Janeiro in 1997. Unpublished.

Pedregulho could only exist at São Cristóvão. Furthermore, the way in which the hill is hugged by the undulating housing block allows it to explode through the open third floor reaching beyond framed views of the bay and surrounding mountains to create an intermediate order between cultural affirmation and natural mimesis.

Contrary to the 'empty formalism' critique of Brazilian architecture of the time, which charged that plastic sophistication came at the expense of true commitment to social equality, current research indicates that there were around 80,000 affordable housing units built between 1942 and 1953. Pedregulho aspired to move beyond the mere provision of shelter towards improving the life of the worker while affirming the nationalistic notion of *novo homem, Brasileiro e moderno* (new man, Brazilian and modern). With an amalgamated architectural language that juxtaposed culture and landscape, Reidy displayed formal mastery in his choice of rectangular prisms for the housing blocks, trapezoidal volumes for the communal facilities and thin shell vaulted spaces for sport-related structures.

The Corbusian 'interior street' dedicated to communal leisure activities is anchored at one end by a small theatre. It horizontally dissects the main housing block in two by virtue of its openness, achieving lightness, duality and superimposition. The layering of the structural rhythm of columns and *pilotis* over the solar shading trellises provides depth and textural counterpoint to an otherwise magnanimous gesture. In the communal facilities, the gardens by Roberto Burle Marx and murals by Portinari activate the blind sides of the gym and school respectively and, with the staging of ramps and stairs, awnings and verandas, playground and garden, the negative space weaves in and out of the figural space creating a spectacle of intersecting solids and voids.

Unfortunately, this utopia was not without its problems —the meeting of lofty spatial aspirations with the preferences of its future inhabitants created many ironic situations. Lauro Cavalcanti points out the specific case of the communal laundry room (Cavalcanti 2001: 36). Inspired by the political agenda of gender equality and in the hope of preventing clothes lines from interfering with the established rhythm of the façade, the individual units were purposely devoid of dedicated water tanks or small sinks. Instead, an automated laundry room was provided. The reality was that for poor *Carioca*[6] women of the 1950s doing laundry was not merely a chore but a bonding ritual. Instead of using the laundry, they opted to use the swimming pool to wash clothes, a practice that was swiftly discontinued and labelled by management as a failed attempt at acculturation.

---

[6] Carioca is the colloquial Brazilian term for a person from Rio de Janeiro.

Conclusion

Despite the painful history relating to the Baroque period and the uneasy relationship Latin America has had with it, when faced with the challenge of self-representation at the dawn of Modernism, a series of events coincide to pave the way for a recycling of Baroque norms within modern architectural production in Brazil. The first is the robust precedent of Baroque architecture that improvised on imported design and construction methods, the best known example of which is without a doubt the work of sculptor architect *Aleijadinho*. His brand of hybrid sculpture architecture —formally *mestizo*, spatially Baroque, and as dramatic as it was theatrical— set the tone for early Brazilian modern architecture.

Similarly, early nationalist avant-garde movements like *Antropofagia* repeatedly put forth the ingestion and digestion of foreign cultural influences as the legitimate way to generate Brazilian modern cultural production. Therefore, the deliberate link to the past is a form of reverse colonisation as has been amply discussed by Gustavo Celorio, who has labelled this cultural strategy a form of 'counter-conquest'. Celorio argues that the Neo-Baroque constitutes a critical practice as well as a theory of New World culture.[7]

Furthermore, the search for original historical precedent was suspect from the beginning. Despite the abundance of documented popular building techniques and spatial relationships, the absence of significant pre-Columbian structures in Brazil disqualified the contemporary Indigenist discourse that was predominant in Mexico and Perú, among others. Thus, the quest for origin points to an innate lack and generates a series of metonymic critical activities that at once conceal and reveal that initial lack. As the Cuban critic Severo Sarduy has aptly argued:

> Lo propio y original americano es tener cosas en principio ajenas que hacemos propias en virtud de que no las teníamos ni podríamos tenerlas. Esa es nuestra originalidad. No tenemos tradición crítica a la manera europea; tenemos crítica en la tradición americana. ¿Y cual es esa tradición crítica americana? La que se genera de la superposición de unas ideas supuestamente universales en una cultura supuestamente peculiar. (Sarduy 1987: 97)

> [The appropriate and original American way is to have things that are originally foreign yet made our own by virtue of not having had them before or not being able to have them. This is our originality. We do not have a critical tradition in the European manner, we have criticism in the American tradition. And what is that critical American tradition? The one generated out of the superimposition

---

[7] For further discussion see Celorio (2001).

of supposedly universal ideas on a supposedly peculiar culture
(author's translation).]

Finally and perhaps most importantly, the theoretical construct
advanced by Costa and other contemporary intellectuals legitimised Brazil's
illustrious colonial past by using nationalist arguments. The past was being
constructed at the same time as the present was being invented and as a result
the relationship between tradition and experimentation is not one of linear
rejection but of contemporaneous translation. The Baroque in fact mediated
the age-old adversarial relationship between technology and culture.

The search for modernity in Brazil travelled inward from the
beginning. This occurred not because of a nationalist desire to connect to
Luso colonial heritage and to attempt to claim a cosmopolitan ancestry, but
as a rejection of imported modern models as foreign and inappropriate
because they required homogeneity and demanded compliance with mass-
production standards. The development of a modern aesthetic came hand in
hand with a search for identity. For cultural production to be relevant it had
to resonate with Brazilian physical reality, its unique topography and climate,
and with its deep connectedness to the past, which made the modernist
premise of breaking with history ultimately unpalatable to its Latin American
temperament.

Works Cited

Benjamin,Walter (2003) *The Origin of German Tragic Drama* (London and New York: Verso).

Cavalcanti, Lauro (2001) *Quando o Brasil era moderno, 1928-1960* (Rio de Janeiro: Aeroplano).

Celorio, Gonzalo (2001) 'El barroco en el nuevo mundo: arte de contraconquista', in *Ensayo de Contraconquista* (Mexico: Tusquets), 81-103.

Costa, Lúcio (1995) *Registro de uma vivência* (Sâo Paulo: Empresa das Artes).

Goodwin, Paul (1943) *Brazil Builds: Architecture New and Old (1652-1942)* (New York: Museum of Modern Art).

Herkenhoff, Paulo (2001) 'Brazil: The Paradoxes of an Alternate Baroque', in *Ultra Baroque, Aspects of Post Latin American Art* (San Diego CA: San Diego Museum of Contemporary Art), 134.

Ortiz, Fernando (1947 [1940]) *Cuban Counterpoint: Tobacco and Sugar*, trans. Harriet de Onís (Durham, NC: Duke University Press).

Sarduy, Severo (1987) *Barroco* (Mexico City: Fondo de Cultura Económica).

Waisman, Marina (2000) 'Introduction', in Kenneth Frampton and Malcolm Quantrill (eds), *Latin American Architecture: Six Voices* (Texas: Texas A&M University Press).

Conclusion

Transculturation: Taking Stock

Mark Millington

Abstract

This essay considers the recent vogue for the term transculturation and critiques a selection of its numerous and divergent uses. That critique enables a return to and a reassessment of Ortiz's theorisation and historical analyses in *Contrapunteo cubano*. While it is important that the term continue to adapt to changing circumstances, many bland and gestural invocations of it have paid insufficient attention to the detail of Ortiz's thinking, which illuminates the whole gamut of different stages and processes involved in cultural encounters and interaction. Without losing sight of Ortiz's strong emphasis on historical analysis, the essay explores why a cultural phenomenon which is universal was theorised and named within Latin America. It also considers the extent to which transculturation can constitute a political position from which in the contemporary world to challenge the hold of global modernisation, which some recent readings have proposed. It concludes that, since the fundamentals of economic and political power have not shifted noticeably since the colonial era, in which transculturation already had a strong presence in one form of another, the idea that it might now bring about democratic interchanges between Latin America and other cultures seems overly optimistic. The kind of analysis which Ortiz brilliantly demonstrates in *Contrapunteo cubano* may illuminate the imbalances and asymmetries of global (inter)exchanges but it is unlikely to do more than that.

* * *

Introduction

'Transculturation' is a term which has been bandied about a considerable amount in certain areas of Latin American studies in the last fifteen to twenty years.[1] But I want to pause to consider some of the issues surrounding its use. As is well known, the term was first seen in print in Fernando Ortiz's book *Contrapunteo cubano del tabaco y el azúcar* in 1940 but, despite the enthusiastic support of Bronislaw Malinowski in his introduction to the book, it apparently did not become a term in common usage in anthropology as he

---

[1] This intensification of interest is mirrored in a revealing, if minor, piece of personal evidence. I recently consulted the 1963 edition of Fernando Ortiz's book *Contrapunteo cubano del tabaco y el azúcar* held by the London University Library. Examination of the borrowing pattern indicates that the book was on loan just seven times in the twenty-six years between 1969 and 1995 (with one gap of sixteen years between 1973 and 1989). In the five years since 1998 the book has already been borrowed ten times.

had hoped. There was a key intervention and adoption of the term 'transculturation' in Angel Rama's book *Transculturación narrativa en América Latina* (1982), a book which narrowed the focus of the term by concentrating on literature and its relation with regional cultures in Latin America. But it is subsequent to that intervention and in the era of the emergence of postcolonial studies in the anglophone academy (and in particular in literary and cultural studies[2]) that transculturation has become a relatively common reference point. In short, the value of stock in 'transculturation' rose in the late 1980s and 1990s as 'investors' climbed aboard. But in the light of this rise, it may be helpful to ask whether the term has any settled meaning: allowing for the evolving and contrastive contexts in which it is used, a significant question would be whether there is any consensus about its meaning. It is not at all clear that the kind of understanding of 'transculturation' which Ortiz proposed coincides with the work currently expected of it. There is, perhaps appropriately, some counterpoint between the meanings which are now in play, and it is therefore important to ask not only when 'transculturation' is used, but also how and why at that particular moment.

One sign of the recent vogue is the desire within postcolonial studies to seek out areas of contestation within cultures of the periphery; transculturation has been seen as a possible way of identifying resistance to hegemonies of all sorts and so of highlighting sources of pluralism and difference. However, given that postcolonial studies represent a strand of critical thinking which, in my experience, has not been significantly embraced within Latin America itself, there must be a strong suspicion that the promotion of 'transculturation' is driven by specific factors within the metropolitan academies, factors which have to do with political anxieties deriving from global structures of political and economic power. In that light, it is important to ask what the academics who take up 'transculturation' and the politics associated with it are thereby performing for Latin America and, perhaps just as crucially, for themselves. Much of the recent debate over transculturation is concerned with modernity, modernisation and postmodernity, notions which were not uppermost in Ortiz's mind as he wrote his book, but which currently appear unavoidable in trying to understand Latin America and its autonomy or lack of it in a global context. Transculturation is potentially a useful term to articulate some of the cultural processes involved in that global context, but the question is whether that term and the processes which it is said to describe are able to deliver on the expectations of those looking for signs of Latin America's difference. It is

---

[2] In principle, transculturation is a term which might be used across a broad spectrum of humanities and social science disciplines, although it seems not to have found its way into many of them. This book represents one of the first attempts to consider transculturation's relevance to architecture and urban space.

worth reminding ourselves that no single term can be expected adequately to deal with the range of cultural processes in play, but my aim will be to go beyond the term itself in order to consider the underlying realities and the arguments put forward in the name of transculturation. So we need to see beyond the term, but we also need to examine the term itself and what is being demanded of it. In reading about transculturation my concern has been to think about a variety of different circumstances in relation to one term. How is it possible to use transculturation in the differing contexts of a burgeoning slave economy in Cuba, in relation to post-Independence Latin America and in contemporary Latin America when cultural interactions within and beyond the region are so diverse and effectively beyond monitoring? Put another way, how can one term be adequate to describe situations ranging from benign mutuality to traumatic exploitation? Each of these different contexts needs to be kept clearly delineated so that the differences in cultural process are not lost from view. My reading of some uses of transculturation is that this kind of differentiation has not been achieved. So what I am proposing to do here is not to offer a new angle on transculturation, nor to reinvigorate it, but to examine some emerging difficulties with it and to problematise its recent vogue. In short, I shall undertake some stocktaking.

Perspectives on Transculturation

A number of recent commentators on and theorists of Latin American culture refer to Ortiz's work, but the emphases in their analyses vary. In what follows I shall take one or two examples from the last twenty years which are indicative of the variety within the field. However, I shall start with Malinowski's introduction to the first edition of *Contrapunteo cubano*.[3] Interestingly, his presentation of Ortiz's book already begins the process that will lead to contemporary readings. Although Ortiz's book undertakes an

---

[3] In the interesting series of letters appended to Santí's edition of *Contrapunteo cubano* (2002), it emerges that Ortiz translated Malinowski's Introduction from English into Spanish (Ortiz 2002: 780, 790). What is not clear is whether Malinowski's original text was printed in the English translation of the book which appeared in 1947. However, for my quotations below from Malinowski I have assumed that this original text was the one printed in 1947 and so I have made no alterations to it. Even though Malinowski was not able to write the Introduction in Spanish it is evident from the letters that he has a reasonable knowledge of the language: he writes the opening paragraph of one or two of them in (slightly inaccurate and unidiomatic) Spanish before apologetically switching to English (or 'gringo', as he puts it). Above all, Malinowski must have had a good reading knowledge of Spanish given that Ortiz writes his letters to him in Spanish and that is the language of the manuscript which Ortiz sent him to read prior to preparing the Introduction.

extensive cultural and historical account of the two main crops cultivated in Cuba, namely sugar and tobacco, Malinowski devotes three of the eight pages of his Introduction to a discussion of transculturation, and a further page to explaining how his own recent work coincides with the thinking underlying Ortiz's term. He then devotes approximately two pages to Ortiz's historical and sociological account of sugar and tobacco (overwhelmingly the bulk of Ortiz's book) and in doing so claims Ortiz for his own school of anthropology, namely functionalism. He ends with comments on Cuban-US relations and the richness of the research presented in the book. Malinowski's emphasis on transculturation is not surprising as Ortiz was conscious of trying to replace the term 'acculturation' which was dominant in Anglo-American anthropology at the time and had precisely sought Malinowski's approval for this innovation. However, the relatively brief attention which he applies to the rest of the book,[4] with its detailed account of the history and sociology of sugar and tobacco on the island, is striking. Malinowski agrees with the view that the term acculturation is inadequate, and indeed he describes it as 'an ethnocentric word with a moral connotation'. And he goes on: 'The immigrant has to *acculturate* himself; so do the natives, pagan or heathen, barbarian or savage, who enjoy the benefits of being under the sway of our great Western culture' (Ortiz 1947: lviii). There is no mistaking here Malinowski's ironic condemnation of an arrogant West imposing its culture on others and blinded by its own self-importance.[5] His approval for the term is based on his feeling that it captures a particular kind of cultural relation and interaction:

> Every change of culture, or, as I shall say from now on, every transculturation, is a process in which something is always given in return for what one receives, a system of give and take. It is a process in which both parts of the equation are modified, a process from which a new reality emerges, transformed and complex, a reality that is not a mechanical agglomeration of traits, nor even a mosaic, but a new phenomenon, original and independent. To describe this process the word *trans-culturation*, stemming from Latin roots, provides us with a term that does not contain the implication of one certain culture towards which the other must tend, but an exchange between two cultures, both of them active, both contributing their share, and both co-operating to bring about a new reality of civilisation. (Ortiz 1947: lviii - lix)

---

[4] It is worth remembering that, in a book of four hundred and thirty-eight pages, Ortiz's theoretical discussion lasts a bare four and a half pages (Ortiz 1978: 92-97) and that the historical section on the transculturation of tobacco, in which the term itself hardly figures, contains eighty pages (Ortiz 1978: 204-84).

[5] In the Spanish translation these words are capitalised —'nuestra Gran Cultura Occidental' (Ortiz 1940: 4)— , which lays on even more irony.

This passage helps to pinpoint my unease with Malinowski's gloss on Ortiz: it seems to me to be simply too abstract —he describes a process without acknowledging any connection with social structures and historical circumstances. In addition, the reference to 'give and take' seems rather bland and indeed problematic given Ortiz's descriptions of colonial slave society. Ortiz's own account, as we shall see, is hardly detailed on a political level, but on some pages it does crucially demonstrate awareness of the human dimension of transculturation and the potential for suffering caused by cultural encounters. In a rather revealing later sentence, Malinowski says: 'Like the good functionalist he is, the author of this book resorts to history when it is really necessary' (Ortiz 1947: lxii). It is as if history were a nuisance which might occasionally have to be dealt with. And he goes on:

> The chapters dealing with the different methods of working the land, depending on whether it is for sugar or tobacco, with the differences in the systems of labor, whether by free workmen, slaves, or hired laborers, and, finally, those having to do with the varying political implications of the two industries are written as much from the historical point of view as from the functional. (Ortiz 1947: lxii-lxiii)

Revealingly, Malinowski ends with a methodological point and not with the pressing question of how different systems of labour might condition the interchange of cultures. What seems to me to be missing here (as quite often in later writers on transculturation) is a sense of the politics and social conditions of actual cultural interaction, which are narrowed into a disembodied and benign 'give and take'. Malinowski does mention the book's political implications but he praises Ortiz for refraining from 'any unwarranted judgements' (Ortiz 1947: lxiii), so that as with history there is a sense of 'bad taste' hovering around politics. But it turns out that the politics referred to have nothing to do with realities internal to Cuba but relations with the USA. Malinowski does not quite say what the political issues of these relations are, but it is clear that he thinks that the USA needs educating about Latin America. However, this political dimension leaves the internal politics of Cuba untouched and the idea of smooth transcultural interchanges undisturbed. It is a tendency towards a similar apolitical perspective that I find unconvincing in some later writing.

The next intervention on the subject of transculturation which I want briefly to consider is Angel Rama's *Transculturación narrativa* of 1982. His may be the most important and sustained deployment of the term since Ortiz, but it is clear that Rama has a rather specific case to argue.[6] He focuses on the situation of literary narrative and its cultural context in the mid-twentieth century. His particular emphasis is on relations between cultural groupings within Latin American nations, in particular between cities/ports (that is major urban centres with strong international connections) and internal regions. In line with the context to which Rama refers, the cultural elements and their dynamic are different from the ones with which Ortiz deals. Where Ortiz was concerned with the effects of multiple cultures all being introduced into Cuba more or less simultaneously without an established local culture, Rama is concerned with defined national situations in which there are well-established internal structures and divisions which come into contact with external practices —in other words, a clearly delineated internal/external polarity. What Rama argues is that there emerged in this period a new kind of reflective regionalism (Rama 1997: 157), one which was more attuned than earlier regional writing to the modernisation reaching Latin America through its major urban centres. He underlines the creative response of writers to new impulses coming from other cultures, which he sees as having led to a transformation of regional perspectives. In line with his actively pro-Latin America stance, he sees the transformation as confirming the existence of societies which are dynamic and distinctive in the interior of Latin America (Rama 1997: 159). He describes the transformation as transculturation, and it does correspond with Ortiz's idea that the outcome of the process is the emergence of new cultural forms. In a key section which figures both in his article (Rama 1997: 158-59) and in his book (Rama 1982: 32 - 34), he quotes an important passage from Ortiz concerned with the preference for the term transculturation over acculturation, and with what is involved in the transculturation process:

> I am of the opinion that the word *transculturation* better expresses the different phases of the process of transition from one culture to another, because it does not only consist in acquiring a culture, which is what the Anglo-American word *acculturation* really means, but the process also necessarily implies the loss or uprooting of a previous culture, which could be called a partial deculturation, and, in addition, it indicates the consequent creation of new cultural phenomena which could be called *neoculturation*. (Ortiz 1947: 32-33)[7]

---

[6] I shall refer to two texts: his well-known book, *Transculturación narrativa en América Latina* (1982), and an earlier article, 'Processes of Transculturation in Latin American Narrative' (1974, translated and reprinted in 1997).

[7] As with most of the quotations from Harriet de Onís' translation of Ortiz's book I have adapted the English for accuracy. In this quotation, it is interesting to note, for example, that she omitted a significant word from the original text. Where Ortiz talks of 'una parcial *desculturación*' (Ortiz

Rama's gloss on the quotation is illuminating.

> Esta concepción de las transformaciones [...] traduce visiblemente
> un perspectivismo latinoamericano, incluso en lo que puede tener
> de incorrecta interpretación. Revela resistencia a considerar la
> cultura propia, tradicional, que recibe el impacto externo que habrá
> de modificarla, como una entidad meramente pasiva o incluso
> inferior, destinada a las mayores pérdidas, sin ninguna clase de
> respuesta creadora. (Rama 1982: 33)

> [This conception of transformations visibly translates a Latin
> American perspective, even in what it may contain of incorrect
> interpretation. It reveals a resistance to consider one's own,
> traditional culture, which receives the external impact which will
> modify it, as a merely passive or inferior entity, destined to suffer
> the most losses, without any kind of creative response.]

Interestingly, although Rama immediately refers to '*this* conception of transformations' (my italics) Ortiz does not use the word 'transformations' in the quotation used. And curiously, and perhaps because of an underlying uneasiness about his assertion, he employs a slightly odd expression — 'visibly translates'— precisely when the term 'transformations' is not to be seen: he is himself striving to *make* the transformations visible.[8] All Ortiz refers to are 'the process of transition' and 'the consequent creation of new cultural phenomena' (neither of which necessarily implies transformation, that is, the mutation of already existing cultural forms or practices). On the other hand, it would be pointless to claim that Ortiz's theory is not fundamentally concerned with transformation, as opposed to destruction or elimination. But it seems to me that, having already narrowed the sphere of references of transculturation to the literary and the regional, Rama is keen to stress transformation because it suits his argument and its specific focus — the effect of modernity on regional cultures and literary practices. The thrust of his argument implies that modernisation and modernity are the future and so what he theorises is the enhancing effect of modernisation on the rural context. In his argument, there is a sense of these cultures moving towards the 'mainstream' of modernity even as they adapt it to their own purposes. That is the compromise formation that Rama is suggesting.[9]

1978: 96, italics in the original) as part of the transculturation process, Onís omits the word 'parcial', thus producing a quite important change in the meaning.

[8] One of the striking things about the debates concerning transculturation is that they seem to invoke automatically a whole series of other terms with the prefix 'trans', although commentators are not always very careful to establish that the prefix signifies the same thing in each case. See below for a further discussion of the etymology of 'transculturation'.

[9] It is also intriguing that Rama's text has an ambiguity in relation to the idea that there may be something 'incorrect' in play. It seems possible to read the quotation above as saying either that

The change of context for the use of 'transculturation' and the ambiguities in the discussion of Ortiz and his term are apparent in later work by other commentators. Ortiz's theorisation is not complex or lengthy but very few later writers bother to pay much regard to the detail of what he says. The tendency in the work of the last decade or so is for many writers to offer a brief (sometimes a very brief) sketch of the idea of transculturation (with or without an explicit reference to Ortiz) followed by an adaptation of it to contemporary contexts or concerns.[10] In itself the adaptation of the term does not strike me as problematic, and indeed it may be considered a strength that it has such flexibility, but what is of more concern is that the term may be understood in different ways.

In her book, *Imperial Eyes: Travel Writing and Transculturation* of 1992, Mary Louise Pratt highlights transculturation in her title, but in practice does not discuss or invoke it very much in her exposition. She makes a brief introduction of the term very early on:

> Ethnographers have used this term [transculturation] to describe how subordinated or marginal groups select and invent from materials transmitted to them by a dominant or metropolitan culture. While subjugated peoples cannot readily control what emanates from the dominant culture, they do determine to varying extents what they absorb into their own, and what they use it for. (Pratt 1992: 6)

Pratt refers generally to ethnographers in this passage, but which ones she has in mind is not stated except in the footnote which comes at the end of the first sentence which refers to one ethnographer, Ortiz, and to Rama, who is rightly said to have incorporated the term transculturation into literary studies. More substantively, and as we shall see in more detail below, Ortiz did not use the term to refer only to subordinate or marginal

---

the conception of transformations or that the Latin American perspective in Ortiz may have incorrect elements ('what it may contain of incorrect interpretation'). To add to the complexity, there is a footnote (Rama 1982: 33 n.22) inserted after the use of the word 'incorrect', but it does not apparently expand on the use of that word but instead introduces a discussion of terminology (*ad-culturation, ab-culturation, trans-culturation*). The very insertion at this point of a footnote about cultural changes implies that the incorrect element resides in the idea of 'transformation' (and perhaps also transculturation by association). In other words, the terms being used may not properly describe the cultural processes involved. This is potentially a complicating and even damaging observation about Ortiz's theory, but Rama does not pursue it. As a result it is not clear in quite what areas Rama sees Ortiz's theory or its application as potentially incorrect.

[10] Santí makes a similar point in his introduction to the latest edition of *Contrapunteo cubano* (Santí 2002: 94). There are exceptions to this tendency, a notable one being Gustavo Pérez Firmat in his *The Cuban Condition*. Pérez Firmat discusses Ortiz in detail and is sensitive to the nuances of his text. However, rather than exploring the range of Ortiz's ideas about history and anthropology, his preference is to focus on the text's style and literary qualities: he analyses the richness of its tropes and the patterns of argumentation which he sees as signs of Ortiz's Cubanness, qualities mirrored in his own slightly arch style.

groups and the ways they relate to and absorb dominant or metropolitan cultures. One of the crucial points about Ortiz is that he is interested in the effects of encounter on both cultures, and I therefore find it rather difficult to square Pratt's initial characterisation of transculturation with his text.

Fortunately, she does move on to a fuller view of transculturation when she suggests that it raises crucial questions:

> [...] with respect to representation, how does one speak of transculturation from the colonies to the metropolis? [...] How have Europe's constructions of subordinated others been shaped by those others, by the constructions of themselves and their habitats that they presented to the Europeans? [...] While the imperial metropolis tends to understand itself as determining the periphery [...], it habitually blinds itself to the ways in which the periphery determines the metropolis. (Pratt 1992: 6)

This passage is a significant addition to the previous one. The first and last sentences, which are broadly focused, coincide with aspects of Ortiz's thinking, given that he emphasises how there is mutual influence in cultural encounters and given his lengthy descriptions of the infiltration of tobacco into Europe. But what Pratt then says about the effect of the periphery's view of itself on metropolitan representations is distinct from and more precise than Ortiz. We are clearly moving beyond Ortiz here (he does not mention such preoccupations as representation), though how the processes of determination of one culture by another relate to deculturation and neoculturation, which are integral to transculturation in Ortiz's description (Ortiz 1978: 96), is not explored by Pratt. But the emphasis on how the periphery infiltrates and shapes the worldview of the metropolis seems to me to be important, and above all it captures a sense of the tense relations and the subterranean processes that can be in play between cultures: all may not be transparent and benign exchange. What the example of Pratt shows is how recent scholars have taken up his ideas without being circumscribed by him.

But one of the perplexing aspects of this tendency 'to go beyond' Ortiz is that scholars end up claiming different things for what transculturation means as the starting point for their different arguments. As an example of that, and in juxtaposition with the first quotation from Pratt above where she stresses how the term is used by ethnographers 'to describe how subordinated or marginal groups select and invent from materials transmitted to them by a dominant or metropolitan culture', we might consider a statement by William Rowe and Vivian Schelling. In the process of a careful consideration of different key concepts used in relation to Latin American culture they say that '[transculturation] is concerned with the mutual transformation of cultures, in particular of the European by the native'

(Rowe and Schelling 1991: 18). The contrast between these characterisations implies an important question about where transculturation occurs, whether in the metropolis or on the periphery. Pratt stresses how subordinated or marginal groups respond to and are creative with metropolitan culture, indicating that transculturation is a defensive and potentially contestatory practice of cultures on the periphery. By contrast, Rowe and Schelling stress mutuality but highlight the transformation of European culture by native culture: the former is transculturated by the latter, a process which, presumably, may occur on the periphery or in the metropolis. It is striking that transculturation in these two versions operates in apparently contrary ways, though Pratt seems far closer to Ortiz's position than Rowe and Schelling.

As a final example of recent trends, I turn to the essay by Felipe Hernández which introduces this book. Near the start of his essay, Hernández says that the term was created 'in order to explore the cultural dynamics in operation between Cuba and metropolitan centres' (Hernández 2004: 3). In fact, Ortiz seems to me to have been primarily interested in the relations and interactions between different cultures (African, European and Asian) which had come into and were finding ways of coexisting within Cuba. Ortiz also considers (in the section of *Contrapunteo cubano* entitled 'The Transculturation of Tobacco') the broad impact of tobacco on European and other cultures. What Hernández's claim highlights is a recent development in the contexts to which transculturation is applied: there is now less attention paid to internal cultural processes and more to Latin America's external relations with the metropolitan nations in the context of multinational capital and globalisation.

Hernández immediately moves on to broaden the focus beyond Cuba, indicating that the term has been applied to the whole of Latin America, and he points out how it has been seen as appropriate to discussions of the cultural economy between peripheries and centres, a move with global implications but still reinforcing the notion of external (rather than internal or regional) relations. He then focuses again on Latin America and the modality of the process of transculturation. He stresses its openness and that it has been used to foreclose the idea that cultures develop taxonomically or unidirectionally. And he moves from references to how transculturation has been used into a bold definition: 'Transculturation refers to a multidirectional and endless interactive process between various cultural systems that is in opposition to unidirectional and hierarchical structures determined by the principle of origin that is always associated with claims for cultural authority'. And he says that the term places 'the theorisation of processes of cultural exchange between peripheries and centres on a more democratic basis' (Hernández 2004: 3). This is a definition which reveals a number of postmodern emphases and on my reading takes us somewhat beyond Ortiz's rather cautious exposition. Hernández might perhaps more justifiably say that this definition is in line with what some commentators have recently taken transculturation to be. Given what Ortiz says in his theoretical chapter about the trauma and desperate suffering of the African slaves in their transportation to and life in colonial Cuba, the idea of a democratic exchange in his theorising would be difficult to sustain. Hernández does later acknowledge the issue of unequal positions of power when he says: 'By "transculturation" [...] Ortiz means that a process of mutual interaction exists between cultures, despite the unequal distribution of power characteristic of transcultural relations' (Hernández 2004: 3). While 'mutual interaction' is indeed what Ortiz is talking about, I would urge that we be careful not to minimise the inevitable influence of 'the unequal distribution of power' on cultural relations. If the phrase 'mutual interaction' is another way of saying 'democratic relations', then I think that Hernández is being too optimistic. And I say this in the light of his explicit later comment that 'it is necessary to reassess the notion of transculturation not only in order to respond to the new realities of Latin American cultures, but also in order to return to the term the critical and political values that it has lost' (Hernández 2004: 7). Hernández argues that Ortiz's theory needs more development if it is to be fully adequate to the context which he himself was confronting, let alone adequate to more recent situations. In broad terms I agree with this assessment (and I suspect that a lot of recent commentators would, though none of them has been as explicit as Hernández about it). He goes on to explore one way forward, which involves post-structuralism (though it seems to me that the post-structuralist position has already informed his exposition of Ortiz). And that way forward may well produce insights (although there are some on the left who would dispute that). But I want to suggest that, while we must pay heed to the history of the term's development, it is important to return to Ortiz because, despite the shortcomings in his theorisation, there are valuable elements in his account which can help to keep our feet on the political ground.

So, having briefly sampled one or two of the recent views of transculturation and of Ortiz's thinking, I want now to turn back to Ortiz himself to try to disentangle him from later accretions. This action is not designed to turn *Contrapunteo cubano* into some kind of scriptural text whose authority cannot be questioned and which has the last word to say on the subject of transculturation. The meaning of the term has needed to develop and will need to continue doing so as circumstances affecting Latin America change. One has only to consider the different contexts in which transculturation has been discussed to see how it has been adapted to circumstance. In the late 1930s, Ortiz himself was writing in a country which had emerged from a colonial regime within living memory and which was still struggling with the high degree of external control exercised by the USA.

By contrast, Rama was writing in the context of faltering modernisations and large-scale urban migrations in Latin America and of urgent debates about economic dependency. Later commentators, like John Beverley and Alberto Moreiras, have responded to more recent discussions about post-colonialism and the effects of globalisation. So, although important aspects of the basic contexts have remained the same across the half century or so covering all these interventions, certain conditions (in economics, politics and communications) have changed and accordingly the terms of analysis have altered. Thinking about transculturation has needed to keep pace. For all that, I think that it is worth looking carefully at Ortiz's text, because I see in it important elements and subtleties that might have a beneficial influence on our current understanding. There can be no denying that the theory of transculturation will have to be re-contextualised but it is also worthwhile re-engaging carefully with Ortiz in order to reveal his strengths and weaknesses, both of which offer salutary reminders to contemporary theorising and analysis.

Fernando Ortiz: *Contrapunteo cubano*

The first thing to be said about Ortiz in *Contrapunteo cubano* is that he is a reluctant theorist. This is quite a long book —the 1978 edition which I have used runs to 438 pages and they contain a wealth of detailed analysis and suggestive description. However, Ortiz gives over just four and a half pages to his chapter on the theory of transculturation (chapter II in the second part, Ortiz 1978: 92 - 97), even though it is an idea underlying much of the book. And not only is Ortiz rather brief in his discussion of transculturation, but he is also rather apologetic about his neologism, craving the reader's indulgence and excusing his 'daring' in proposing this new term. He is quite clear that he is introducing the new term in order to replace the well-established 'acculturation', which he defines as meaning the process of transit from one culture to another more powerful one and the social repercussions resulting from that movement. It is paradoxical that, in defining the term to be replaced, Ortiz employs a word —'transit' ('tránsito') (Ortiz 1978: 93)— which incorporates the prefix which is the crucial marker of the difference of his new term. This overlap may already suggest that the terminology being used has its problematic aspects, as I will explain more fully below. His argument for the new term is that it expresses the highly varied phenomena which came about in Cuba as a result of complex *trans*mutations of cultures, without appreciating which it is impossible to understand the evolution of the Cuban people in key areas of social life: the economic, institutional, juridical, ethical, religious, artistic, linguistic, psychological, sexual and so on. It is significant that he uses the plural form 'cultures' to allow space for the complex impacts of all those elements involved in what Pratt has called 'the contact zone' (Pratt 1992: 6-7). He goes on to give an example of the transculturations so essential to Cuban history which, rather oddly, involves something more like cultural destruction than transmutation: he talks of the transculturation of the Palaeolithic Indian to the Neolithic and the subsequent disappearance of the latter because of a failure to adapt to the impact of Castilian culture. Transculturation clearly failed at that point.

Ortiz then moves to a discussion of the elements involved in the cultural process in Cuba (Ortiz 1978: 93). What is very striking in this passage of the theoretical chapter is the emphasis on human beings as the bearers of culture and frequently as the victims of cultural change (an emphasis which is less apparent elsewhere in the the book).[11] It is this human dimension which has often been overlooked in commentaries on both Ortiz and transculturation. He is at pains to establish the cultural diversity of both Spaniards and Africans. He speaks of Spaniards 'with distinct cultures' (Ortiz 1978: 93), and that plural is evident again in his characterisation of the Africans arriving in Cuba, whom he describes as 'of diverse races and cultures' (Ortiz 1978: 93). Moreover, he talks of the Spaniards as 'torn' ('desgarrados') from their peninsular societies and *trans*planted into an unknown situation demanding that they adjust to 'a new syncretism of cultures' (Ortiz 1978: 93). This reference to the taxing experience for the Spaniards is followed by a description of that of the Africans, who were 'uprooted from their originary social nuclei and, with their cultures destroyed, oppressed beneath the weight of the dominant cultures here, as the sugar canes are crushed between the rollers of the mills' (Ortiz 1978: 93). He makes it clear that, while there is a degree of comparability between Spaniards and Africans (the 'torn' applied to the Spaniards finding its equivalent in the 'uprooted' applied to the Africans), the violence and suffering experienced by the Africans is clearly greater than that of the Spaniards. It is implied that there are different intensities of transculturation according to social status, though this variety and unevenness are not explored further by Ortiz and rather rarely by later commentators. In that respect it is tantalising that Ortiz does not say more about how the 'destroyed' cultures of the Africans then become involved in transmutations via contact with other cultures, but this is just one example of how the brevity of his discussion leaves areas of imprecision. Nonetheless, the implication here concerning varying forms of transculturation and its unevenness are points to which I shall return. Ortiz stresses the sheer variety and fluidity of the movements involved, and so he speaks of 'sporadic waves' and 'continuous flows' of immigrant cultures, 'ever flowing and influential'

---

[11] The strength of this contrast was drawn to my attention by Jon Beasley-Murray.

(Ortiz 1978: 93).[12] He finishes this crucial paragraph with a sentence summarising the major elements of the cultural experience which he is exploring: 'every immigrant [is] like one uprooted from their native land in a double, critical moment of disjunction ('desajuste') and realignment ('reajuste'), of *deculturation* or *exculturation* and of *acculturation* or *inculturation*, and in sum, of *transculturation*' (Ortiz 1978: 93).[13] This sentence encapsulates both the human dimension and the cultural processes which he has been talking about. However, the bunching of terms here under one master term distinguished by the prefix 'trans' is somewhat confusing and does not fully correspond with a later passage defining transculturation. In this passage, the term seems to be an overarching description of different cultural processes involving radical loss (deculturation or exculturation) and movement to another culture (acculturation or inculturation), but there is no mention of the vital, later 'neoculturation' (Ortiz 1978: 96), a term which indicates the potentially creative aspect of cultural encounters. It is as if the end of the process here were the movement into another culture, in other words acculturation, which is precisely the term which Ortiz began by arguing needed to be superseded. At this point it seems that 'transculturation' does not so much replace 'acculturation' as subsume it.

In the next part of his explanation of the realities which justify the coining of a new term, Ortiz gives a brief cultural history of Cuba starting with the earliest inhabitants. Much of this history focuses on the human aspects of the process of transculturation, so he makes it quite clear what acute suffering was caused for all those involved. When transculturation failed it is evident that the alternative was the simple and rapid destruction of the culture of the weaker group, whether it be that of the indigenous 'taínos' or that of one of the African groups brought in. Ortiz underlines the rapidity of the processes (what had taken four millennia in Europe happened in less than four centuries in Cuba [Ortiz 1978: 94]) and the provisionality and impermanence of the experience:

> There were no human factors more important for cubanness than these continuous, radically contrasting geographical, economic and social transmigrations of the settlers; than that perennial transitoriness of their objectives and than that life in constant rootlessness from the land they inhabited, constantly in misalignment with the society which sustained them. Men,

---

[12] In her English translation, Harriet de Onís comes up with a rather misleading phrase for Ortiz's 'fluyentes e influyentes', for which she has: 'always exerting influence and being influenced in turn' (Ortiz 1947: 98). This suggestion of reciprocity is not justified by the context, where Ortiz has just indicated certain equivalences and also disparities between the peoples and cultures arriving in Cuba. It is just such an unproblematised reciprocity which some later commentators have stressed.

[13] De Onís' translation simply omits mention of 'exculturation' and 'inculturation'.

economies, cultures and anxieties, everything here was felt to be
foreign, provisional, changing, 'birds of passage' over the country,
at its cost, against its wishes and to its detriment. (Ortiz 1978: 95)

Ortiz goes on to lay particular emphasis on the appalling experience
of disconnectedness and disorientation of the Africans. The intensity of this
description marks out the difference of their experience from that of the rest:

> More uprooted than any, they were crowded together like animals
> in a cage, constantly in a state of impotent rage, constantly longing
> for flight, for freedom, for change and constantly in a defensive
> state of inhibition, of dissimulation and of acculturation to a new
> world. (Ortiz 1978: 96)

However, having established the appalling nature of the Africans'
suffering, Ortiz rather oddly reintroduces all the other immigrants into his
description in such a way as again to suggest equivalence. The following
sentences immediately follow the last quotation:

> In such conditions of uprooting and social amputation, from
> continents across the ocean, year after year and century after
> century, thousands and thousands of human beings were brought to
> Cuba. To a greater or lesser degree of dissociation both negroes
> and whites lived in Cuba. All living together, above and below, in
> the same atmosphere of terror and force; terror of punishment for
> the oppressed, terror of revenge for the oppressor; all outside
> justice, misaligned, beside themselves. And all in a painful process
> of transculturation to a new cultural environment. (Ortiz 1978: 96)

This paragraph therefore has a rather odd progression, at one stage
seeming to single out the particular hardships of the Africans, at another
indicating shared suffering and transculturation. There is a sense of
equivalence between the races at the end of the paragraph (despite the phrase
'to a greater or lesser degree'), which sees the Africans involved in a painful
process of transculturation where barely four sentences before they were
undergoing acculturation. Such discrepancies as these make Ortiz's
theorising in these pages seem less than fully evolved.

After these two pages dealing with the human dimension of the
cultural processes in Cuba, Ortiz turns away from subjective experience to
end his theoretical discussion by returning to the impersonal dimension of
terminology. This oscillation, which is left in a rather unresolved state,
between the personal and the impersonal is characteristic of Ortiz's account.
It is at this point that he comes closest to a full explanation of
transculturation, and his reasons for rejecting 'acculturation', which

apparently have something to do with its Anglo-American status.[14] In his opinion (and again he becomes defensive), the term transculturation provides the best expression of the different phases of the process of transition ('el proceso transitivo') from one culture to another. We might recall that he also used the word 'transit' [tránsito] in the second paragraph of this whole section in his definition of 'acculturation' [Ortiz 1978: 93], which again indicates the closeness of the two terms. He suggests that 'transculturation' goes beyond the mere acquisition of a different culture to embrace other elements: 'the loss or uprooting of a previous culture, which could be called a partial *deculturation*,[15] and, in addition, it signifies the consequent creation of new cultural phenomena which could be called *neoculturation*' (Ortiz 1978: 96). Although not very detailed and perhaps not wholly coherent (it is not self-evident, for example, how a *partial* deculturation fits with the notion of the loss of a previous culture), this explanation gives some sense of the phases through which an individual might pass in the transcultural experience (even though Ortiz is talking of cultural processes, it is people who must live them out). That experience involves both loss and gain though neither is absolute: the loss is partial and the gain is of new cultural phenomena (and not of a complete new culture). The implication at this point must be that Ortiz sees acculturation as involving the complete loss of a previous culture and assimilation to another, already existing one (no creative, new phenomena here, apparently). Although Ortiz has, somewhat confusingly, also suggested in this chapter that transculturation subsumes acculturation (Ortiz 1978: 93), it seems to me that the kind of differentiation between the two terms which I have brought out here is important. The distinction certainly distances Ortiz from a number of recent commentators, who, in using the term in connection with contemporary circumstances, pay little attention to the initial phase of partial deculturation (not to mention all the suffering associated with it) and stress creative interplay between cultures, perhaps echoing Malinowski's 'give and take'.

To end his definition of transculturation Ortiz introduces a simile: '[…] in any embrace (abrazo)[16] between cultures there occurs the same as in individuals' genetic reproduction: the offspring always has something of both progenitors, but is also always distinct from each of them' (Ortiz 1978: 96-97). I must admit to finding the simile of the 'embrace' rather bland and

---

[14] De Onís' translation shifts the emphasis here by calling acculturation an English term, a shift which rather loses the implicit point about the contemporary disciplinary dynamics of anthropology.

[15] De Onís' translation omits the crucial word 'partial' here, a significant error not noticed by the translator of Rama's article (Rama 1997: 158), who simply reproduces de Onís' version of the quotation from Ortiz.

[16] De Onís' translation disconcertingly uses the word 'union' here, which, while it appropriately captures the idea of sexual intercourse implied in the simile, suggests a complete joining together which is profoundly at odds with the cultural experience described by Ortiz.

unconvincing at this stage, so it would be interesting to hear more about how the Africans in Cuba 'embraced' the cultures of Europe and how the Spaniards on the island 'embraced' African cultures. What is undoubtedly significant here for future theory is the space which this genetic metaphor allows to the notion of hybridisation. But the use of this simile is a sign of how Ortiz's exposition does not achieve a thoroughly worked out explanation of the variety and nuance of the cultural processes involved in transculturation. While undoubtedly suggestive, his theory as expounded in this brief chapter of *Contrapunteo cubano* is undermined by certain gaps in its explanation and also from internal inconsistencies which close reading brings to the surface.

Given the uneven nature of Ortiz's theorising, it is worth giving brief consideration to the import of his practical analyses and historical descriptions. After all, the overwhelming majority of his book is devoted to those analyses and descriptions, and Fernando Coronil has stated that: 'It was through his analysis, more than through his brief formal definition, that Ortiz showed his understanding of transculturation' (Coronil 1995: xxvi). I intend to comment on a few points in his account of tobacco, since it is this commodity which receives most attention in the second part of *Cuban Counterpoint*, and indeed the ninth chapter in the 1978 edition is entitled 'On the Transculturation of Tobacco'. Ortiz explains that tobacco spread from Cuba to Spain and then around Europe, despite the opprobrium attached to it by the Catholic Church because of its place in indigenous religious practices. That spread was sometimes justified on contemporary medical grounds. The use of tobacco soon also reached Africa and beyond. He talks of this movement as transculturation, sometimes as if its mere introduction somewhere effected transcultural changes, but he does not always explain what the transculturation consisted in. So he says, for example, that Africans of every sort found it easy to adopt tobacco and did understand its narcotic and magical properties, though it was not incorporated in religious rituals (Ortiz 1978: 215-16); on the other hand, the Africans adopted the Indian practice of collective pipe-smoking (Ortiz 1978: 218). What seems hard to be sure about is what precisely transculturation was in the different contexts which Ortiz describes. It is not self-evident, for example, what kind of transculturation took place in Europe when it adopted the taking of snuff and the smoking of cigars. On the description provided, these activities look like a social practice *added on* to already existing leisure activities, and an initial process of deculturation and a subsequent neoculturation (that is, the creation of new cultural phenomena out of the 'embrace' of two cultures) are difficult to discern.

Something more like transculturation seems to have happened in Cuba, where white settlers visited 'shamans' ('behíques'), despite the opprobrium heaped on them by the Catholic Church:

> [...] the whites in these regions of the Indies had no hesitation in having recourse to the *behíques* and to their ceremonies, prophecies and spells when they thought that by their mysterious effect they might gain some benefit, satisfaction or consolation. Europeans began to use tobacco, to 'drink up' its smoke, to inhale its powder, to 'bewitch' themselves with its aromatic smoke and even to swallow its concoctions and emetics, knowing full well that this was a sinful practice, a departure from orthodoxy, a heresy against traditional customs, an act of daring for which they would be held responsible; in short, falling into satanic temptation. (Ortiz 1978: 209-10)

Here the early European settlers can be seen to adopt 'alternative medical' practices, though again one might wonder what element of neoculturation was involved. It seems likely that neither the experience of the Africans in Africa nor of the European settlers in Cuba can compare with the combination of cultural erosion and subsequent adaptation undergone by the African slaves in Cuba. In this case, the nature of transculturation is likely to have been qualitatively different from that of these other groups, hence my preoccupation with differentiating between kinds of and contexts for transculturation.

Indeed, Ortiz makes it clear that the Europeans came to have a quite specific relation with tobacco. He describes the destruction of indigenous shrines and images and the elimination of local priests during the conquest and colonisation of Cuba, and he then refers to the disappearance of the whole indigenous population as a way of contextualising how the local religious connotations of tobacco died out (Ortiz 1978: 211). Nonetheless, he says that the use of tobacco spread amongst the settlers, but that the main reason for the extraordinary increase in its use was its commercial potential:

> [...] in order to explain the extraordinary spread of tobacco amongst the white men, it is necessary to consider other factors based on the real values of the plant, which the Europeans thought adaptable to their customs, in certain curious social repercussions which I shall soon indicate and, above all, because of the new economic, commercial and tax-yielding significance which tobacco acquired in the white men's civilisation. Tobacco, which, aside from its physiochemical nature and its individual physiological effects, had amongst the American Indians an original social structure of a predominantly religious character, acquired amongst the European Americans and then amongst other peoples a structure of a principally economic character, brought about by a curious, rapid and complete phenomenon of transculturation. (Ortiz 1978: 211)

This is an interesting passage. At the start the key point is that the Europeans thought tobacco adaptable to their customs, in other words that tobacco could be assimilated to European culture. And the principal reason is that tobacco is identified as a commodity with commercial and tax-yielding potential. On the evidence here, it is feasible that tobacco in fact changed nothing in Europe but simply became one more commodity alongside a host of others within the European context. While this assimilation appears to change the way in which tobacco was treated within a culture (Ortiz's point seems to be that tobacco was not a commercial or taxable crop before it went to Europe), there is no indication yet of how it changed European culture (he promises that this will come later). At this point it is not clear to what his reference to transculturation applies, whether it is that European culture underwent it or whether the culture of tobacco did. If the latter is the case, that introduces an intriguing idea, namely that a product of nature which is assimilated and given significance by one culture and then is absorbed by another is thereby itself transculturated, as opposed to the emphasis being on the effect of transculturation on the cultural practices of human beings as they shift between cultures. It is this latter, human dimension which seemed to be central in Ortiz's early theorising of transculturation (Ortiz 1978: 92-97).

Ortiz indicates that there is one way in which tobacco introduces a new ingredient into social life in Europe. He explains that governments became alarmed by the rapid spread of the use of tobacco amongst all classes and by the burgeoning economic activity associated with it, so that significant social repercussions ensued. It was feared that the effect of this new economic activity would upset existing social hierarchies:

> This apparently trivial novelty of tobacco gave rise to several problems and a danger. They had to be controlled. If on its appearance in the old Eurasian world tobacco inspired surprise, curiosity and desire, it also awoke very deep suspicions and covetousness. Some feared that serfs, by becoming small cultivators of lucrative crops, could achieve emancipation. [...] That is why, in the countries of the Old World, tobacco was hunted down as soon as its immense mercantile and agricultural potential revealed itself and in those countries with absolutist government, or ruled by tyranny, feudalism and servitude [...], the persecution was carried out with violent fury, even with the death penalty and with the most terrible vilifications. (Ortiz 1978: 253)

Here is evidence of the impact of tobacco on the social, economic and political life of Europe and beyond (Ortiz refers to Turkey, Russia, Persia, China and Japan). Similarly, Ortiz has already explained that there was a massive impact within Cuba brought about by the imposition of capitalist practices in the cultivation of the plant, with foreign control of production ensuring that Cuba's return on trade was minimal. In fact, because of the foreign take-over of production and subsequent migrations by tobacco workers in search of better wages in the USA, Ortiz talks of the decubanisation of the industrial aspects of production (Ortiz 1978: 75-76). The impact of the commercial development of tobacco production was evidently enormous both in Europe and in Cuba. Although he does not explain the detail of how cultures changed alongside these economic developments, it is scarcely conceivable that they did not. However, what is clear is that the dynamics and effects of transculturation are highly varied and that specific attention to local contexts is essential if the cultural processes are to be understood. This is not, it seems to me, a point which Ortiz explicitly makes, but it is implicit in the examples which he provides.

Whither Transculturation?

Coinciding with some of my concerns, a number of recent commentators — for example, Silvia Spitta (1995), John Beverley (1999) and Alberto Moreiras (2001a and 2001b)— have pointed out difficulties with Ortiz's theory and with current trends in the development of the theory of transculturation. It is evident that there are problematic elements in Ortiz's theorisation and his linking of the theory with historical realities: a certain lack of specificity, at times a sketchiness about the cultural processes and at others a less than clear fit between theory and circumstance. One aspect of the difficulties with Ortiz's theory of transculturation is the etymology of the term itself. A crucial step in his thinking is the move away from the term acculturation on the grounds that it is an Anglo-American term which refers to too narrow a cultural process. But the question is how much better the new term is, in which much depends on the substitution of the prefix 'trans' for the prefix 'a' or more fully 'ad'.[17] How far does etymology justify the move? About all that commentators agree on as essential to the meaning of the term is movement, but that idea is already contained in the prefix 'ad'. What commentators point up is that the term transculturation captures a sense of the plurality of movement between cultures (Malinowski's 'toma y daca'). However, the prefix 'trans' indicates movement across, beyond or through, and there is no

---

[17] Santí takes Catherine Davies to task for 'misunderstanding' the etymology of the word 'aculturación' when she suggests that the prefix 'a' signifies movement towards something. Santí argues that the prefix in Spanish signifies the absence of something (Santí 2002: 86 n.97), which is, of course, a meaning which the prefix can also have in English. What is in play here is the difference between the idea of moving into a culture and that of having no culture. In fact, discussion of a Spanish etymology may be beside the point since it seems most likely that the word has simply been borrowed from English, where the etymology derives from the latin 'ad' and indicates movement into a culture, or assimilation. An analogous construction in Spanish might be 'abrillantar' (to add lustre to).

clear relation with reciprocity or a movement back and forth. One might look at other words which contain the same prefix to confirm that this is the case. A transition is a passage from one place, state, stage, style, subject or musical key to another. Ortiz himself uses the word 'transmigrate' (Ortiz 1978: 94) to refer to the bringing into Cuba of a new population of Europeans and Africans after the disappearances of the indigenes, but he makes no reference to return journeys. Even the word 'translate' —a favourite with a number of recent commentators— is concerned with shifting from one language into another. As Spitta says: 'Etymologically, translation implies the carrying over, displacing, and transferring of meaning from one language into another' (Spitta 1995: 13). At one point Ortiz uses the word 'transmigraciones' (Ortiz 1978: 95) and links it to the idea of the transitoriness of purposes and the uprooted life of the colonists in Cuba and he seems to have in mind that the Europeans often returned home after a period on the island. But etymology does not ground that sense any better than it does 'transculturation'.[18] And that finally is the point: it is not so much what the term might mean in a contextless etymology that matters but the meaning which Ortiz wants to give to the term in the contexts which he is describing. What the prefix 'trans' ultimately signifies in Ortiz's argument is not a watertight lexical derivation but, on the one hand, as Pérez Firmat indicates, 'the processual, imperfective aspect of culture contact' (Pérez Firmat 1989: 23), and, on the other, a will to differentiation from another term and another tradition. This is an important aspect of his work on which we need to keep a firm grasp because, in recent uses of the theory of transculturation —which have begun to risk overexploitation and an emptying out of meaning— , key aspects of Ortiz have drifted out of focus. One thing which seems to me to matter in Ortiz's account as a whole is the reality of complex interactions and their political and social freight. He may broadly concentrate on cultural processes but in places he does acknowledge what happens to human beings as those processes are unfolding.

In addition, I would suggest that Ortiz also has an acute sense of why transculturation is a term coined in Latin America. The kind of cultural processes which the term refers to are hardly unique to that region —in fact they must have been a constant back into prehistory: wherever peoples and cultures have met and interacted, transculturation will have occurred. And yet, this term was coined in Cuba in the twentieth century. It is here that Ortiz's political and historical sense is important in reminding us of the intensity of certain Latin American realities, which have pushed a conscious and strategic transculturation to the forefront. Latin America's lengthy colonial history of exploitation and manipulation and its simultaneous,

---

[18] Pérez Firmat also has doubts about the etymology of transculturation: see Pérez Firmat (1989: 22).

sustained assimilation to Iberian modes of thought and governance mean that it has been engaged in a search for resistance that may be accounted a cultural constant. That search for resistance may have been more or less conspicuous, more or less explicit, but it was not a superficial or modish embrace of heterogeneity —it was a matter of fundamental importance and self-respect. Of course, that search has almost always run in parallel and even intertwined with the desire for assimilation or acculturation to the other — that is germane to the cultural ambivalence of Latin America. It also needs to be stressed that, given the range of cultural forces and players in the historical field, transcultural processes take myriad forms with micrological and macrological effects. The way in which those processes occur —in colonial or neo-colonial circumstances, in urban or rural locations, between the classes of colonial or national society, between the colony and the metropolis, between the new nation states and global empires, between national institutions and transnational bodies and corporations, in economic, agricultural or literary contexts, and any number of other ways— needs to be borne in mind so that one's understanding of transculturation can be kept finely tuned.

In the light of some recent commentaries on transculturation, which have linked it with autonomy and resistance to global and neo-colonial forces, it seems important to ask how feasible in fact such autonomy and resistance are in a globalised world. A degree of scepticism seems to me to be in order about how much autonomy might be achievable, and about the extent to which the idea of a resistant self-identification might be mystificatory. These questions are about where transculturation might take a society or culture, and about the political efficacy of neoculturation. In his discussion of Ortiz and Rama, John Beverley argues that they both conceive of transculturation as a teleology connected to modernity and the nation-state: 'For both Rama and Ortiz transculturation functions as a teleology, not without marks of violence and loss, but *necessary* in the last instance for the formation of the modern nation-state and a national (or continental) identity that would be something other than the sum of its parts, since the original identities are sublated in the process of transculturation itself' (Beverley 1999: 45). And he goes on to be even more explicit in relation to Rama: 'For Rama, transculturation is above all an instrument for achieving Latin American cultural and economic modernity in the face of the obstacles to that modernity created by colonial and then neo-colonial forms of dependency' (Beverley 1999: 45). Moreiras says something similar when he argues that, for Rama, successful transculturation is about assimilation to modernisation as unavoidable reality, as world destiny (Moreiras 2001a: 188). On these readings, Ortiz and Rama saw transculturation as a necessary 'doing business with' and therefore acceptance of powerful global forces, presumably via local adjustments (though neither Beverley nor Moreiras mentions the neoculturation that was central in Ortiz). Beverley's and Moreiras' readings identify effectively Latin America's ambivalence, as it is caught between the desire for assimilation to global trends and the desire for the (relative) autonomy which the condition of the nation-state implies. But Beverley goes beyond a critical view of this way of positioning Latin America in *external* realities, and also underlines the shortcomings of the notion that the *internal* effects of transculturation might be to further the '"incomplete" project of Latin American modernity' (Beverley 1999: 46) by increasing social integration. He is utterly dismissive when he says: 'The idea of transculturation expresses in both Ortiz and Rama a *fantasy* of class, gender, and racial reconciliation [...]' (Beverley 1999: 47).

The fundamental question which writers like Beverley and Moreiras raise is whether transculturation in the contemporary world can challenge the hold of global modernisation. Now, perhaps even more than in Ortiz's time, this is the framework which must be addressed. And the answer to that fundamental question may depend on the location and nature of the transculturation that occurs. But it may also be that the notion of 'challenging the hold of global modernisation' is simply overambitious. Much of the time, transculturation is local, a tactical adaptation to external forms, though nonetheless significant at that level. But this limitation reveals what is the core of the question about the effectiveness of transculturation and that is whether it is conceivable that it might operate strategically. The negative view would be that, current political and economic structures being what they are, transculturation is and can aspire to be no more than a survival technique. On this view, transculturation localises and partially mitigates dominant political and economic realities. The positive view would be that, such is the creativity and diversity of cultural practices, transcultural forms will constantly emerge to open up new spaces and possibilities, including elements of critique and self-determination. There are at least two ways in which this positive view might be argued, one being via a conscious attempt to create a variant cultural logic or autonomy and the other via an emphasis on the potential impact of the practices of subaltern cultures. I have doubts about both kinds of positive argument. In the case of creating a variant cultural logic, while the will to creativity is revealing and may cast light on the oppressive logic of modernisation, the attempt to create a local cultural specificity may be no more than a reaction to dominant practices and as such leave them in place, thereby changing nothing fundamental. In the case of emphasising subaltern cultures, there may be a danger of assuming that those cultures embody some absolute difference or are the repository of some 'untarnished truth'; and beyond that, there are major ethical concerns to do with presuming to represent subaltern points of view and values and mobilising them for the cause of other less marginal groups.[19] Nonetheless, both lines of argument serve the salutary purpose of reminding us of the need to question global acculturation and may enable the examination from a new perspective of the impact of global economic and political realities.

A sceptical approach might lead one to the view that transculturation is no more than an angling on the basic process of conforming with modernisation, a process in which the effects of neoculturation are at best relatively minor. One way of putting the claims for the reach of neoculturation to the test is to ask whether there is evidence in the contemporary world that current examples of transculturation have any impact beyond Latin American borders, in other words whether there is any real reciprocity in the cultural dynamic. I would hazard a guess that a deep impact is only felt where there is also migration, in other words, from the Latin American point of view, largely in the USA (but others will be more qualified than me to gauge the degree of that impact and how it might affect the realities of global power). If the reciprocity in transculturation is important it may also be fair to say that in current global conditions it is probably harder for peripheries to make an impact than in the colonial period. And that is because the post-modern capitalist world is a decentred network providing no clear pressure points, while, as Arif Dirlik has argued, Euro-US values are still ingrained in it (Dirlik 1994: 350). Another way of testing the claims of neoculturation is to look from a different angle and inquire whether the weak and poor are or have been empowered by transcultural innovation. The answer seems to me to be both 'yes' and 'no': 'yes' to the extent that critique and deflection are potential destablising resources; but 'no' to any large-scale, structural impact, even though that negative does not remove the value of exposing the truth. So, in asking whether transculturation can aspire to any impact, the point is to ask about the relative positions of the cultures involved in any encounter. Spitta highlights precisely this kind of issue in critiquing Ortiz's use of the term 'counterpoint', which in music indicates equality between melodic lines (Spitta 1995: 5). And she questions the appropriateness of the idea of equality to the cultural relations which Ortiz was examining, and that query is just as relevant to current relations between Europe/USA and the peripheries. Such is the flexibility and strength of metropolitan cultures that it is conceivable that, when they are not simply appropriating other cultures to turn their products into consumer commodities, they could indeed absorb elements from the periphery, adapt

---

[19] Carlos Alonso forwards a not dissimilar argument about the use of the 'optic of the subordinate cultural party' (Alonso 1998: 28). He goes on to make a further important point when he says that this emphasis on the subordinate optic does not entail 'any concrete exploration of the plurivocal, self-contradictory, and open-ended dimension of metropolitan discourse, which is therefore left to stand as the self-same, monolithic authority it purports to be, regardless of its supposed disfigurement in the periphery' (Alonso 1998: 28).

them, thereby strengthen themselves and return with a renewed capacity to infiltrate or manipulate the periphery.

It is also vital not to overlook the structure of power internal to Latin America which conditions the dynamics of transculturation. Neil Larsen has argued that transculturation offers a mystificatory and therefore false solution to the underlying problems of the extreme social duality in the region: 'such duality subsists not only in the empirical fact of the deep divisions separating rich and poor, city and country, elite and popular culture, etc., in societies such as Brazil or Mexico but in an historico-ontological condition that fundamentally alters the social ground of national and regional experience itself' (Larsen 2001: 139). In that context, Larsen argues that transculturation does not address the fundamental conditions of social division:

> The essential point [...] is to grasp the cultural duality that separates rich and poor, city and country, etc. as a problem that cannot be solved on its own cultural terms. Its solution must be social, historical —and ultimately political. Thus, while transculturation may enable a more precise, empirical description of cultural life on its most immediate level in Latin America, it cannot give even the slightest indication of how to resolve the cultural dualities that are and continue to be the historically inevitable result of colonisation and a persistently enforced neo-colonial relation to the global economic order. The very historical forces that have produced the deep cultural divisions reflected [...] in transcultural theory continuously reproduce these same divisions even as the spontaneous tendency to transculturation blunts their edges. (Larsen 2001: 139)

In short, for Larsen, claims for the effectiveness of transculturation are a culturalist indulgence and he dismisses any idea that it might substantially modify social, historical or political conditions. It may blunt the edges but cannot begin to effect change.

It is no accident that scepticism about transculturation derives from the left and from those who observe how institutionalisation reduces the radicality of most discourses and terminologies. A vital aspect of the leftist critique, with which I am fundamentally in sympathy, derives from an awareness that Latin America is *always already* in a global system, in a specific place and on specific terms, and against such a reality the shifting of culturally conditioned perceptions of how the world can work and the values inherent in those perceptions is only a first step towards something different. And history bears out this point of view. After all, considering Ortiz's attention to the colonial roots of transculturation, it is evident that, in several hundred years, it has not equalised relations between Latin America and the metropolitan powers. Aspects of the content and dynamics of the relationship may have changed, but one may wonder whether the fundamentals of the relationship are substantially different today. It is from this perspective that the idea of benign or democratic interchanges between Latin American and other cultures seems wide of the mark.

Conclusion

The prime concern which motivated this essay was that the recent, varied use of the term 'transculturation' had stretched its meaning rather thin. It seems that 'investors' have climbed aboard and that, in so doing, the focus and critical usefulness of the term have begun to be diluted. There must be considerable doubt as to whether the promotion of the term is not driven by the Euro-US Academy's desire to authenticate a line of postcolonial criticism via the incorporation of a Latin American term which can be turned to its own ends. I am not at all clear that, beyond one or two high-profile Latin American exponents, the term has achieved much validity within broad cultural debates within Latin America itself. What this might tell us about the academic dimension of global cultural production and ownership hardly needs to be spelt out, though the ironies involved and the discrepancy between declared purposes and effective practice deserve to be pondered carefully. The benefits to individuals within the Euro-US Academy of the transculturation of 'transculturation' should not be overlooked. At the heart of the concern about this particular transculturation is that it has often seemed to pay insufficient attention to the political and economic structures subtending any cultural transaction and therefore to have lost one of the key (perhaps implicit) elements in Ortiz's original conceptualisation. It is undeniable that the content and dynamic of global cultural interaction have changed since Ortiz was writing and an inevitable part of that change is that thinking about the meaning of transculturation has evolved, but a key virtue of his work was its attention to the detail of specific, contextualised case studies and we lose that grounding at our peril.

Certain recent commentators (notably, Beverley, Moreiras and Larsen) have raised doubts about how transculturation affects ways of thinking about and perceiving Latin America. I share many of these doubts, but it is also important to acknowledge that the whole nexus of cultural processes which Ortiz described —deculturation, acculturation, neoculturation, transculturation— is probably in constant operation in every contemporary culture. It is barely feasible to imagine a world without these processes in some form. So the sense in which it might be possible simply to celebrate transculturation should be examined carefully. Few, I imagine, would argue against the notion that a world in which acculturation was less routine and accepted would be a better place, but one needs to be equally careful about a rush to invest in the idea of transculturation, given that it does not occur in a vacuum and, as I have been at pains to underline, needs to be seen in its interweaving with structures of power and the range of mutual influences between different cultures. There are very diverse and uncontrollable flows of information and networks of cultural interaction in operation today, but the questions are how those flows and networks operate, how information is moving, where and how the influences are absorbed, how cultures institute and disseminate value, what degree of deculturation is occurring and what kinds of neoculturation are emerging. There has been some emphasis in recent discussions of transculturation on interaction, but I think that we need to be clear about what we take that term to mean: interaction may not imply equality and mutuality. Influences may operate back and forth between cultures but be asymmetrical in quantity and quality, be highly imbalanced and still take place with well oiled efficiency. Above all therefore, we need to understand how these processes affect people's lives and the social relations in which they live.

And that leaves us with the vital issue of what can be done about imbalanced, asymmetrical influences where they impact negatively on the lives of those in one of the cultures involved. Given continuing global conditions of inequality, the question of how to resist cultural hegemony remains pressing. In general, I am not optimistic in the short term about the prospects for any far-reaching challenge. It seems to me wishful to look to indigenous or marginalised cultures as a basis for resistance. I agree with Alonso when he writes: 'In Spanish America there has been no autochthonous sphere that could be configured and opposed overtly to the West as a strategy for containment, since cultural identity has been so inextricably bound to modernity' (Alonso 1998: 35). The indigenous and the marginalised and their experience are at best urgent reminders of the work that needs to be done. Any moves to oppose dominant cultures will be severely challenged to find a way to go beyond a reflexive relation with it: opposition might simply solidify cultural relations into a polarity and, as a reactive strategy, ultimately reconfirm the dominant culture as the driving force, without isolating its own heterogeneity and internal contradictions. One needs to stress and stress again that all cultures are heterogeneous, potentially contradictory (both internally and in their interrelations) and constantly in transformation, however slowly. Dominance is often partial and reliant on processes of transculturation which are *reciprocally*, if differentially, transformative.

In my view, the best way of redrawing the cultural-political map is not to shrink back into narrow self-affirmations, but to expose what the dominant cultures are and how they work, both in the metropolis and on the periphery. We need also to continue trying to understand how peripheral processes of transculturation function both to accommodate and to deflect the effects of the global and how the cultural sphere adapts to and re-evaluates shifting economic and political pressures. It may be that the leverage to carry out a broad critical analysis comes from the local or the regional, precisely because the global and the local are intertwined and not simply polarised against each other. But the need is to achieve a critique which avoids generalised condemnation of the West and engages with the specific problems of its cultures and their effects. Such critical analysis may not itself change the world but it can advance our understanding of what is happening in it. And, it is in his critical restraint and his careful examination of specific processes of local cultural transformation, that, I think, the ultimate value of Ortiz's *Contrapunteo cubano* lies.[20]

---

[20] I should like to thank Fabricio Forastelli, Felipe Hernández and Bernard McGuirk for their helpful comments on a draft of this essay.

Works cited

Alonso, Carlos (1998) *The Burden of Modernity: The Rhetoric of Cultural Discourse in Spanish America* (New York and Oxford: OUP).

Beverley, John (1999) *Subalternity and Representation. Arguments in Cultural Theory* (Durham and London: Duke University Press).

Coronil, Fernando (1995) 'Introduction to the Duke University Edition. Transculturation and the Politics of Theory: Countering the Center, Cuban Counterpoint', in *Cuban Counterpoint. Tobacco and Sugar* (Durham and London: Duke University Press), ix-lvi.

——— (1996) 'Beyond Occidentalism: Toward Nonimperial Geohistorical Categories', in *Cultural Anthropology* 11.1, 51-87.

Dirlik, Arif (1994) 'The Postcolonial Aura: Third World Criticism in the Age of Global Capitalism', in *Critical Inquiry* 20, 328-56.

Hernández, Felipe (2004) 'Transcultural Architectures in Latin America: An Introduction', in Felipe Hernández and Mark Millington (eds), *Transculturation: Cities, Space and Architecture in Latin America* (Amsterdam: Rodopi), 1-16.

Larsen, Neil (2001) *Determinations: Essays on Theory, Narrative and Nation in the Americas* (London and New York: Verso).

Malinowski, Bronislaw (1978 [1940]) 'Introducción', in Fernando Ortiz, *Contrapunteo cubano del tabaco y del azúcar* (Caracas: Biblioteca Ayacucho), 3-10. (English version in Ortiz 1995 [1947].)

Moreiras, Alberto (2001a) *The Exhaustion of Difference: The Politics of Latin American Cultural Studies* (Durham and London: Duke University Press).

——— (2001b) 'A Storm Blowing from Paradise: Negative Globality and Critical Regionalism', in Ileana Rodríguez (ed), *The Latin American Subaltern Studies Reader* (Durham and London: Duke University Press), 81-107.

Ortiz, Fernando (1978 [1940]) *Contrapunteo cubano del tabaco y del azúcar* (Caracas: Biblioteca Ayacucho). (There are several notable editions of the work. The first was: Havana: J. Montero, 1940, with a prologue by Herminio Portell Vilá and an introduction by Bronislaw Malinowski. Among subsequent revised and enlarged editions are: Las Villas: Universidad Central de Las Villas, 1963; Caracas: Biblioteca Ayacucho, 1978, with a Prologue and Chronology by Julio Le Riverend; Madrid: Cátedra, 2002, edited and introduced by Enrico Mario Santí. The English translation is: *Cuban Counterpoint. Tobacco and Sugar*, translated by Harriet de Onís, New York: A. A. Knopf, 1947 [republished: Durham and London: Duke University Press, 1995]. This translation abridges the 1940 edition; it goes without saying that it does not include the revisions and enlargements of the 1963 edition.).

Pérez Firmat, Gustavo (1989) *The Cuban Condition. Translation and Identity in Modern Cuban Literature* (Cambridge: Cambridge University Press).

Pratt, Mary Louise (1992) *Imperial Eyes: Travel Writing and Transculturation* (London and New York: Routledge).

Rama, Angel (1982) *Transculturación narrativa en América Latina* (Mexico: Siglo XXI).

———— (1997 [1974]) 'Processes of Transculturation in Latin American Narrative', in *Journal of Latin American Cultural Studies* 6.2, 155-71.

Rowe, William and Vivian Schelling (1991) *Memory and Modernity. Popular Culture in Latin America* (London and New York: Verso).

Santí, Enrico Mario, 'Introducción', in Fernando Ortiz, *Contrapunteo cubano del tabao y del azúcar* (Madrid: Cátedra), 23-110.

Spitta, Silvia (1995) *Between Two Waters: Narratives of Transculturation in Latin America* (Houston: Rice University Press).

Notes on Contributors

Michael Asbury is a research fellow based at Chelsea College of Art and Design. His PhD thesis is entitled 'Hélio Oiticica: Politics and Ambivalence in 20th Century Brazilian Art.' As a fellow at Chelsea College of Art and Design he is responsible for the management of the AHRB-sponsored project entitled 'Modernity and Identity in Art 1850s-1940s: India, Japan and Mexico', which is run jointly by the University of Sussex, Chelsea College of Art and Design and Camberwell College of Arts. He has organised and curated a number of exhibitions and was associate-curator responsible for the architecture and photography display at the 'Rio de Janeiro 1950 - 1964' section of 'Century City: Art and Culture in the Modern Metropolis', the inaugural temporary exhibition at Tate Modern in 2001. He is the author of various articles and reviews on Brazilian art and is currently translating a publication on Brazilian architecture for Phaidon Press.

Anny Brooksbank-Jones taught at the Universities of Nottingham, Southampton, Nottingham Trent and Leeds before moving in January 2001 to Sheffield, where she is currently Hughes Professor of Spanish and Head of Department. She has taught and published widely on Spanish and Latin American cultural studies and gender studies. Publications include: *Latin American Women's Writing: Readings in Theory and Crisis* (co-edited with Catherine Davies, Oxford University Press 1996); *Women in Contemporary Spain* (Manchester U.P. 1997); *Cultural Politics in Latin America* (co-edited with Ronaldo Munck, Macmillan 2000). She is currently completing a study of visual culture and risk in Spain Latin America.

Luis Carranza received his PhD from Harvard University. He is Assistant Professor of Architecture and Architectural History and Theory at Roger Williams University, Bristol, RI. He is currently completing a book on Mexican avant-garde architecture.

Ricardo L. Castro, MRAIC, received the degree of *Arquitecto* from the Universidad de Los Andes in Bogotá. He obtained an M.A. in Art History and an M.Arch. at the University of Oregon. He has taught at the Universidad de Los Andes, Bogotá, the University of Oregon, Kansas State University and L'université Laval. He is currently an Associate Professor of Architecture at McGill University in Montreal, where he has taught since 1982. He was the director of IRHA (Institut de recherché en histoire de l'architecture.) from 2000 to 2003. In 1990, Castro was awarded the Prix Paul-Henri Lapointe in the category 'History, Criticism and Theory' by the *Ordre des architectes du*

Québec. He has been the recipient of several research grants from the Canada Council as well as two grants from the Graham Foundation for Advanced Studies in the Fine Arts: in 1995 for his work on Colombian architect Rogelio Salmona and in 2001 (in collaboration with Nicholas Olsberg) for a monograph on the work of Canadian architect Arthur Erickson. Castro contributes architectural criticism and photographs to national and international architectural publications. He has participated in numerous photographic exhibitions in Canada and the United States and has also been a contributing writer for various collections of architectural essays. In 1998 his book on Colombian architect Rogelio Salmona was published by Villegas Editores, Bogotá.

Carlos Eduardo Dias Comas qualified as an architect at the University of Pennsylvania and got his doctoral degree at the University of Paris, with a thesis whose title is 'Précisions: Architecture Moderne Brésilienne 1936-45'. Besides running a small architectural practice, he is Professor of Architectural Design at the Faculdade de Arquitetura, Universidade do Rio Grande do Sul, Porto Alegre, Brazil. He was a Visiting Professor at the University of Miami and the Catholic University of Chile. Schools where he lectured include the Architectural Association, London, the Ecole d' Architecture Paris-Malaquais, the Escuela Técnica Superior de Arquitectura de Barcelona, Harvard University and the Universidad Central de Venezuela. He co-authored with Miquel Adrià *La Casa Latinoamericana Moderna* (Mexico City: 2004) and contributed essays to several books, among which 'Le Corbusier y Suramérica' (Fernando Pérez Oyarzun, ed.; Santiago de Chile: 1991), 'Le Corbusier-Rio de Janeiro, 1929-1936' (Yannis Tsiomis, ed.; Rio de Janeiro: 1999), 'Arquitetura Brasil 500 años' (Roberto Montezuma, ed.; Recife: 2002) and 'Les Amériques: Utopies et Cruautés' (Jean-François Lejeune, ed.; Brussels: 2003).

Adrian Forty is Professor of Architectural History at The Bartlett School of Architecture, UCL. His published works include *Objects of Desire: Design and Society Since 1750* (1986), *The Art of Forgetting* (published in collaboration with Suzanne Kuchler in 1999) and *Words and Buildings: A Vocabulary of Modern Architecture* (2000).

Felipe Hernández is an architect and Lecturer in Architectural Design, History and Theory at the University of Liverpool. He has an MA in Architecture and Critical Theory and received his PhD from the University of Nottingham. He has taught at the Bartlett School of Architecture (UCL), The Universities of Nottingham, Sheffield, East London as well as at the School of Art and Design, Nottingham Trent University. Felipe Hernández has published numerous essays and articles examining architectural practices in

Latin America through contemporary cultural theory. He is editor of 'Spaces of Transculturation: Architecture and Identity in Latin America', *Journal of Romance Studies* (Winter 2002), and is currently completing a book on contemporary Latin American architecture.

Monika Kaup is Assistant Professor of English at the University of Washington, Seattle. She is the author of *Mad Intertextuality: Madness in Twentieth-Century Women's Writing* and of *Rewriting North American Borders in Chicano and Chicana Narrative*. She is also co-editor (with Debra Rosenthal) of *Mixing Race, Mixing Culture: Inter-American Literary Dialogues*. Currently she is working on the New-World Neo-Baroque.

Peter Kellett is a Senior Lecturer in the Global Urban Research Unit of the School of Architecture, Planning and Landscape, University of Newcastle upon Tyne. His PhD was based on an ethnographic study of informal housing processes in northern Colombia. His main research interests continue to focus on housing, particularly on the dwelling environments of disadvantaged households in cities in the developing world. Currently he is co-researcher on a large DFID-funded international comparative research project examining the use of the home for income generation in informal settlements in four developing cities.

Mark Millington holds the Chair of Latin American Studies in the University of Nottingham and is currently Dean of the Arts Faculty. In 1998, he was a Rockefeller Fellow at the Universidade Federal de Minas Gerais, Brazil. His research focuses on Spanish American narrative fiction in the twentieth century and on issues in critical theory. He has published books on Juan Carlos Onetti and co-edited others on literary and cultural theory. He has also published numerous articles and chapters on the following writers amongst others: Gallegos, Borges, Felisberto Hernández, Monterroso, Donoso, García Márquez, Cabrera Infante, Vargas Llosa, Osvaldo Soriano and Tomás Eloy Martínez. He has a book forthcoming on the representation of masculinity in Latin American fiction. He is currently working on the role of the public intellectual in post-revolutionary Mexico.

Robert Mugerauer is Dean and Professor of the College of Architecture and Urban Planning at the University of Washington, Seattle. He is the author of *Interpretations on Behalf of Place* and *Interpreting Environments*, as well as co-author (with Lance Tantum) of *High-Tech Downtown*. In addition, he co-edited (with David Seamon) the book *Dwelling, Place, Environment*. His present work focuses on the impact of technology and tourism on traditional environments.

Jane Rendell is a Reader in Art and Architecture at the Bartlett School of Architecture (UCL). And architectural designer, historian and theorist, she is author of *The Pursuit of Pleasure* (Athlone Press, 2002), editor of 'A Place Between', *Public Art Journal* (October, 1999) and co-editor of *Strangely Familiar* (Routledge, 1995), *Gender, Space Architecture* (Routledge, 1999), *Intersections* (Routledge, 2000), and *The Unknown City* (MIT Press, 2000). She is currently completing a new book for Reaktion Press, *From Art to Architecture* and is working on 'Writing Aloud', a project of site specific writings and readings.

Helen Thomas first became interested in Latin American architecture while practicing as an architect in Seville. Subsequently she completed a Ph.D. on mid-twentieth-century architecture in Mexico, in which she explored articulations of the site at El Pedregal, including some of those discussed in her essay in this volume. She is currently the Architecture Education Officer for the V&A+RIBA Architecture Partnership, based at the Victoria & Albert Museum (V&A).

Sandra Vivanco is an Associate Professor of Architecture at the California College of Arts and Crafts. Her teaching career spans the North-American East and West, while her sphere of professional activity includes Japan, Italy, Peru and Portugal. Her main research interest is Latin American Modernism, specifically the post-war condition of Brazil. Her company, A+D (Architecture + Design), specialises in building educational multi-unit residential projects. Through her work with several non-profit organizations in San Francisco, she aims to bridge the gap between education and practice.

Index

New from
The MIT Press

The Era of Choice
The Ability to Choose and Its Transformation of Contemporary Life
Edward C. Rosenthal
"Once men and women had hardly any choices in life, and now there are so many that choice itself has become a source of anxiety. Switch off your 500 cable channels and read Edward Rosenthal's important new book." — Gregg Easterbrook, author of *The Progress Paradox*
336 pp. $32.50

Mexican Modernity
The Avant-Garde and the Technological Revolution
Rubén Gallo
"Vividly captures the sense of excitement that accompanied the introduction of modern technology into twentieth-century Mexican culture." — Gustavo Pérez Firmat, Columbia University
248 pp., 10 color, 71 black & white illus. $29.95

Suspect
edited by John Knechtel
Essays, graphic novels, films, and commentary examine the figure of the suspect and the politics of suspicion in a post 9/11 world.
288 pp., 80 color, 50 black & white illus. $15.95

Making Things Public
Atmospheres of Democracy
edited by Bruno Latour and Peter Weibel
Redefines politics as a concern for things around which the fluid and expansive constituency of the public gathers.
1000 pp., 550 color illus. $50

now in paperback
Requiem for Communism
Charity Scribner
Examines the politics of memory in postindustrial literature and art.
320 pp., 39 illus. $17.95 paper

Enduring Innocence
Global Architecture and Its Political Masquerades
Keller Easterling
How outlaw "spatial products"—resorts, information technology campuses, retail chains, golf courses, and ports—act as cunning pawns in global politics.
208 pp., 20 illus. $24.95

now in paperback
Balkan as Metaphor
Between Globalization and Fragmentation
edited by Dušan I. Bjelić and Obrad Savić
"Rich and varied in its exploration of Balkan identity . . . and challenges the reader to think in new ways about the region."
— *Slavic and Eastern European Journal*
350 pp. $19.95 paper

now in paperback
Spectral Evidence
The Photography of Trauma
Ulrich Baer
"A very thought-provoking contribution to the theorizing of photography and memory, both collective and individual." — *Metapsychology*
216 pp., 31 illus. $19.95 paper

Zone Books

Death and the Idea of Mexico
Claudio Lomnitz
"Examines the Mexican people's in many respects unique relationship to death throughout several centuries." — Friedrich Katz
Distributed for Zone Books
450 pp., 52 black & white illus. $34

now in paperback
Publics and Counterpublics
Michael Warner
An investigation of how the idea of a public as a central fiction of modern life informs our literature, politics, and culture.
Distributed for Zone Books • 318 pp. $19.95 paper

To order call **800-405-1619**.
http://mitpress.mit.edu

Producing the Pacific
Maps and Narratives of Spanish Exploration (1567-1606)

Mercedes Maroto Camino

Amsterdam/New York, NY 2005. 144 pp. + 34 ill.
(Portada hispánica 18)

ISBN: 90-420-1994-8   € 40,-/US $ 54.-

Producing the Pacific offers the reader an interdisciplinary reading of the maps, narratives and rituals related to the three Spanish voyages to the South Pacific that took place between 1567 and 1606. These journeys were led by Álvaro de Mendaña, Pedro Fernández de Quirós and Isabel Barreto, the first woman ever to become admiral of and command a fleet.

Mercedes Maroto Camino presents a cultural analysis of these journeys and takes issue with some established notions about the value of the past and the way it is always rewritten from the perspective of the present. She highlights the social, political and cultural environment in which maps and narratives circulate, suggesting that their significance is always subject to negotiation and transformation.

The tapestry created by the interpretation of maps, narratives and rituals affords a view not only of the minds of the first men and women who traversed the Pacific but also of how they saw the ocean, its islands and their peoples. Producing the Pacific should, therefore, be of relevance to those interested in history, voyages, colonialism, cartography, anthropology and cultural studies.

The study of these cultural products contributes to an interpretive history of colonialism at the same time that it challenges the beliefs and assumptions that underscore our understanding of that history.

USA/Canada: 906 Madison Avenue, Union, NJ 07083, USA.
Fax: (908) 206-0820 Call toll-free: 1-800-225-3998 (USA only)
All other countries: Tijnmuiden 7, 1046 AK Amsterdam, The Netherlands.
Tel. ++ 31 (0)20 611 48 21, Fax ++ 31 (0)20 447 29 79
Orders-queries@rodopi.nl   **www.rodopi.nl**
Please note that the exchange rate is subject to fluctuations

The Theater of Transformation
Postmodernism in American Drama

Kerstin Schmidt

Amsterdam/New York, NY 2005. 230 pp.
(Postmodern Studies 37)

ISBN: 90-420-1895-X   € 46,-/US $ 64.-

The Theater of Transformation: Postmodernism in American Drama offers a fresh and innovative reading of the contemporary experimental American theater scene and navigates through the contested and contentious relationship between postmodernism and contemporary drama. This book addresses gender and class as well as racial issues in the context of a theoretical discussion of dramatic texts, textuality, and performance. Transformation is contemporary drama's answer to the questions of postmodernism and a major technique in the development of a postmodern language for the stage. In order to demonstrate the multi-faceted nature of the postmodern theater of transformation, this study draws on a wide range of plays: from early experimental plays of the 1960s by Jean-Claude van Itallie through feminist plays by Megan Terry and Rochelle Owens to more recent drama by the African-American playwright Suzan-Lori Parks.

The Theater of Transformation: Postmodernism in American Drama is written for anyone interested in contemporary American drama and theater as well as in postmodernism and contemporary literary theory. It appeals even more broadly to a readership intrigued by the ubiquitous aspects of popular culture, by feminism and ethnicity, and by issues pertaining to the so-called 'society of spectacle' and the study of contemporary media.

Kerstin Schmidt is currently Assistant Professor of American Studies and Intercultural Anglophone Studies in the Department of English at the University of Bayreuth, Germany.

USA/Canada: 906 Madison Avenue, UNION, NJ 07083, USA.
Call toll-free (USA only)1-800-225-3998, Tel. 908 206 1166, Fax 908-206-0820
All other countries: Tijnmuiden 7, 1046 AK Amsterdam, The Netherlands.
Tel. ++ 31 (0)20 611 48 21, Fax ++ 31 (0)20 447 29 79
Orders-queries@rodopi.nl   **www.rodopi.nl**
Please note that the exchange rate is subject to fluctuations

Poverty
A Philosophical Approach

Paulette Dieterlen

Amsterdam/New York, NY 2005. VII, 176 pp.
(Rodopi Philosophical Studies 6)

ISBN: 90-420-1975-1   € 40,-/ US $ 56.-

In *Poverty: a philosophical approach*, the author studies various philosophical issues concerning poverty in the Program for Education, Health and Food (PROGRESA) that was in effect in Mexico, from 1997 to 2002, and shows how theoretical discussion is necessary to clarify some ideas concerning the application of a social policy.

Poverty is one of the main problems concerning economics, political philosophy, and ethics. It is an ethical problem because of its relationship with self-esteem. Since poverty is intimately related to social policies, the philosophy of poverty must consider the distribution criteria used to attend to people in situations of extreme poverty. This would involve attention to their needs, preferences, capabilities and "well-being" rights.

The book considers social policies applied to poverty, and their occasional abuse of utilitarian instruments. Many are implemented without considering cultural differences, including varying patterns of conduct in diverse communities.

Equality also matters. Since poverty and inequality are not the same, the study of the latter allows us to target groups found in the lowest levels of "the playing field".

USA/Canada: 906 Madison Avenue, UNION, NJ 07083, USA.
Call toll-free (USA only)1-800-225-3998, Tel. 908 206 1166, Fax 908-206-0820
All other countries: Tijnmuiden 7, 1046 AK Amsterdam, The Netherlands.
Tel. ++ 31 (0)20 611 48 21, Fax ++ 31 (0)20 447 29 79
Orders-queries@rodopi.nl   **www.rodopi.nl**
Please note that the exchange rate is subject to fluctuations

Intercultural Explorations.

Volume 8 of the Proceedings of the XVth
Congress of the International Comparative
Literature Association *"Literature as Cultural Memory"*
Leiden 16-22 August 1997.

Edited by Eugene Eoyang.

Amsterdam/New York, NY 2005. IV, 292 pp.
(Textxet 32)

ISBN: 90-420-1636-1   € 60,-/ US $ 75.-

Divided into four sections: "Asian-Western Intersections," "Intercultural Memory," "Intercultural Perspectives on Women," "Genre Studies," and "The Intercultural Arts", these essays from diverse hands and multiple perspectives illuminate the intersections, the cross-sections, and the synergies that characterize significant literary texts and artistic productions. Individually, they exemplify the insights available in an intercultural perspective; together they remind us that no culture - even those that claim to be "pure" or those that might be regarded as isolated - has escaped the influence of external influences. As a result, this volume is doubly synergistic: one, because it focuses on intercultural phenomena within a specific culture, and two, because they represent multiple perspectives on these phenomena.

USA/Canada: 906 Madison Avenue, UNION, NJ 07083, USA.
Call toll-free (USA only)1-800-225-3998, Tel. 908 206 1166, Fax 908-206-0820
All other countries: Tijnmuiden 7, 1046 AK Amsterdam, The Netherlands.
Tel. ++ 31 (0)20 611 48 21, Fax ++ 31 (0)20 447 29 79
<u>Orders-queries@rodopi.nl</u>   **www.rodopi.nl**
Please note that the exchange rate is subject to fluctuations

Mitos e identidades en el teatro español contemporáneo.

Bajo la dirección de Mᵃ Francisca Vilches de Frutos.

Amsterdam/New York, NY 2005. 113 pp.
(Foro Hispánico 27)

ISBN: 90-420-1806-2   € 25,-/US$ 32.-

Con un telón de fondo internacional de desorientación generalizada, han triunfado en el ámbito español, durante las últimas temporadas teatrales, espectáculos comprometidos con la indagación sobre la identidad humana. Uno de los caminos elegidos por los escritores dramáticos ha sido la recreación de mitos, a los que dotan de una nueva configuración para dar respuesta a los problemas y dudas del ser humano contemporáneo. En este volumen se reúnen seis trabajos originales, de María-José Ragué-Arias, Diana M. de Paco Serrano, Pilar Nieva de la Paz, Mᵃ Francisca Vilches de Frutos, Wilfried Floeck y Anita Johnson, especialistas en la materia, que ofrecen un panorama sobre la manera en la que destacados autores dramáticos han recreado en lengua española algunos de estos mitos.

USA/Canada: 906 Madison Avenue, UNION, NJ 07083, USA.
Call toll-free (USA only)1-800-225-3998, Tel. 908 206 1166, Fax 908-206-0820
All other countries: Tijnmuiden 7, 1046 AK Amsterdam, The Netherlands.
Tel. ++ 31 (0)20 611 48 21, Fax ++ 31 (0)20 447 29 79
Orders-queries@rodopi.nl   **www.rodopi.nl**
Please note that the exchange rate is subject to fluctuations